Charles Thomas Paske

Life and Travel in Lower Burma

A Retrospect

Charles Thomas Paske

Life and Travel in Lower Burma
A Retrospect

ISBN/EAN: 9783337077792

Printed in Europe, USA, Canada, Australia, Japan

Cover: Foto ©Andreas Hilbeck / pixelio.de

More available books at **www.hansebooks.com**

Photo by F. Oertel.

A BURMESE TEMPLE.

From Major Temple's collection.

LIFE AND TRAVEL IN LOWER BURMAH

A RETROSPECT

BY

DEPUTY-SURGEON-GENERAL C. T. PASKE

LATE OF THE BENGAL ARMY

EDITED BY

F. G. AFLALO

(*Authors of* "*The Sea and the Rod,*" *&c.*)

LONDON
W. H. ALLEN & CO., LIMITED,
13, WATERLOO PLACE, PALL MALL, S.W.

EDITOR'S PREFACE.

WHEN my friend asked me to read through these reminiscences in their original form, with a view to editing them, I had to tell him at the outset that the remoteness of the retrospect might probably prove a serious obstacle.

But, being neither a history nor geography, and dealing lightly with a number of topics that should be of interest to many Englishmen, it soon occurred to me that they might perhaps find readers in spite of not being up to date.

It is the fashion nowadays—and it seems to me a somewhat injudicious practice—to publish the record of one's travels and experiences within a few weeks after returning home, whereas many opinions that the writer would naturally hold while still under the unsettling influence of travel, might be at least very considerably modified, were the final proof corrected ten years later, without losing in value.

The present form of these retrospective glances, which skim lightly over half-a-dozen years in some kind of chronological order, has been prepared from a manuscript that has during the past two years received many amendments; so that the reader has at least an unbiassed account of a few years' official residence in one of the most promising of our Eastern possessions.

EDITOR'S PREFACE.

The appalling multiplication of English books is probably destined to continue until Macaulay's New-Zealander contemplates the ruins of St. Paul's, and it would almost appear that the classes and masses are alike following Dr. Johnson's advice : " Read anything for five hours a day and you will soon be learned."

In spite, however, of the modern facilities for publishing, had there been no further object in view than the narration of a few personal experiences, the author would never have launched another venture on the troubled sea. Our legislators have for some time past been contemplating a distant and hazy vista of Utopia, though faulty navigation has carried the vessel far wide of the destination, and will, not improbably, land her some day on the rocks.

Of particular and terrible interest is their future Indian policy; and those who are good enough to read the following pages will find not a few startling instances of how far such policy has hitherto been based on sound practical lines.

In some cases, the author has maybe expressed his convictions with candour rather than discretion; but as he has ever stood by his guns, I think it would have been exceeding what was expected of me, had I modified one or two expressions of opinion that are almost certain to meet with stormy weather in certain latitudes.

So tiny and insignificant a craft, however, may surely hope to ride the angry waves and arrive safely in port.

London, October, 1892.

F. G. A

CONTENTS.

	PAGE
EDITOR'S PREFACE	V

CHAPTER I.
THE VOYAGE 1

CHAPTER II.
STILL UNDER CANVAS 22

CHAPTER III.
THE CITY OF PALACES 36

CHAPTER IV.
ON THE MOVE ONCE MORE . . 46

CHAPTER V.
FIRST IMPRESSIONS . . . 57

CHAPTER VI.
THE TEACHINGS OF BUDDHA 69

CHAPTER VII.
RIVER-LIFE UNDER DIFFICULTIES . . . 85

CHAPTER VIII.
UNDER ORDERS 110

CHAPTER IX.
PROME 123

CONTENTS.

CHAPTER X.
A Secret Expedition . . . 137

CHAPTER XI.
Further Details . . . 149

CHAPTER XII.
"El Dorado" . . . 161

CHAPTER XIII.
Cloudy Weather 175

CHAPTER XIV.
"Leave of Absence" . . 188

CHAPTER XV.
Moulmein . . 201

CHAPTER XVI.
Amherst 214

CHAPTER XVII.
Tavoy 224

CHAPTER XVIII.
The Mergui Archipelago . . . 233

CHAPTER XIX.
Mergui 241

CHAPTER XX.
And Last . . . 252

Index 263

MYAMMA:

A RETROSPECT OF LIFE AND TRAVEL IN LOWER BURMAH.

CHAPTER I.

THE VOYAGE.

> "So long
> As he could make me with this eye or ear
> Distinguish him from others, he did keep
> The deck with glove, or hat, or handkerchief,
> Still waving, as the fits and stirs of his mind
> Could best express how slow his soul sail'd on,
> How swift his ship."
>
> SHAKESPEARE, *Cymbeline*.

THE conditions under which we now plough the ocean or fly through continents present so remarkable a contrast to the state of affairs half a century back, that we who are in the autumn of life, with the signal of the "sere and yellow leaf" fluttering feebly at the masthead, can scarce realize the old coaching days, with their thirteen hours' travel to every hundred miles, as more than an old dream.

Time in those days was, to all appearances, of less commercial value than it is now, when it represents the Golden Calf, and commerce is conducted by means of electricity and steam. The merchant had to wait patiently for months before learning the fate of his argosies; Clive was eleven months reaching India; experience and nautical skill reduced the time to six, and improved routes to four months; while one month now suffices, through the agency of steam, from Southampton to Bombay. The arrival is then flashed home through that "girdle" which Puck offered to put "round about the earth in forty minutes."

When the Victorian era takes its place in the pages of England's history, the revolution effected by electricity and steam in its commerce, its battles, and its treaties, will occupy a large and important part of the interesting and glorious chapter.

Long voyages under canvas are nowadays therefore, except as a means of recuperating one's health, the exception; and it is not surprising that the employment of steam power should be so universal, whether from considerations of time and business, or of sea-sickness and pleasure; a steamer moves through fifteen or twenty miles an hour day and night, independent of wind and weather, whereas a sailing vessel is heavily handicapped, having to quadruple the distance in constant "dogs' legs," besides being becalmed in certain latitudes for days together.

The rising generation greet any allusion to the voyages so common in the palmy days of the now defunct East India Company with *fin-de-siècle* contempt; living, as they do, in an atmosphere of perpetual excitement and unrest, they are almost incapable of comprehending the frame of mind in which their forefathers plodded through their allotted span of life.

But as "many things by season season'd are to their right praise and true perfection," so the human mind seems able to adapt and accommodate itself to the varying circumstances of this transient sphere. A century or so hence the people of this country will probably look on our modern naval and mercantile craft with as critical an eye as that with which we contemplate the *Victory*, or the first steamers of the P. and O. We pride ourselves on the combination of size, speed, and comfort, and the graceful lines of our floating palaces, on their electric lighting and luxurious saloons; we feel confident that not much more can be accomplished: yet could we but " revisit the glimpses of the moon " in 1992, we should find ourselves in the midst of a new creation.

On the 1st September, 185—, a majestic old frigate-built East Indiaman lay moored off Spithead, all ready to weigh anchor and awaiting only the arrival of the pilot and one or two passengers, detained by accident or otherwise. She was surrounded by numerous small craft, some laden with various articles for sale, others waiting to convey ashore those who had come aboard to see the last of sons and daughters about to seek their fortunes in the glorious East, where money was reputed to be easily made, and men hungered for wives of the European pattern.

Very mixed were the feelings of the passengers at the moment of parting: regret on the one hand at being separated from loving parents, severed from the tried companions and indelible associations of early youth; on the other, a certain feeling of independence and freedom, and the natural ambition to get on in the world.

Many shook hands for the last time on this side of the grave; and as the tiny craft pulled away and were lost in the distance, the solitude of the cabin was sought, and a blessing implored on the dear ones left behind.

There may be a reluctance on the part of many to utter a prayer under normal conditions, but in an unusual state of things there are, I believe, few who will not deviate from the beaten track and intuitively ask aid from a higher power.

Sorrow, however, takes but a passing hold of the elastic nature of youth; and when the shrill whistle of the boatswain and the stamping of many feet on deck proclaimed that the anchor was being weighed and the canvas loosened, curiosity soon gained the ascendancy, and, in spite of eyes still red with weeping, passengers as yet unknown to each other might be seen occupying every coign of vantage, and watching the sailors as they sped round the capstan to some familiar air played on the fiddle; and anon looking up as sail after sail was loosened, then drawn home and bellied by the freshening breeze. That she was moving soon became evident from the noise made by the water and the gradual diminution of familiar objects ashore. Glasses were brought into requisition, and closed with a sigh when, even with their aid, all was blurred, hazy, indistinct.

So faded that "white-faced shore, whose foot spurns back the ocean's roaring tide"; and before the end of the year we were to look upon another of a very different complexion, low, swampy, and muddy; fringed with cocoanut trees, at the foot of which jackals shrieked, making night hideous, and around which mosquitoes buzzed and bit, as with the avowed mission of scaring away nature's sweet restorer.

To the officers and crew all the bustle of getting under weigh was of course familiar; but to some fifty passengers, starting for the most part on their first voyage, it all seemed chaos: anon a stentorian voice gave an order, resulting in a tramping of feet and the thud of ropes falling on the deck, to the accompaniment of "Cheery, boys, oh!" or some other ditty that was prime favourite in those days.

Having made a fair offing, the good old ship bore steadily down channel, the pilot entering his boat somewhere off Start Point, and his "God speed!" seemed to sever the last link that bound us to the mother country.

Even in a comparatively calm sea the movement of an East Indiaman was sufficient to test one's sea-going qualities, so that, when the bells had been struck for meals, the cuddy table presented numerous gaps, while certain ominous sounds proceeding from the direction of the private accommodation announced to the happy few the advent of that terrible ordeal *mal-de-mer*. Happily for the majority of mortals it soon wears itself out; and the stomach, conforming to the law that "use is second nature," soon becomes tolerant of the new order of things, and ceases to resent the innovation of digesting under conditions of perpetual motion. I only came across one case in which sea-sickness became a source of positive danger. The sufferer, a hale and healthy man on coming aboard, was reduced in the course of a couple of months to a mere bag of bones. What medical aid failed to do was accomplished by nature; his sickness ceased, and in lieu thereof he acquired an insatiable appetite which distressed him. He apologized for the amount that he ate at meals, and for filling his pockets with biscuits afterwards; but he was powerless to restrain himself, so that by the time we arrived at our destination he was the counterpart of his original self. I never saw him again, but I imagine that, if he did ever return to Europe, his path lay through unexplored regions, as I believe he would have attempted to traverse them on foot rather than again enter a cabin.

Personally, I never experienced sea-sickness; the

only influence that the motion of the ship had over me was that I fell asleep on the least provocation, which was very many times a day, as reading and writing were equally out of the question.

By the time the dreaded Bay of Biscay had been crossed, and the ship had entered warmer latitudes, the deck presented a more animated appearance, and the cuddy table became devoid of gaps. All sorts and conditions of both sexes had now acquired their sea-legs, and their sea-stomachs too; for the most part they ate, I am convinced, more than was good for them. Sea-air enjoys the reputation of stimulating the appetite, and it undoubtedly had that effect in this particular instance, assisted, maybe, by the seductive variety presented at each meal. It was surprising, indeed, how such a number could be so catered for day after day, extending to the third part of a year: mutton, pork, fowls, ducks, and geese were always forthcoming, to say nothing of the ubiquitous ham; nor was there any falling off in fresh bread and pastry, while the cows in the long boat kept up the supply of milk. After each meal the water astern became dotted with empty bottles—for passengers, who could have as much ale, &c., as they pleased, *did* please—which, as they sank to great depths, were probably shivered into fragments ere they reached the bottom by the increasing pressure. Supposing, indeed, the waters had dried up, the Cape route to India could, I doubt not, have been easily traced by these innumerable fragments of glass. The captious critic, commenting on what we had done for that vast continent extending from the Himalayas to Cape Cormorin, was wont to remark that, had the Mutiny been successful, empty bottles alone would have remained as monuments of a century's dominion. Thus we should have had the same memorial from Spithead to the Hooghly, and might have figured as a nation in whose administration glass figured as an important ingredient, the captious one ignoring in all probability such insignificant achievements as the Grand Trunk Road, and suppression of Infanticide, Thuggee, and Suttee.

The only article on which any restriction was placed was the fresh water allotted for the purpose of ablution, more than a given quantity being obtainable only under peculiar conditions. But temptation, like slander, " rides on the posting winds, and doth belie all corners of the earth," and even old East-Indiaman stewards were hardly above its subtle influence.

Unrestricted access, then, to everything save fresh water, was the old order of things; and the P. and O., besides having kept abreast of the requirements of the present day in the matter of shipbuilding, speed, and comfort, deserve more credit than they actually got for being the pioneers of so admirable an innovation as lowering the passage-money, and charging extra for wine, beer, and aërated waters.

Many of my contemporary travellers will remember how from start to finish of a voyage the table was crowded at breakfast, lunch, and dinner with bottles containing various wines; in addition to which there were frequent descents to the cuddy to slake an imaginary thirst with a B. and S. This inordinate and imaginary thirst died a natural death under the new system of paying for what is ordered. A bottle of claret on the breakfast table became the exception rather than the rule: few made it "eight bells" to any extent, and the pop of soda-water bottles became very rare.

From the suspicious way in which we English approach each other, whether in a private room or in a public conveyance, it would seem as if there lurked in our composition some of that cautious mistrust so characteristic of the wild beast. But after having been a week or so in each other's company, the passengers positively began to thaw towards one another; a welcome change that was, however, succeeded by a still harder frost. For a time, indeed, we constituted a happy family, dancing, singing, and acting together; but this temporary and unstable fusion of minds was doomed to resolve itself into two antagonistic elements, an untoward state of affairs that culminated only as the good ship drew near her destination. There were two ways of accounting for this division in the camp; my own view of the matter was that we saw too much of each other from "rosy morn till dewy eve," which, besides breeding contempt, gave birth to that " green-eyed monster," jealousy. But the sailors ascribed all that went wrong to the presence of so many clergymen, whom they looked upon as the *fons et origo* of storms and everything undesirable. It is, however, a melancholy yet undeniable fact that a number of human beings herded together for any considerable length of time will be sure to fall out, behaving in all probability rather less charitably than so many tigers and jackals.

But on the whole, much as there was to lament in the matter of ruffled tempers and petty ways, the outward-bound vessel represented a perfect paradise during the four months' voyage, compared with the ordeal of a similar period aboard a homeward-bound Indiaman. To give even a faint idea of the angry conflagration of passions by which the passengers in the latter were wont to distinguish themselves, one would have to borrow from the "Inferno" of Dante, and conjecture what must be going on in Pandemonium, where the evil spirits meet in council!

The living freight was of the most volatile and combustible nature, while the perpetual friction of its conflicting elements—swarms of noisy children, and touchy old men with disordered livers—kept the ship in perpetual danger of destruction. But a merciful Providence has tempered the wind to the Anglo-Indian by pointing out an overland route, and consigning the homeward-bound Indiaman, in so far as passengers are concerned, to the pages of history; so that the danger of spontaneous combustion is now confined to the cargo.

To resume our outward voyage. By the time we had finished taking stock of each other, conjecturing why So-and-so was going out to the East, the beautiful island of Madeira hove in sight; but to our united earnest entreaties to be allowed to land for a few hours at Funchal the captain turned a deaf ear, expecting the wind to change at any moment to a more favourable quarter. For some time, however, it continued dead against us, and the repeated tacking enabled us to obtain different views of the peaceful isle, so near and yet so far, with the land sloping up from the sea to some 6000 feet, and patches of cultivation appearing here and there amid the thick woods.

With all the selfishness of youth, I fervently hoped to remain weather-bound in such a paradise for an indefinite period; but my hopes were literally blown away by the wind itself, which "chopped" round, and Madeira faded from view.

The beautiful is said to be a joy only as long as it lasts; but my recollections of this island on which nature has been so lavish have outlived so evanescent a period, and I have often dreamt of it in later days. Had it only fallen in with the eternal fitness of things to have made it a part of the outlying British Empire, English capital and enterprise would have developed its resources, seconding the efforts of Nature's prodigality, instead of counteracting them. We may possibly have already acquired more than our share in all *five* quarters of the globe without casting longing eyes on Naboth's vineyard; our possessions may reasonably excite the jealousy of other powers, but no one can deny that we are specially adapted, both physically and mentally, for colonization far above any other nation; and that Madeira would have shone with especial brilliancy in the British Crown is a foregone conclusion.

On my first return voyage, years after, we landed at St. Helena, which, interesting as it is from its historical associations, cannot in my opinion compare with Madeira in natural beauty.

Among the least pleasant experiences of the whole voyage was the ordeal of being becalmed near the line, where an oily sea sent back the glare of perpendicular rays: several days of this sort of thing proved too much for the tempers of the passengers, without evoking very choice selections from the copious vocabulary of the crew.

Ths cuddy table was patronized in stately silence, and at any time, indeed, conversation became as spasmodic and laconic as the merest courtesy would allow. We of the civilized persuasion have somehow drifted into the notion that it is imperative on us to talk at all times and seasons, so that few tongues ever rest from morning to night, when the timely interference of Providence paralyzes for a time our power of speech.

Being becalmed in such a spot has its ludicrous as well as its painful side; and few could help feeling amused at the sight of the ship's bows pointing at different times to every direction of the compass, as the under-currents made us drift where we would not, intensifying our utter helplessness.

Then, too, the captain would come on deck, look around and aloft, whistle, and betake himself once more to the sacred precincts of his cabin. The officer on watch would imitate his chief with pious precision, especially the whistle, in which he had the faith peculiar to sailors in need of a favourable wind. But the son of Astræas remained in obdurate seclusion in his Thracian cave, and passengers and crew rose to the verge of desperation.

One early hour out of the twenty-four contained, indeed, some element of enjoyment, and that was when the decks were undergoing the beneficial process of "holy-stoning," which consisted in rubbing them from stem to stern with a species of pumice and a plentiful supply of sea water. Then it was that the early bird could get a most enjoyable bath, not in the sea, indeed, which was infested with sharks, but on deck under the full play of a hose.

The bath was customarily followed by a cup of tea, extracted by bribery and corruption from the cook; and then we generally paced the deck barefoot and with just a suspicion of clothing, until the *levée* of El Señor Sol, whom, from his nasty habit of insinuating himself under the brim of one's hat, I have always found most trying at daybreak. The bath, the cup of tea, and an anteprandial pipe were not the only advantages of early rising, as one also escaped thereby the extremely trying noise of "holy-stoning" directly over one's cabin.

No Hindoo, Mohammedan, or Buddhist ever went

through his religious ceremonies with such unerring regularity and unshaken faith as inspired the sailors in their "holy-stoning," in which process they seemed to take especial delight, so that it almost amounted to fetichism; and the face of the chief mate, who usually presided at this daily celebration, would assume an angelic expression that apparently stimulated the men to further efforts.

Unquestionably great as are the benefits conferred by the modern appliances and improvements in the art of shipbuilding, in one respect at least the old Indiaman had the whip-hand of its successor, and that was a roomy cabin, a bed- and sitting-room combined, amply, if not elegantly, furnished. Contrasted with the berth —or "pigging"—system of modern ships, this was a prodigious advantage, compensating to a great extent for the length of the voyage. Being caged up with several utter strangers, passing, for example, through the Red Sea, and in a state of insufferable heat, is an ordeal that one is not likely to forget; having to climb at nights into an upper shelf, and, if one is fortunate enough to sleep through the night without being pitched out, putting one's bare foot on the bald head of the gentleman below, who also wanted to get up at the same moment—these are instances of the luxury of modern travel of which one hears so much. And we bear it all with a patient shrug worthy of Shylock!

Another digression! But how can one help philosophizing on board ship?

Whether from whistling or more natural causes, the wind at last sprang up, and there was a visible accession of spirits to the cuddy table—animal-spirits, I mean; for the health of the breeze was drunk by one and all in sparkling champagne.

"Holy-stoning," too, proceeded on the following morning with unexampled vigour, and the chief mate's face positively beamed.

And now we crossed the line. The elaborate and rather cruel ceremonies with which a previous generation used to celebrate the "crossing" were by this time considerably modified; though even now it was made an opportunity for levying blackmail and inflicting personal discomfiture on such as were in little favour with the rest. We do not know for certain whether nectar was intoxicating—though we should shrewdly suspect such to be the case, considering the unaccountable behaviour of some of the gods in Olympus—but it is certain that Neptune, who shortly arrived on board, was not superior to a mundane predilection for Jamaica rum, an extra allowance of which was meted out to all; so that he probably fell asleep in his chariot, leaving his horses to find the way home by themselves.

Homeward-bound vessels were rarely visited by the sea-god, from whose unwelcome attentions one was exempted by having once crossed the line.

The next diversion on board was created by the capture of a large shark that had been hovering in our wake for several days, and suspected of having purloined more than one joint of sailors' pork, suspended from the bowsprit to wash out superfluous salt. At last he was caught in the act and duly reported; a deputation waited on the chief mate, and, averse as captains are as a rule to the mess that such a capture makes on the "holy-stoned" deck, the dire decree went forth for his punishment. This involved the sacrifice of yet another leg of pork, and in a few moments he was on deck, his spine being at once severed at its caudal extremity with a blow from an axe.

The shark, though in reality but little out of harmony with the law of Nature, which is "one with rapine," has acquired with all nations, civilized and barbarian, a reputation even worse than that enjoyed by its terrestrial prototype—the tiger. It would be superfluous on my part to describe the arrangement of his fins, or the size and number of his serrated, lancet-shaped teeth; for do they not nowadays teach Natural History even in Board schools!

Still more remarkable than anything about the shark itself is the presence of the two pilot-fish that almost invariably flank its head on either side. These interesting creatures instantly swim towards anything that is thrown on the water, swim round it, and then return to their patron; if it be a bottle, or any other inedible object, all three then remain aloof, but if fit to eat, the shark immediately makes for it.

When he is captured, indeed, they will swim for days on either side of the rudder, with the fidelity of dogs; and on one occasion I managed, after several hours' hard work, to entrap them both in a bucket. Belonging, as they do, to the Scomberidæ, they bear in shape a pronounced resemblance to the mackerel; the average length is one foot, and the body, which is of a silvery gray, is marked with five transverse dark bands; while the dorsal fin, when erect, reminds one forcibly of the perch, but the family to which they belong, and which includes the albacore, bonito, and mackerel, has no representative in fresh water.

Fried steaks cut from the tail-end of the defunct shark were served that day at the Junior Officers' Mess, of which I was elected an honorary member; and I must say that the dish was palatable in spite of the associations that clung to the monster. The sailors of those days had a firm conviction that the appearance of a shark forecasted a death on board. A lady occupying a cabin next to mine was rapidly nearing her end from the ravages of consumption, and I never looked out upon the warm, still sea without perceiving a huge shark swimming leisurely round the ship as it crept slowly on. It was, of course, the merest coincidence, and a word of encouragement from the captain would have again placed shark-steaks on the *ménu;* I was so impressed, however, with the hideous idea, that only the presence of several invalids on board and the consequent necessity for avoiding all unnecessary disturbance, prevented me from putting a rifle-bullet into him as he neared the surface.

At last the unfortunate lady succumbed, and the shark immediately dived after the coffin, which was, however, extra-heavily weighted at one end and pierced with numerous holes; whether he accomplished his nefarious purpose after the coffin rested amongst seaweeds, strange crustaceans, and nautili, who shall say? Anyhow, we saw no more of him.

Traversing the ocean in a modern steamer would give one the idea that it is but scantily inhabited; the churning of the screw is heard some way ahead, and all the fish are scared away to the depths, so that an occasional school of porpoises, too eager in the pursuit of flying-fish, is about the only sight worth recording, and then it only lasts a few moments, while the affrighted creatures tumble headlong over one another in their frantic endeavours to escape. Of a sailing vessel, however, they take but little notice, gambolling around in the most leisurely manner. They are gregarious, not unlike the dolphin, but with a less elongated snout, well armed with teeth adapted for seizing the small fish that form their staple article of food.

Another fish partial to the wake of a sailing-ship, on account of the amount of animal refuse which is thrown overboard, is the bonito, closely allied to the tunny, though smaller and more graceful. The average length is between two and three feet, and it is, for its size, the strongest fish I ever met with. Like the mackerel, its congener, it is most beautiful directly after its removal from the water; its back is steely-blue, which grows lighter at the sides and eventually shades off into silver under the belly, along which run several horizontal lines of darker hue. The sailors harpoon it for sport rather than for the sake of its flesh, which is coarse and somewhat rank. When the ship is only creeping along with but little wind, it is possible to take bonito on a spinning bait; but very strong tackle is requisite for bringing it on board. I have seen a successful (?) handliner, who hooked a large bonito while fishing from a small boat, towed in every direction for a considerably exciting time before he could come to closer quarters with his capture.

On one occasion I enjoyed some excellent mackerel-fishing off St. Helena, catching enough to fill two ship's buckets in a very short time and with no other bait than a few shreds of red rag. Suddenly the biting ceased, and as the water was beautifully clear, one could plainly discern the approach of a dim figure, large and powerfully built—in fact, a bonito—which just sniffed at the hooks and passed on majestically, after which the terrified mackerel returned—to the buckets!

This novel sport was very enjoyable, lasting until I was called away to conduct a party over the island and make a few purchases. The scenery was certainly lovely, and the various spots connected with the brief imprisonment of Napolean Buonaparte excited the interest of the entire party; yet I must confess that I should not care about it as a place of residence for any length of time: it is not to be compared with Madeira in any one particular.

The albacore, another of the Scomberidæ, is also frequently caught or harpooned; it is a much thicker and deeper fish than the last-named, sometimes attaining to an enormous size. Its flesh, too, is in much higher repute, and was equally appreciated by the nations of antiquity who dwelt upon the shores of the Mediterranean, in which sea it thrives along with its near relative the tunny. The dorsal fin, which is situated rather far back, graduates somewhat abruptly, vanishing into a number of small finlets up to its unusually crescentic tail with the same arrangement of finlets underneath.

Very interesting to the voyager are the performances of those creatures called flying-fish, which probably cause more amusement to passengers round the Cape than any other members of the finny tribe.

The apparatus by which they are on special occasions propelled for a short time through the air is nothing but an unusual development of the pectoral fins; but it is at least extremely doubtful whether they employ these exactly as a bird uses its wings. I have many a time observed them most carefully, but have always failed to detect any flapping motion: the fins were merely extended, and I noticed that in the direction of the wind they could move through the air for some distance, when they would fall back abruptly into their own element, as if their muscular energy was suddenly expended; while any attempt to proceed against the wind invariably resulted in failure. I am, therefore, of opinion that as they emerge from the water with considerable " way " on, the pectorals fully expanded, the wind drives them as long as the latter keep moist; so that the whole proceeding is a *vis a tergo* rather than a flight, though it is doubtless extremely useful in escaping from their greedy enemies, much as small fry will often take to the air when pursued by a large jack.

For the most part, they only rise a short distance from the water, though often sufficiently high to fall upon the deck. Illustrations of the flying-fish generally depict it as if about to mount up in the air and ascend to the altitude patronized by larks, where, in company with its fellows, it flits to and fro across the disc of the sun like a swift. I like these illustrations; they show a considerable power of imagination and not a little impudence: unfortunately, however, the flying-fish is not quite so amphibious. One variety—the *Exocœtus volitans*—has now and again been found in British waters, having presumably lost its way; or perhaps, after all, the afore-mentioned illustrations are based on fact, and the creatures have indeed flown overland from the Mediterranean, where they abound along with the flying-gurnards and similar species.

Occasionally, in the warmer latitudes, the ship would be surrounded by a fleet of argonauts, or paper-nautili, which, if one excepts the fairer portion of the passengers, are quite the prettiest creatures to be seen during a voyage. The creature can easily quit the shell, which resembles in shape that of the true nautilus, not being attached to it as is the case with the majority of molluscs. Beautiful as the creature unquestionably is, yet it reminds one of the hideous octopus, in that both are provided with a number of tentacles, two of which, dilated to a circular membraneous expansion and raised above the water, bear a decided resemblance to sails, while the others, which move under water, suggest the action of oars. Hence arose the idea, which, still prevalent at the time of which I am writing, has only been combated comparatively recently, that they actually sailed and rowed about.

The membranes, when unfurled, as it were, in the rays of the sun, certainly display a variety of delicate colours, that the famous " Judson " himself might envy but could never imitate ; but they are only seen to perfection on a calm sea ; the least disturbance sends them precipitately into the inmost recesses of their shells, when they instantly sink to the depths, presumably by some specially devised apparatus, that enables them to exhaust the air, since they cannot contract the volume of their habitat. Perhaps the same arrangement permits of their generating some kind of gas when they feel inclined to go to the surface for a sail and a " look round."

Sailors not infrequently confuse them with the so-called " Portuguese man-o'-war," which is, however, a much lower and headless organization, living by suction, and bearing but slight resemblance to the delicate and many-coloured argonaut. This name will doubtless recall to the reader's mind that fabulous band of Greek heroes who, under the leadership of Jason—not the aforesaid Judson !—sailed forth to Colchis for the lofty purpose of hoodwinking the sleepless dragon and stealing the ram's Golden Fleece.

At the time when the Exhibition of 1851 gave such an impetus to Science and Art, the " argonaut," " Portuguese man-o'-war," " Paper "-, and True-Nautilus were very much confused in the minds of men generally, and of sailors in particular. The shell of the last named was sent from the East, and its nacred interior excited the admiration of all. In lieu of the discs common to the cephalopods, it is provided with calcareous mandibles with which it crushes the numerous small crustaceans, on which it feeds as greedily as the octopus of the Mediterranean and Southern Seas, or the "squid" that plays such havoc in the Channel trawl-nets.

The only other sight worth recording was the occasional blowing of a whale, that curious marine mammal, whose incongruities have puzzled even eminent biologists. There are many interesting questions in the life-history of the whale of which we are in almost total ignorance; such are, for example, its average age, which conjecture has extended to centuries, and the period of gestation before it launches its baby on the troubled waters—think of it, a "baby" whale of some ten or twelve feet in length! But what has always appeared to me the most interesting point in the whale is the extraordinary disproportion of its tiny throat—a throat not two inches in diameter, so that an ordinary herring would choke the largest whale. It behoves us, however, in all justice to the most remarkable book that has ever appeared as the universal delight of castle and cottage, to disregard the emphasis with which its scientific detractors are wont to decry some of its more remarkable assertions, and to exculpate it, at least in this case—I refer, of course, to the famous history of the rebellious prophet—where it makes no mention of the exact species to which the "great fish" belonged; the whale having been associated with the story in later days by romancers whose intellect is scarcely less remarkable than that of a somewhat puerile clergyman, whom I once heard endeavour to prove that the "great fish" was simply a common alligator, which is about as abundant in the Mediterranean as the whale itself!

In excessively warm latitudes, where certain winds are contending for the mastery, waterspouts are not uncommon, and are, of course, dreaded in proportion to their proximity to the ship. They are analogous to the whirlwind on land, the ascending column in the latter being charged with particles of dust, instead of, as at sea, with condensing vapour.

In either case, distance lends enchantment!

Such, then, were a few of the sights and speculations afforded, in the days when journeys were calculated by months, by the great world without, as a means of beguiling the time when wind and weather permitted one to stay on deck.

Scarcely less remarkable were the diversions of the little world within; the shifts to which we were put in our unflagging endeavours to relieve the monotony of "life below stairs;" but I must leave these to another chapter, in which I hope to reach the end of my voyage.

CHAPTER II.

STILL UNDER CANVAS.

"O'er the glad waters of the dark blue sea,
  Our thoughts as boundless, and our souls as free,
  Far as the breeze can bear, the billows foam,
  Survey our empire, and behold our home!"
                                    BYRON, *Corsair.*

SOME portion of the time, however, was necessarily spent below. Dancing was the favourite pursuit with the majority, but was only practicable when the wind was light and the sea calm.

Although Terpsichore was my least beloved of the Nine, one had but little choice when the promenade deck was cleared, and the pale light of the moon supplemented by all the lanterns that could be spared.

Music, too, furnished a deal of enjoyment, both to those who could perform themselves and to the majority who could only appreciate the performances of others.

A large stern cabin, almost the only one unoccupied by passengers, was turned into a saloon, where singing could be indulged in without fear of disturbing others. The custodian of this sanctum was the captain's wife, herself a well-trained musician; and she only issued invitations on the strict stipulation that there was to be no flirting. And I think, indeed, that the few flirtations were strictly of the Platonic order; and that most of the young ladies were led to the Hymeneal alter within a few weeks of their landing, not—be it observed—by any of their shipmates, but by older residents in the country; some may have succumbed in the "City of Palaces," but the majority were probably in request farther up country.

Yes, India was a famous place for matrimony in those days. The supply almost equalled the demand: the arrival of an Indiaman sent a thrill of excitement through many a manly breast; and much manœuvring was resorted to in order to see the young ladies land.

But the whirligig of time and the agency of steam have considerably modified the Furlough Rules; and men come to England to marry the women, instead of the women going to India to marry the men.

Without meaning to be hypercritical, one is tempted to wish that Indiamen were freighted as of yore!

The efforts of those who most did congregate in the music-room soon led to a concert, which was an undeniable success. The great feature of the evening was an Ethiopian entertainment, preceded by a prologue given by Bones and Banjo, part of which still lives in my memory, especially a borrowed epigram, levelled at a certain individual who laboured under the delusion that he was no mean vocalist:

> "Swans sing before they die: 'twere no bad thing
> Should certain persons die before they sing."

A higher flight in the intellectual domain was now attempted in the shape of a weekly paper, over which a man of erudition, one at least who had successfully climbed the rungs of a University career, was soon persuaded to preside, while his wife undertook to provide a manugraph.

Contributions, signed only with a *nom-de-guerre*, had to be placed in a box affixed to the mainmast, of which the editor had the key; and, from the conspicuous absences, it soon became evident that many were deep in the agonies of composition.

But even this flower of promise was nipped in the bud; and the captain showed his experience of the ways of passengers when he prognosticated that it would share the fate of any other nine days' wonder.

Before its extinction, however, this unhappy organ fanned into a flame the smouldering embers of cliqueism, which had originated with dancing.

Except during the prevalence of the trade-winds, our "runs" varied very considerably. These particular winds, however, brought contentment to all; they are uniformly cool and steady by day and night; every stitch of canvas is set, and the ship heels over to a certain angle and there remains for days together, so steady, indeed, that on a specially inclined table one could with comfort indulge in billiards.

The officers and crew have a comparatively easy time of it as long as these winds last, being exempt from all necessity of furling, reefing, or bracing of yards—while the enjoyment extends even to the dumb portion of the "live stock," the cows in the long-boat, the sheep in their pens, and the poultry—everywhere.

To the uninitiated it appeared strange that we should, when outward bound, have to proceed so far south in order to round the Cape, while on the homeward journey we could hug it so closely as to see the low-lying coast; but the phenomenon was easily to be accounted for by the prevalence of certain winds and oceanic currents.

The history of the art of navigation, from the mariner's compass of the fifteenth century, when Columbus discovered its variations, down to the perfect instruments of the present day, has always seemed to me highly interesting. Even in the sailing days the captains practised it with wonderful accuracy. Far out in mid-ocean, we were bearing right on an island laid down in the chart, and I asked the captain whether he intended altering the ship's course. "Not at all," he replied; "we shall sail right over it." We did so. An early navigator probably saw a dead whale there, which he duly entered on the chart. And unquestionably as logarithms and modern instruments have simplified matters, it is even now not quite so easy as it appears.

We had now entered colder latitudes, where we were glad to put away the easy-chairs and fold up the awning, and in lieu thereof pace the decks in a vigorous manner enveloped in warm clothing. But we were not unprepared for the change, which came on gradually; and, even in its extremes, did not approach that which was once experienced by a Bishop of Newfoundland, who had to visit a small island in his diocese that lay right in the Gulf Stream. He left his main charge, so he told me, enveloped in furs, but the moment his steam yacht crossed the line of demarcation—perceptible by the change of colour in the water—he had to exchange them for the thinnest garments he could muster. The exact readings of the thermometer plunged in on either side the line, as he told them to me, I no longer remember; but I do recollect being struck by the great difference—so great, indeed, that, had the information not come from such a source, I should have been incredulous. Great as are the irregularities in the weather that one experiences during a sea voyage, they vanish when compared with the caprices of the true British climate. And yet we take a kind of gloomy national pride in it;

and I have known homeward-bound Englishmen quite looking forward to a "Channel fog" from the moment they left Bombay. A juster appreciation of its merits is shown by our Yankee cousins, one of whom said of our atmosphere: "No climate, not even weather; nothing but samples"; while another is responsible for the following excellent parody of a well-known rhyme :

"Dirty days hath September, April, June, and November;
From January to May, the rain it raineth every day;
From May until July, there's not a dry cloud in the sky;
All the rest have thirty-one, without a blessed ray of sun;
And if their days were two and thirty, they'd be just as wet and quite as dirty."

The evenings were now long, and our share of daylight was curtailed, so that a still greater proportion of our time was spent below in conversation, cards, chess, &c.

Our habits with regard to "turning-in" were somewhat primitive; all lights had to be out by 10 p.m., and a responsible officer went the rounds to see that the dictum was scrupulously carried out.

The very thought of "fire" on a wooden ship well saturated with tar, and far away in mid-ocean, was enough to make one's blood run cold; and so it is not to be wondered at that the captain showed his teeth on one occasion, when one of the passengers was reported for infringing this law, and threatened to place him in irons for the rest of the voyage. Need I say that the offender gave no further cause for complaint?

We may be thankful that nowadays the chances of a fire breaking out on board ship are, thanks to the electric light and the less combustible materials of which our ships are built, reduced to a minimum.

The ladies were invariably the first to retire, though

they probably continued prattling until long after we were in bed and asleep; a habit which, as Dundreary said, "No fellow could understand." Precept and example have been tried in vain: for as it was in the beginning, &c., &c.

After we had been at sea for some time without seeing a living thing other than fish, the air suddenly became alive with Cape pigeons and albatrosses; and I managed to capture one of the latter on a stout hook baited with a piece of pork. After a little hesitation, he pounced upon the prize, and, raising his beak, swallowed it at a gulp.

I was fully prepared for his taking flight, and, indeed, had he got my line foul of the rigging, I should soon have been in difficulties. But, discarding such a course, he planted his webbed feet firmly before him, offering thereby such resistance to the water that it was no easy matter to get him alongside. At last, after I had received timely assistance from a passing sailor, the bird stood on deck, and was at once violently sick, vomiting great quantities of a clear, oily liquid. I have since learnt that all sea-birds are sick on board ship, and quite unable to use their wings.

According to my invariable practice of despatching my victims as quickly as possible, I killed this one immediately—one might almost add painlessly—with a small dose of prussic acid. He turned out to be a very plump bird, measuring fifteen feet from tip to tip of his outspread wings. By an unfortunate misunderstanding on the part of one of the sailors, my capture was thrown overboard before I had set up the skeleton; the only use that was made of it being the employment of a few of the feathers to show the direction of the wind, or, as one of our passengers with a poetical turn of mind put it:

"Oh! bid them beware of ships that go from London to the Indies,
Else they'll be caught, and their feathers plucked to show which
way the wind is."

By far the most graceful of the many other species of sea-birds that were continually hovering about the ship were the stormy petrel, or, as the superstitious sailors call them, "Mother Carey's Chickens." Their wonderfully rapid flight, now in the hollow between two waves, anon on the foaming crest of another, really looks more like walking on the water; and I understand that petrel is only a corruption of Peter. Among the sailors they have a bad reputation, and are regarded as birds of ill omen, a superstition which, on the principle of "give a dog a bad name," &c., has clung to them, but which is in reality quite undeserved. Ignorance and tradition have, in fact, placed the cart before the horse: the stormy petrel follows storms, but cannot possibly foretell them.

By a modification of my albatross line, I managed to capture several of them; a proceeding, however, which had to be conducted with great secrecy; as, had the sailors got wind of it, and a storm followed by coincidence, I should probably have figured as the hero in a repetition of Jonah's history—minus the "great fish"; and I am by no means sure whether even that important detail would have been wanting.

About this time we fell in with an emigrant ship; signals were exchanged under Marriott's Code, and it was intimated that the presence of our captain was wanted on board. Both ships accordingly hove to; and in a weak moment of impulse I sought permission to occupy a place in the captain's gig. The request was readily acceded to, and, if confession be at all desirable, I am quite prepared to confess to a slight degree of nervousness, as the small craft rose and fell in the most frolicsome manner, as if indeed she were glad to feel herself once more in the water. All sorts of horrible fancies coursed through my mind : what if the wind suddenly shifted, causing those flapping sails to belly out and carry both the ships farther away! We were hundreds of miles from land, and we had not so much as a biscuit or a drop of fresh water in the gig. Then I reviewed mentally all the terrible stages—casting lots, glaring at each other, &c., &c., and—we were alongside. The captain disappeared below, but I of course stayed on deck talking to the emigrants. How brave and sanguine they were ; how little they seemed to heed the dreary prospect of a far-off country full of privations, where all would be up-hill work for many a long year. They saw Hope pointing to the bright to-morrow, to fields ripe with golden corn, the fruit of their labour, and homesteads made glad with the merry laughter of children. I wonder how many realized the vision ! They crowded on deck, and their "Cheer, boys, cheer," gradually waxed fainter and fainter as we neared our own ship.

When standing once more amongst my fellow-passengers, who plied me with all manner of questions, my thoughts reverted to those brave emigrants, and I dwelt with almost selfish complacency on the great difference between their prospects and our own.

Most of us were going out in the employ of a Company that reputedly paid its servants handsomely, and treated them kindly ; we were to be enrolled as units in an administration never equalled in the world's history : where all grades performed their duty *con amore*, and where officers were happy and contented, knit together by ties of brotherhood.

I will not sigh for the old order of things : it would

be unseemly in one who has served under the new ; but one cannot help remarking that it was the Mutiny which swept away the old peaceful era, substituting one of an opposite nature both in the European and the native elements. The Company gauged and respected the prejudices of the community over which it ruled ; and, if it was not exactly loved, it was at least respected.

Now, however, Western ideas and Western methods of thought have, in spite of protest, been forced upon the aborigines. Up to the end of 1858-9 their respect for us was as sincere as could be expected from the people of a conquered country ; but since that time the gulf has gradually widened, till, if another Mutiny were to break out, the whole of the population would be against us, instead of, as on the former occasion, for us. Under the cloak of giving them a *quid pro quo* for all the incalculable benefits which they have, however involuntarily, bestowed upon us, we continually force ourselves into places which they hold most sacred, and add insult to injury by endeavouring to propitiate them with dolls and other refuse of our fancy bazaars !

As to the Mutiny, the exciting cause was undoubtedly the manner in which home influence and interference undermined the discipline of the army : the annexation of Oude and the episode of the greased cartridges were but handles to lay hold of. But of this more anon.

One evening a circumstance occurred which for the moment aroused the monster envy, that had, for a time at least, slumbered peacefully, and overthrew all our confidence in our captain and our pride in our vessel. A bright light was reported astern, which rapidly loomed larger and larger, bearing down upon us with most astounding speed. Some thought it must be a pirate, and propounded ingenious and reassuring questions as to the latest fashion in "walking the plank."

Presently, two more lights were reported just above the horizon, which gained upon us equally rapidly, and then it dawned upon the mind of one of the passengers that the Cape route was to be essayed with a large steamer, of which the first was the pioneer.

She came, she saw, she conquered; and we, who had hitherto regarded our ship as a veritable hare, now discovered, to our intense chagrin, that she was but a tortoise after all.

Added to this discomfiture, we had to listen to such banter as: "Can we do anything for you in Calcutta, besides telling them that you're coming some day?"

Her lights soon vanished far ahead! Was it a phantom vessel, the creature of a distempered brain?

For some time we maintained a significant silence round the cuddy; after which, thanks to the genial influence of the *old* system of provisioning, tongues were loosened and opinions freely expressed.

For my own part, I was in no hurry for the voyage to draw to a close; not only did the dangers of being at sea appear to me no greater than those with which we are beset on land, but I looked upon it as a respite from the pestilence that was ever strutting about the land for which we were bound.

What if the steamer did arrive many days before us; would it make any practical difference in the life ahead? Others, I regret to say, thought differently; they fretted and fumed; vilified sailing vessels in general, ours in particular, and made themselves generally miserable, frowning whenever their eye fell on the unoffending sails, and sneering at the "run," which, seeing that it kept a steady ten or twelve miles an hour, was hardly to be grumbled at.

Man is a strange creature, and he exhibits himself under a variety of phases; but nowhere, perhaps, so remarkably as during a long sea-voyage.

We had now reached our southernmost point, and were steering in a north-easterly course.

The only break in the monotony of this part of the voyage was made by our passing the extremities of these deserted volcanic islets, St. Paul's and Amsterdam, of which I attempted a sketch, which occasioned no little amusement.

These dreary oases of fused rock are said to contain two springs in juxtaposition, one of boiling and the other of cold water. These might, as I reflected, afford invaluable assistance to a shipwrecked mariner, who could possibly boil a fish or a stray gull's egg in the former, while the latter would supply the means of performing his ablutions and quenching his thirst. The only geographical interest attaching to these spots is that they are equidistant from the Cape of Good Hope, Ceylon, and Tasmania.

Meanwhile the ship was rapidly approaching her destination; the days of the voyage were already numbered, and it was resolved to give a grand fancy dress ball on the first evening that we should spend at anchor in the river. From the difference in the colour of the water, it soon became apparent that the remainder of the voyage might be counted by hours; the Gangetic delta was pouring forth its mud from many gaping mouths; and the water grew more and more uninviting, till we at last passed the Pilot Brig, and anon came in sight of a low-lying, muddy-looking coast, fringed with cocoanut trees. In an hour or so we were in the

Hooghly; and I cannot say that either the river or its banks impressed me very favourably.

We were now in the month of December, which, being the coolest season of the year, is the favourite time of arrival for all sorts and conditions of ships; and it was probably in consequence of this that no steam tug was at first available to tow us the remaining hundred miles. Very reluctantly, therefore, we had to let go the anchor only a short distance from the mouth of the river.

That night we were to have enjoyed the fancy dress ball for which so much preparation had been made, when an untoward accident put an end to all our merriment. A young middy, a promising lad and a great favourite on board, fell from the mizen-top—

> "To die! to sleep:
> To sleep! perchance to dream."

Such is fate! William III, whose diseased and emaciated form had survived the thickest of a dozen frays, dies through his horse stumbling on a mole-hill in his own park; a great African explorer is killed by the accidental explosion of his own gun; so, too, our poor little middy, after having many a time helped furl a sail in mid-ocean, with the billows raging in their fury, and the lightning playing about the yards, must needs fall here, with the vessel riding at anchor in a very duck-pond! He was probably a victim to sunstroke. Never shall I forget the thud that brought me up from below, caused by his head being shattered against the deck. One of the ship's boats conveyed his remains to a small European cemetery not far from the shore, where others of his countrymen had preceded him—a lonely spot, around which the jackal yelled and the tiger prowled.

As the tug could not be with us till the following day, I seized the opportunity of going ashore in one of the native craft with which European ships are invariably beset on entering an Eastern river.

I proceeded on foot through a small village, very clean and regularly built, composed of well-thatched, one-storied houses. Something—I suppose it was the manner in which the men were lolling about and smoking, while the women did all the work—reminded me of small villages that I had seen in Ireland.

But what first attracted my attention was the ubiquitous sparrow, just as impudent and pugnacious-looking as ever. I now came to a tract of dried-up rice-fields, as hard as brick-bats, where the trees were few and far between, and were for the most part alive with parroquets of gorgeous plumage, chattering and jabbering, as if, forsooth, they had to settle the affairs of the whole country. I therefore varied the monotony of the walk by shooting an occasional bird, which, however, proved quite useless for culinary purposes. As it grew late in the day, I turned back towards the shore; and it appeared to me a favourable opportunity for returning the kindness of the junior officers, at whose hospitable mess I had discussed many a leathery piece of salt pork and weevil-eaten biscuit, washed down with rum and water. By means of a great deal of gesticulating—for I knew not a word of the language—I became the proud possessor of a goodly store of live fowls, eggs, and plantains, for what I afterwards discovered to be about three times the correct price. I was received with thanks on board, and, from my doubtless grotesque appearance, armed with a gun and umbrella, and surrounded by my provisions, was forthwith dubbed "Robinson Crusoe."

While anchored in the lower reaches of the river, we experienced a slight foretaste of some of the pleasures that awaited us in the land we were about to reside in ; our night's rest was ever and anon disturbed by the weird and startling cry of a jackal ; and the dermic irritation caused by mosquito-bites was a source of great pain to novices.

At last the tug arrived, and we once more got under weigh, rapidly bridging over the remaining part of the voyage, and perhaps, too, the most dangerous, on account of the St. James and Mary shoals, and many others almost equally hazardous. But these were passed in safety ; the river became narrower and narrower—crowded, too, with all manner of small craft freighted *en route* to market. The whole scene was certainly striking, rendered, indeed, still more picturesque by the setting sun ; so that, as we passed up that suburb of Calcutta so appropriately called "Garden Reach," the entire bank was bathed in a flood of light, while our ears were assailed by the chants of natives pulling at their oars—chants not devoid of a weird kind of beauty. Not far above this we dropped anchor, and the ship swung round with the tide. All was bustle and excitement ; and with a shake of the hand, and a hurried "Good-bye ; mind you call on us soon," &c., &c., the passengers dropped one by one over the side ; and in this wise the voyage of those days came to an end.

CHAPTER III.

THE CITY OF PALACES.

"Experience keeps a dear school, but fools will learn in no other."
FRANKLIN.

FOR my own part I remained on board till the deck had assumed a less chaotic appearance, when I resolved to migrate temporarily to one of the hotels. This, however was not to be; for an old friend, anticipating my resolve, and bent on frustrating it, suddenly appeared on board with the welcome information that he had hired a room for me at his quarters. Nothing loth, I bundled my traps into the boat, and prepared to accompany my friend, bidding *au revoir* to the officers with no little regret; they had throughout the voyage treated me with the utmost courtesy, and I had almost grown to look upon the old ship as my home. Nor was the City of Palaces just then calculated to impress a new arrival very favourably, or to raise his spirit-barometer. Darkness was coming on apace, as it always does in the East, and the dim, weird light afforded by the few oil lamps scattered about was considerably obscured by the dense mist that was rising from a large open space, through which we drove in my friend's "buggy." This sombre picture was completed by the dusky figures that flitted hither and thither; and, taken altogether, I found it gruesome and depressing.

The house in which my friend resided was a boarding-establishment (with *table d'hôte*), very convenient for temporary sojourners of the male persuasion; we sat up till a very late, or rather, early hour, as there was much to chat about; and eventually my friend consigned me to the care of his own special valet, with the most detailed instructions—for I knew not a word of the language—and wished me "Good night." With sundry misgivings, I followed my swarthy attendant, who glided noiselessly in front of me. The room that had been assigned to my use was evidently very spacious—one can tell somehow when one is in a large room, even in total darkness—but as it was only very dimly illuminated by a small wick steeped in oil, I was unable to ascertain its exact dimensions until the next morning. I remember that it also struck me as chilly and damp, and I wished myself back in the cosy cabin in which I had enjoyed many an uninterrupted night's rest for the last four months. In the middle of the apartment I discerned a bed, surmounted by an enclosure of netting; on one side was a strip of carpet, and close at hand stood a chair. Now, my friend had particularly impressed on me that the mosquitoes were just now very strong on the wing, and as hungry as hunters; also that on the manner in which I got under the netting depended all my chances of sleep. He further instructed me to sign to the "bearer" when I was ready, who would, he said, just raise the edge of the curtain, when I must jump in. The eventful moment arrived: I signed to the "bearer," and pointed to the bed, whereupon he commenced beating the air around with a kind of switch, and lifted a corner of the net.

By this time I began to realize in the whole proceeding a pleasurable element of excitement, and as he raised the net, I darted in. Alas! it was but to fall out the other side. I felt myself going, and as a drowning man will clutch at a straw, I held on to the bedclothes, dragging them along with me, curtains and all. When I had at length got clear, there was the " bearer" staring at me as if I were a wild beast or a lunatic ; then he fled—returning shortly afterwards with another set of curtains, after which he once more made the bed. This *entrée* was successfully accomplished ; but my troubles did not end here. The fact was, I felt uncommonly cold ; suddenly a happy thought occurred to me, and stealthily thrusting out an arm from under the curtains, I dragged in my clothes and the strip of carpet. I slept soundly, but woke betimes—as who, indeed, even of the Seven Sleepers, would not have ?—for of all the discordant uproars I had ever heard, the *réveille* of the feathered tribe—crows, minahs, and other villains—certainly stood first.

Shortly afterwards the "bearer" entered, noiseless as a tiger, and proceeded to open the shutters and admit the morning light. He next advanced to my couch with the evident intention of rousing me, but seeing the additions that I had made in my bed-clothing, stopped short. I pretended to be asleep, but watched him carefully. The poor fellow opened his eyes to their widest, looked round the room, thought for a moment, and then fled as before ; returning this time in the company of my friend, who glanced at the bed, and immediately roared with laughter. It was all very funny, no doubt ; but, not being quite able to appreciate the joke, I took refuge in pretended sleep. Later on, at breakfast, I gave a detailed account of what had happened, which my friend supplemented with the "bearer's" version. Poor bearer! In spite of repeated explanations, he avoided me as much as possible, and evidently considered me dangerous. A day or two after I was claimed by a relation, and that domestic at least was greatly relieved by my departure! There is, gentle reader, a right and a wrong way of getting INTO bed as well as OUT OF it, as I found to my cost on more than one occasion; as, for example, the first stormy night at sea, when I made use of my swing-cot.

Ignorance both of the language of the country and of the vast vocabulary of Anglo-Indian expressions was a sad drawback to anything like real enjoyment in those early days; as, besides feeling a bore of the first-water, having to ask so many questions, one felt more or less at every one's mercy.

At my first dinner-party I well recollect a gentleman inviting me to take "simkin" with him; politeness constrained me to accept "with pleasure"—and also with some secret misgivings; and some coagulated stuff was shot into my glass, which, on melting, turned out to be champagne—a word beyond any native's power of pronunciation, and, in consequence, corrupted into "simkin" by natives and Europeans alike.

Another friend begged me to call on him at some house in "Mango Lane." I promised to do so, but, unfortunately suspecting a practical joke, I retaliated by telling him that my abode was "Pine-Apple Alley." Had I only inquired, matters would have turned out otherwise. As it was, the poor fellow drove all over the town in search of a place that did not exist; while I never took the slightest trouble to find out his abode, though it was situated in one of the most important thoroughfares in Calcutta, where merchants most did congregate. Shortly afterwards we met out driving; and after the ensuing explanation, I made the *amende honorable*.

I have already said that Calcutta did not impress me

favourably at first; and after each subsequent visit I disliked the place more and more.

The event of the day, to which all looked forward with great eagerness, was the evening drive up and down a road running parallel with the river; but its duration was of the briefest. As if by magic, the place would suddenly swarm with all sorts of conveyances, from the well-appointed barouche to the modest buggy. The ladies, one and all, looked cadaverous, so much so that I felt quite concerned about them; but was somewhat reassured by my friend's reply to my inquiries: "Oh! no, they are all ill; they all get like that after they have been out here a short time."

As far as I could judge, the aim of each native coachman was to outdrive his fellow Jehu, for we certainly moved at a break-neck pace. Consequently, I seldom saw any of my shipmates there. That rapid transit for a brief hour in an open conveyance, with occasionally an hour's visiting and shopping in a closed one, seemed to me all the outdoor exercise that the ladies had, and this accounted in a great measure for the extreme pallor of their complexions.

In the way of contrasts, I do not think I ever beheld anything so pronounced as the fresh, rosy, and yet bronzed complexions of the new arrivals, and those of the more acclimatized specimens of the gentler sex; yet at the same time, where there prevailed any redundancy of colour and tendency to coarseness, the climate appeared to exercise an ameliorating effect, imparting grace and refinement.

I thought, of course, that every one would be abroad in the early morning, but the Europeans were conspicuous by their absence; and, during the colder months at least, the state of the atmosphere was none too inviting, as a chilly mist invariably hung over the place like a pall, to be dispersed only when the sun was too high to render going forth at all agreeable.

Notwithstanding, I used to make my way through it from one end of the large, open space—the "Maidan"—to the other, returning home with my hair and moustache covered with dewy moisture.

I used on these occasions to meet with one countryman, who, like myself, felt bound to have his morning "constitutional" at any price; and after various stages of recognition we became closely acquainted. I came across him a year ago—nearly forty years after the time of which I write—in Richmond; we were both *walking!*

During the day, with the sun shining upon it, the City of Palaces looked somewhat imposing, especially the business quarters, alive with people of almost every nationality, and the most heterogeneous collection of conveyances, foremost among which was the indigenous "Palkee." It was pleasant to watch—from a distance; in fact, the perfumes of Arabia did not predominate; and, as water-carts were an unknown quantity, the dust and the glare combined to produce headache and thirst, the latter being temporarily quenched by various American drinks, in which, as my head told me, rum predominated.

There was an amazing demand for these drinks; and, without wishing to enlarge on their merits or the reverse, I must say they were honest drinks, compounded of the best materials, and very unlike those that I have tasted under similar names at certain of our Exhibitions.

The most appalling thing about the Calcutta of those days was the nauseating effluvium that arose from all parts of it; this was a smell *sui generis*, noticeable indeed in and around "Chowringhee," the European quarter; still more so in the neighbournood of the best shops; and reaching its climax in the China Bazaar, a den of the most arrant thieves to be met with in any country. I imagine that it was a peculiar distillation of sewage, brought about by the action of a hot sun; and I remarked its peculiar intensity at daybreak, and just after nightfall. On one occasion, I mistook the hour for a funeral, and arrived a great deal too soon at the rendezvous, which was close to that exceedingly filthy river the Hooghly; I was, I remember, well-nigh poisoned—a dissecting-room could hardly come up to it. I had almost said that, on the part of the residents, familiarity with the odour had bred contempt; but that would be falling short of the mark, inasmuch as I believe they had positively learned to like it.

The mention of smells associated with sewers brings to my mind the "bandicoot" rat, one of which, to my considerable discomfiture, I saw making its way across my friend's "compound." It appeared to me quite as large as a leveret, and considerably more formidable, nor was I greatly reassured by the information, "Oh! that's *only* a bandicoot; plenty of them about." The term "bandicoot" is a corruption of the native name *pandikoku*, which signifies pig-rat. It is a clean feeder living on grain and roots, and is said to be as delicate eating as the porcupine. The internecine "war of the rats," waged in our country between the black and the brown, terminated in favour of the former, those useful scavengers that, for the most part, live in our sewers; but in the East—from which they were, like most other nasty things, originally imported—they swarm everywhere, and are most destructive. For the sake of the grain, which my sheep would turn out of their troughs, each in his eagerness to obtain the lion's share, they positively honeycombed my field. Having in vain tried extermination by means of drowning and smoking, I bethought me as a last resource of phosphorescent paste, and by spreading it on pieces of native bread and placing it near their holes, I killed heaps of them, which were buried under my vine with good effect.

I thoughtlessly tried the same experiment in my bungalow; this time, however, instead of coming out to die as they had done in the field, the rats preferred to die in retirement. I consequently had to vacate the house for six weeks, during which time it was thoroughly dismantled and purified. They not unfrequently show fight. On one occasion, going to a cupboard late at night, in search of some supper for a friend and myself, I found everything in the possession of rats. We drove them off for a time, but they returned to the charge, and even came on the table in numbers, literally fighting with us for the mastery. Carving-knives, however, gained the victory, but not until a dozen or so had been disposed of. Fortunately the bandicoot is not aggressive, otherwise not knives but swords would be necessary.

During the first few weeks at Calcutta I had occasion to make a few purchases in the way of light clothing, and boldly dived into that unsavoury locality the China Bazaar. The dealers recognized the novice by their own inherent instinct, and set to work accordingly.

No. 1 informed me that he was an honest man, the only one indeed to be found in the place; would I step inside his shop and see the wares, that were very good and ridiculously cheap; he also very kindly and emphatically warned me against dealing with the man over the way, "one d—— big thief!" No. 2 came up and vituperated No. 1: told me that the articles offered were worthless, but that *his* shop, &c., &c. No. 3 next arrived on the scene, and in a patronizing tone vilified Nos. 1 and 2; they were both thieves, and in league to cheat me. At length, sick at heart, I took refuge in my conveyance and drove home, sending my servant for the articles I required, a thing that I ought to have done at first.

The whole thing was on a par with the mercantile qualifications of a native who once sold a bird to a friend of mine on the Upper Congo, and who, by way of summing up all the warbler's good qualities, exclaimed,—

" Father cock, mother cock, sing from three in the morning till late at night—so help me!"

All Calcutta was wrapt at night time in impenetrable gloom; I occasionally drove to the Barrackpore end of the town, the deserted streets only lit by the faint glimmer of an occasional oil lamp, and the stillness broken now and again by a troop of jackals yelling, and then scampering off, as if pursued by the Prince of Darkness. On such occasions one of the troop is supposed to say— and it certainly sounds remarkably like it—" I smell the body of a dead Hindoo," when the rest join in with, " Whe-re, whe-re, whe-re!" in a very shrill voice.

Of places of amusement, theatres and the like, there seemed absolutely none. I soon discovered too that *everything* in the East was diametrically opposed to our Western notions, and, among other instances, it was customary for new arrivals to call on the residents, instead of *vice versa*, as at home.

I derived much amusement from the spectacle afforded by a ball, where the dancers of both sexes partook for the most part of the " shadowed livery of the burnished sun." White dresses and gay colours contrasted rather strangely on the female form divine, though evening dress was not altogether unbecoming on the males. The women were, on the whole, remarkably good-looking, and displayed faultless figures, as well as being very graceful dancers. They also had an eye to the main chance, and were somewhat less reserved on such matters than is sanctioned by the usages of society elsewhere; and an old chum told me that a coloured beauty, with whom he had danced several times during the evening, without being aware of having held her more tightly than usual, murmured to him, as she was leaving, "Why for you squeeze my chumrah (skin) and not propose me matrimony?"

Bad as Calcutta was from a sanitary point of view, it would have been ten times worse but for the huge army of nature's scavengers that swarmed in the atmosphere, chief among which were the kites and crows. But the most dignified was the *Argala*, or "Adjutant," a wading bird, not unlike the stork, especially in its preference for human society. This species particularly affected the roof of Government House. They are about five feet high, and their head and neck almost destitute of feathers; and the beak is so large as to enable them to seize and swallow a dead cat or bandicoot.

The new arrival in the East has, it will be seen, much to see and learn, and still more to unlearn. He buys his experience at a considerable cost, for, although the sky may change, the mind is too indelibly stamped with old impressions for them to be easily effaced. For some time he is a very helpless being, tossed about in a sea of trouble, and dependent for assistance on those around him.

I most unexpectedly came across kind friends, else I should indeed have felt a fish out of water. They have joined the great majority—peace to their souls!

CHAPTER IV.

ON THE MOVE ONCE MORE.

" Mark ! where his carnage and his conquests cease !
He makes a solitude, and calls it peace ! "

BYRON.

JUST as I was getting more reconciled to the new order of things it was ordained that I should move farther south ; move, too, in light marching order, for the dogs of war were already astir in a land flowing with milk and honey, the inhabitants of which professed that wonderful faith that takes its name from Buddha, about which I shall have more to say anon.

A week's steaming brought us to Rangoon, the then head-quarters of the conquering army, which was located within a stockade several miles in circumference, protected by a deep, broad ditch, then upright massive timbers backed by earthwork eight feet broad. The story of its capture is too well known to bear repetition.

I now found myself confronted with a new phase of Eastern life, and on the whole infinitely preferred it to what I had just quitted: the one was civilization grafted, so to speak, on an alien stock ; the other was to all appearance still the abode of " primeval primitiveness."

There were, of course, many—those especially with wives and children far away—who thought otherwise ; and while some regretted the comforts of civilization, which they never appreciated until they had experienced the want of them, there were others who pined for the soothing influence of female society.

The space enclosed by the stockade was sufficiently large to accommodate all the barracks, besides affording room for short walks and rides. It was also possible to venture a short distance beyond, though the unsettled state of the country rendered it the height of imprudence to travel far; indeed, a friend and myself, who had ridden on one occasion to a native village beyond the vast plantation of Jack-fruit and pine-apples, gathered from the unmistakably hostile proceedings of the inhabitants that discretion was the better part of valour, and urged our ponies somewhat precipitously homeward.

I have called Burmah a land "flowing with milk and honey," in allusion to Nature's prodigality in the animal, vegetable, and, in all probability, mineral kingdoms, though the resources of the underground wealth had at that time but little prospect of speedy development.

In comparison with its area, the country was very sparsely populated, the majority of its inhabitants living on the immediate banks of its many rivers, and leaving hundreds of square miles in undisputed possession of the most luxuriant forests and the creatures that lived therein.

There was only as much in the way of cultivation as just ministered to their immediate wants, which were the most modest, the more so, as they were for the most part vegetarians, and the soil and climate brought forth abundantly with a minimum of trouble.

Then, too, the ubiquitous *bamboo* furnished material for their dwellings, for holding water, and a host of other purposes. The bamboo stands, indeed, in much the same relation to the Burmese as coal to us, and any cessation in the supply would be attended with consequences scarcely less calamitous.

The pine and custard-apples, plantain or banana, and Jack-fruit grow to perfection.

A well-grown and thoroughly ripe custard-apple, eaten when just ready to fall to pieces on the slightest provocation, is certainly a pleasant and enticing fruit, which may be eaten with impunity, but which, like the rose, is not without its thorn, in the shape of a very unpleasant after-taste. The hills on the right bank of the Irrawaddy, opposite Prome, were celebrated for them, and the plantations, tastefully laid out, formed quite a feature in the landscape.

The plantain of the East, or banana of the West, grows to perfection in Burmah; those of Bengal are vastly inferior, while those grown under glass in this country are sickly exotics, forming but a very poor substitute for that which they pretend to be.

The Jack-fruit did not commend itself to the palate of Europeans: in smell and taste it closely resembles the *durian*, which abounds in the Malay Archipelago. The taste of both resembles that of the Jargonelle pear; and both, strange to say, smell like rotten eggs.

There was a perfect forest of Jack-fruit trees extending many miles to the west of the stockade. This was a favourite resort, both on account of its numerous shady groves, in which the pine-apple grew in wild luxuriance, and by reason of the number and variety of birds, reptiles, insects, etc., which it afforded to the observant naturalist.

To ride or walk there required, however, some degree of caution Below lurked scorpions and snakes; above, running along the branches, were numbers of very large and fierce black ants, furnished with formidable nippers, which they did not hesitate to use most effectually whenever they chanced to alight on the nape of one's neck.

The fruit of these trees sometimes attains to an enormous size; one suspended at either extremity of a bamboo being as much as a strong man could carry.

Another creature that abounded in these forests was the kalong, or flying fox, a large bat, which sleeps the whole day, hanging head downwards from the branches, to which it clings with hooked claws.

Nothing could, perhaps, be more marked than the differences, both physical and mental, that exist between the Burmese and the Hindoos and Mohammedans of India. They have not a single feature in common—customs, religion, ways of thinking are equally different. Burmah, as it was—for I know not how far the conquering hand may have altered the spirit of its dream since I knew it—was infinitely preferable. The pages of history furnish us with proofs as abundant as they are sad, that no nation can advance as long as the hand of the conqueror weighs it down; there may be a spasmodic and artificial progress, but in reality the conquered races recede, since there is in the East no possibility of their absorbing and assimilating their conquerors, as did the Greeks and Saxons of old, which is the only chance of their deriving lasting benefit from the victors.

It would be about as easy "to make a silk purse out of a sow's ear" as to bring aborigines round to our way of thinking and acting; they acquire the vices of the dominant power, but unhesitatingly eschew its virtues.

In the days that I am recalling, the Burmese were by no means faultless, yet they acted up to their own idea of the eternal fitness of things; and were, I doubt not, happier in their way, under their own form of government, bad as we profess to consider it, than under ours.

Men and women were alike characterized by an independence of spirit, the like of which I have never yet encountered in any other race; they absolutely scorned any form of menial employment, so that Burmese domestics were then unknown. This was sheer love of freedom, and not merely the pride attaching to caste, which has no existence in Burmah; their independence was visible in every action, so the yoke must bow these haughty necks very low.

In average intelligence, too, they are infinitely above most of the inhabitants of Hindostan: while the latter would merely pass one by with a "salaam," the Burmese used frequently to stop and speak, perchance asking for a light, and always evincing the most undisguised gratification if you but let them have a peep at the mechanism of your watch.

The physical advantages are scarcely less striking; the men are not handsome, and the women may be far from pretty, but the former were sturdy, muscular specimens of humanity, and the latter possessed a good figure and a striking head of raven hair, and were besides extremely graceful.

Both were seen to the best advantage when trooping *en masse* to the pagoda with offerings to "Gautama," the most imposing sight of its kind that I ever witnessed in the East.

All were scrupulously clean, and dressed in their best, while the women set off the blackness of their hair by interlacing with it the blossoms of a white, waxy flower.

A little in advance of each group marched a *Pongyee*, a priest or monk, sounding a loud gong; otherwise the silence was unbroken. One remarked a total absence of the drumming, shouting, dancing, and general turmoil that characterize most religious rites in India, rendering them an unmitigated nuisance, for they necessitate police supervision and sanitary precautions on an extensive scale. On these occasions the sexes were separated, the men and women marching on different sides of the road, both going and returning.

Their code of morality was said to be of a not very exalted order; but, I blush to own it, this has become much a matter of opinion—

> "And two in fifty scarce agree
> On what is pure morality."

Anyhow, they can in all probability compare very favourably in this respect with any other Oriental nation, and, for the matter of that, with many a European one.

Their detractors, or rather the preachers of the disinterested process of civilization, have made capital out of their practice of parting with their daughters for a pecuniary consideration; but this came into vogue only when the European arrived on the scene and offered prices for the girls that to their simple fathers appeared fabulous.

Nor, in their opinion, did the transaction cast the slightest slur on the young lady's character, since she was always at liberty to return home and resume her old place in the family, if such were the desire of the principal parties concerned. Moreover, Anglo-Indians are—I apologize, *were*—unfortunately among those who, in some encounters at all events, could not afford to throw stones; it used to be emphatically impressed upon young ladies that a civilian was worth so much, "dead or alive;" while the market-value of a military man was fixed at considerably less.

Marriage was represented to them as a mere matter of £ s. d., a form of social barter; they were to pass by the "red coat" on principle, concentrating all their blandishments on the "black" one. In our insufferable egotism, which drivelling patriots dignify with the name of insular pride, we are very apt to lay down a code of ethics for others, without thinking it at all necessary to practise the morality we preach.

As is customary in the East, most of the work fell to the lot of the women, their lords and masters only condescending to lend a helping hand whenever resources threatened to fail. The besetting vice of the Burmese was gambling and betting, as much, in fact, a part and parcel of their nature as with "Mr. John Chinaman;" on the whole, indeed, I am of opinion that they cast the Celestial into the shade. At a certain popular boat-race I remember sitting beside a Burmese of some position, whose proceedings were veritably those of a lunatic; he danced and cried, he undid his long black hair and tried to pull it out.

I too, so he deigned to inform me, should have behaved likewise, if I had had such a bet on the race as he. In reply to my interrogation as to the extent of this wonderful bet that appeared so to affect him—"What have I betted? Oh! only my wife, children, house, clothes and furniture!" He positively lost all, and disappeared.

Cock-fighting was another amusement at which large parties would gladly assemble. The birds came of a good stock, were large, heavy, well-spurred, and carefully bred, with, as I suspected, a strain of the "jungle-fowl," a shapely bird, which abounds in the jungle, though difficult to get at on foot, and which, if hung for the proper time, eats as well as pheasant.

The fanciers, each with his bird under his arm, would resort of an evening to any convenient shady spot, clear a ring, and set to work amid prodigious excitement. One never, perhaps, thoroughly grasped the utter brutality of this sport until he had seen it practised by those poor "savages;" in this case, however, it would have been too glaring a case of "glass houses," etc., etc., to have even criticized it!

The one physical exercise of which the Burmese had but a very imperfect idea was the art of horse-riding. As they used very short stirrups, and consequently kept their knees right above the saddle, their seat was extremely insecure, only practicable indeed at the "amble," a pace peculiar to their ponies, horses being unknown.

The European eye measured the qualities of that indigenous animal, with the result of soon placing it beyond the reach of ordinary mortals. I bought one for 3l.; in five years the price rose to 30l. In fact, one of those crazes for which our society is famous, took that direction; it suffered from "Pegu ponies" on the brain, talked of them, dreamed of them.

The enthusiasm of Phaeton the ill-starred to emulate Jehu was scarcely greater or more unfortunate than that of all sorts and conditions of both sexes to drive a pair in a well-appointed, low carriage.

They were certainly well-bred animals, yet withal most docile; many a night did mine carry me home with unerring instinct, when, owing to a darkness that could be felt, I could not see his head.

The natives looked with undisguised amazement on our cavalry and artillery horses: to begin with, the process of mounting sorely puzzled them. Later on, when it was decided to weed them out, a few, sold by auction, came into the possession of ambitious and adventurous Burmese, one of whom I watched with great amusement in his fruitless endeavours to mount. The climax was reached when, in despair, he tied the animal to one of the posts of his verandah, and climbing over the railing from inside, lowered himself into the saddle. Delighted beyond measure at the success of his stratagem, he cautiously proceeded to "cast adrift," and doubtless enjoyed a famous ride, of which the element of excitement was by no means the least attraction.

There was a peculiar kind of football in which these people excelled, which in so far resembled our own "Association" that the use of the hands was strictly forbidden. There, however, the resemblance ceased: the ball, about the size of those used at croquet, was constructed of strips of cane, and consequently very light; some thirty players would form a large circle, and would keep the ball going from one to another, with toes, heels, and knees, with wonderful skill and accuracy.

But the most striking of their national amusements was the theatrical performance known as a "Pooay," which was given in a kind of large "Punch and Judy" show.

Seats were literally *taken* early; that is to say, every one brought a brick, deposited the same according to fancy, and forthwith squatted upon it.

The *dramatis personæ* were dolls dexterously manipulated by a complicated arrangement of wires, while the men behind proved no mean ventriloquists; the performance, too, was as lengthy as it was excellent, for I have seen the audience assemble of an evening, and break up when I have passed that way again *next morning!*

Any clever joke would be received with uproarious mirth, and—let the reader be lenient in his judgment of these poor, untaught savages!—the broader the allusion, the more they relished it.

Comparisons are, as a rule, odious, but the pharisaical suppression of many native Burmese modes of recreation gives rise to reflections that will find expression ere long in the outcry of an injured people. We lay the flattering unction to our souls that we are not as others; *we*, forsooth, forbid the natives to bet and gamble. Why can we not at least have the honesty to admit that we hold India and Burmah solely and entirely for the sake of the "loaves and fishes," without descending to cant about our duty as the pioneers of a religion with which such races can have but little real sympathy, and a civilization that—if, indeed, it be nothing worse—is at least no improvement on their present state?

The new arrival is at once struck by the large number of places of worship scattered broadcast over the country. They generally culminate in a pagoda, a wonderful tapering structure, very solidly built, and covered from the base upwards with gold-leaf, while the apex is generally surmounted by an umbrella, the insignia of royalty, or some other fantastic device. They were built in honour of Buddha, the labour and material being voluntary gifts of the people. If offerings of produce could be relied on as a measure of their devotion, then were the Burmese an essentially religious people. Plantains, boiled rice, curiously concocted native dishes, flowers, umbrellas—all were presented in profusion, and all—not excepting the more perishable portion of even the umbrellas—were disposed of by swarms of crows, the more adventurous of which pounced upon the good things while the worshippers were still busy with their devotions.

Of the many wondrous natural phenomena that so puzzle us Europeans in the far East, the extraordinary instinct possessed by vultures and other birds of prey is by no means the most inconsiderable. But a few moments need elapse after a bullock falls dead on the march, and one already sees black spots not far above the horizon, which soon prove to be vultures making straight for the carcase with unerring precision. Naturalists are divided in opinion as to whether this extraordinary power of perception owes its origin to some unusual development of the sense of vision, or to an equally unintelligible transcendency of the olfactory organs: one fact, I believe, speaks strongly in favour of the former hypothesis, and that is, that the birds as often as not approach from windward.

The numerous roadside temples offered unlimited opportunities for "looting," the panacea for all military hardships; though the occasions were indeed better than the prizes, which consisted for the most part of images of Gautama covered with gold and silver foil.

All is, I imagine, fair in war; though in how far that rule admits of modification in the case of a war declared by a dominant power against a race of half-naked Orientals, I do not care to inquire. The Burmese certainly bore the pillage of their temples in a philosophic spirit, not to be met with even in a Christian country; they bowed to the inevitable, they made a virtue of necessity, they trusted to the teachings of their faith, rendering good for evil, so as to ultimately reach Nirvana, the goal of all their earthly and spiritual ambition, in the hope of which life was alone worth living.

CHAPTER V.

FIRST IMPRESSIONS.

"He hears, alas! no music of the spheres,
But an unhallowed, earthly sound of fiddling."

"A spark neglected makes a mighty fire."

THESE temples were by no means good specimens of Burmese architecture, which perhaps culminated in the *Kyoungs,* or resorts of the priests: a large quantity of elaborately carved timber entered into the construction of these edifices, the roof of which gradually diminished from below upwards, and were on this account far more pleasing to the eye than the more abrupt style adopted in Chinese temples.

They were for the most part raised in quiet and secluded groves, whither the pious *Pongyees* could retire for purposes of contemplation, in humble imitation of the founder of their creed.

These *Pongyees,* who were always clean-shaven, and clad in yellow robes, transcended in purity of life and devotion to their sacred cause any others of like persuasion that I ever came across. They were, moreover, courteous, unassuming, and affable to a degree, always ready to impart any information that lay within their ken, and supporting it with such written documents as they possessed.

The people at large held them in the greatest veneration, and the funeral obsequies of any distinguished member of the order were of an elaborate and somewhat costly nature. The first process was the embalming, in which art the Burmese must have been little inferior to the ancient Egyptians. When this process had been completed and the limbs were bound up and covered with a kind of varnish, the body was placed in a *kyoung*, where it lay in state for a month or six weeks, during which time there was always a light burning within the building, while prayers, intercessions, and offerings of every kind were made by devotees from all parts.

The last rite of all, cremation, I had the good fortune to witness, on a very important occasion, amid a large concourse of worshippers. The mummified remains were reverently laid on an iron grating between two low parallel walls, and a fire was ignited below, fuel being added as required; and although the wood was dry, and both it and the body burned furiously, the latter took a considerable time to incinerate.

While the deceased was lying in state, some foolish Europeans, possessed, I regret to say, of more zeal than honesty, made off one night with a few of his ornaments, and escaped only by the skin of their teeth.

Thus, even to Burmese philosophy there was a limit; they could endure with stoical indifference the spoliation of their temples; they uttered no audible protest against the unholy appropriation of pagodas sacred to Buddha, "the Wise," "the Enlightened," but when their offerings for the repose of a high priest's soul were surreptitiously made away with, then their anger was kindled. The images were coveted, not for their intrinsic value, but because they were clever caricatures of the invader, both the civil and the military element being represented. Thus the resentment of the marauder predominated over even his cupidity; though no one who knew the character of the Burmese could ever suppose for one moment that they intended this as an insult, for, being themselves almost proof against the shafts of ridicule, they not unnaturally concluded that a nation so superior in intellect would be above such trifles. And here they erred; their intercourse with Europeans had hitherto been fragmentary—limited to a casual trader, and it had consequently never dawned on them that the sensitiveness of a race varies directly with its organization.

But for the stockade, the pilferers' chance of escape would have been small indeed, and even as it was, they reached the main gate not a moment too soon. The sentry on duty shut it in the faces of the enraged pursuers and called out the guard. By restoring the images, and vouchsafing some sort of explanation, an episode which might have been attended with serious consequences was thus happily tided over.

I have already contrasted the Burmese with the natives of Hindostan, and I am constrained to compare them with the *Mongolidæ*. They closely resemble the Chinese in their features and habits; their language, too, is monosyllabic, and they also remain in a stationary condition for all time. This latter feature of their national existence is due to the generosity of nature; we northern races are engaged in an everlasting pitched battle with the elements, and where nature adds difficulty she adds brain; but with a warm climate, an abundant fauna and flora, rivers teeming with fish, and just enough intelligence to appreciate these gifts, besides a religion which fitted in with their mode of thought, what need had the Burmese of progress?

Their misfortune lay in being interfered with, because they did not understand the customs of what we are pleased to call "civilization," and their country was wrested from them in consequence by the superior force of might. The rubbish indulged in as regards "improving and elevating them" I have but little patience with; it is, in the first place, right down dishonest, and it is, moreover, impossible even were it desirable.

In the "commercial advantages," which were—let us be frank—the mainspring of the whole movement, there figured largely certain mines that had for years dazzled our eyes and excited our thirst for gain : well, we took them as the price of our "improvements," and how have they been manipulated?

I have already had occasion to discuss the variety and strength of Oriental smells ; one could, in fact, very well do without the sense of smell while in the East ; the scent even of the flowers, of mango, orange, lime, and dedonia, is oppressive in the sultry atmosphere. But the "artificial" smells are something to experience; that of an Indian bazaar—a compound of assafœtida, decayed produce, and stagnant drains—clings to a person for ever ; that of a Burmese market is delightfully enhanced by the perfume of Gua-pu, a speciality of the country, in which stale fish, lime, and other similar ingredients are incorporated *secundum artem*.

The display in the Rangoon market included meat, fish, poultry, fruit, vegetables, and flowers, in variety and abundance ; but every other odour was assimilated and overcome by Gua-pu. Yet who shall ridicule so acquired a taste ?

The alderman likes his green turtle, the Chinaman his birds' nests, and the Frenchman his frogs' legs ; so, too, the Burmese will have his Gua-pu.

The fact is, there is Gua-pu and Gua-pu !

On one occasion, proceeding up the river with the

Commissioner, the late Sir A. Phayre, I was roundly abusing this native delicacy; he fetched a stone jar and begged that I would taste the contents. When I had done so and reported favourably, he informed me to my astonishment that it was a superior quality of the compound I had been vilifying. Had he not been so perfect a gentleman, and so considerate to all that had the pleasure of acting under him, I should have suspected that he inwardly enjoyed my obvious discomfiture at having so erroneously condemned anything *in toto*.

He was certainly far above the ordinary run of rulers in all those qualities that adorn a man and a Christian. It was my good fortune to be near him for weeks together, when heavy responsibilities weighed upon him: we had to traverse wild tracts of country with dangers at every turn, and the end—if ever reached—bristled with difficulties. To be acquainted with him was a matter for congratulation; to serve under him was a privilege; to know him was to love him.

When circumstances had parted us, I had very undesirable occasions for studying the reverse of the medal —egotistical, fussy, fault-finding men, to please whom was beyond the range of human attainment; men primed with theory, but worse than useless in practical administration, whose one object seemed to be to offend and estrange their fellow-countrymen, and to oppress and outrage the natives.

The one type elevated the service; the other lowered both the service and all concerned therein, causing the tide to ebb to a very low mark.

The words of the Bard concerning the good and evil deeds of mankind have no application to the lamented Commissioner; he left no evil deeds to survive him, nor were his many good ones lost with him, for as long as

Burmah is inhabited—and there is not at present any very startling prospect of a decrease in its population—his memory will be revered by Native and European alike, a monument more lasting than stone or brass.

For a conquered race the Burmese certainly held their heads remarkably erect, looking the usurper straight in the face without any shame for their own position. The fact was, a very superficial acquaintance with our habits and mode of living had convinced them of our superiority in every respect—save one.

It is very curious that every Eastern native looks down on our music with undisguised contempt. Our bands might discourse the gems of Chopin, Beethoven, and Balfe, but only the veriest loiterer would stop to listen, and, to judge by his expression, it fell as flat on his ear as a penny trumpet would on ours.

Real music was too refined and complicated for nerves accustomed throughout generations to coarser measures in harmony. This was the same all over Hindostan; and it is therefore surprising that our regimental native bands were remarkably good before the Mutiny.

A Burmese band consisted of a number of drums in a circle, and diverse brass instruments, awful to look upon, and still more awful to hear; though what they lacked in harmony they certainly made up for in noise. With the exception of the ubiquitous and irrepressible mosquito, the whole of the lower creation fled before it; and only a sense of dignity prevented many of us from following suit.

The performers must have been animated by extraordinary zeal, if the manner in which they hammered on the drums and blew through the wind-instruments be any criterion. As I invariably hastened in a direction opposite to that which was taken by the performers,

I never witnessed the climax of the celebration; but if it continued for long on the same *crescendo* principle as that with which it passed me, I should think it must ultimately have resulted in rupture of the drum-heads and explosion of the remaining instruments.

The effect of music on nations, and through them on individuals, certainly furnishes matter for a deal of interesting study and comparison. In the primitive state it is simple and natural: Eastern nations make use of it to produce temporary excitement, a method that we have retained in our military bands, or, combined with dancing, as the food of love.

It has always been inseparably connected with religion and religious observances, from the organ and choir of Western religions to the drum and cymbals of the East. If the imagination of the poet can give to "airy nothing a local habitation and a name," music has a yet greater power; and they are indeed twin sisters, poetry and music raising the civilized mind far above the ordinary range of things earthly. There will doubtless always be some mortals, even in the highest stage of civilization, who are nowise susceptible to the beauties of music; of them our poet for all time has spoken in uncomplimentary terms, perhaps harshly; but, if such a being is not to blame, he is at least incomprehensible.

Among the many disadvantages under which Eastern nations labour, is the absence of melody in the voices of the feathered tribe. Our nightingale, thrush, and lark are all birds of sober plumage; but in the East there are no vocal artists; no lark poising itself in mid-air warbling forth in the early morn, and gladdening the heart of man with its song; no thrush singing to its lady-love from the topmost branch of a may-tree; no nightingale to lend its charm to a summer twilight—nothing but gaudy plumage and burnished colours that dart hither and thither "brief as the lightning in the collied night."

The birds utter for the most part harsh, discordant sounds; and it appears to me that the reason for this want of vocal sweetness is to be found either in the climate or in the number of carrion-eaters. A nightingale, for instance, singing from the leafy branch of a tamarind tree, with a pack of jackals yelling beneath, would be a contrast repugnant to nature, a dislocation of the fitness of things.

Our English vanity enables us to tolerate peacocks in the gardens of the wealthy. For the sake of seeing them strut about terraces and spread their tails in the sunlight, people will endure their torturing cry at daybreak, and even turn a deaf ear to the complaints of the gardener, who soon loses all patience with this most mischievous of birds. I do not remember them in Burmah, but in India they are very numerous, affecting in particular the denser jungles frequented by tigers.

An idea prevails indeed among the natives that the peacock follows such animals, but its only foundation lies in the coincidence that both love solitude. I remember on one occasion coming upon some hundreds of these beautiful birds committing rare havoc in a cultivated field. But they soon took cognizance of the intruder, and I had only just time to shoot a male and a young female, when all traces of them had vanished; the former for the sake of his feathers, the latter for the table. Certain shady trees bordering a canal near our encampment turned out to be a favourite roosting-place for them, but ere they could settle down for the night a general scrimmage would take place for the best seats:

fine feathers may make fine birds, but do not always cover amiable dispositions—not, at least, in the *ornithological* biped!

Oh, my digressions! You wanted to hear about Burmah and its inhabitants, and here I have been discoursing on music and peacocks!

Being subject to a heavy annual rainfall, all their dwellings are built on piles, and are thereby raised to several feet above the ground. This expedient, a sanitary precaution against damp floorings and emanations from the soil, a *sine quâ non*, in fact, under such climatic conditions, gave a special character to their villages, which were constructed for the most part of bamboos.

But while steering clear of Scylla, they ran into Charybdis. Fire played great havoc with them, and its annual course was "short, sharp, and decisive." The wonder was that it did not occur a dozen times a year instead of once; and I doubt whether a hydrant close at hand, with an unlimited supply of water, would have been of any real service.

They never took the least precaution with regard to fire, although their houses, furniture, and mats, and all consisted of nothing but bamboo; perhaps they thought that the annual fire was as inevitable as the annual moonsoon. Indeed—to borrow an illustration from our own historians of the seventeenth century—I am strongly of opinion that this annual conflagration stifled the origin and prevented the spread of epidemic disease. Witness the fact that, a few years later, when more substantial buildings had taken the place of these flimsy wooden structures, thereby reducing such visitations to a minimum, cholera raged with great virulence, a disease hitherto almost unknown to the country,

F

where doctors had been occupied chiefly with cases of fever and dysentery.

I have known a regiment up to its full strength so ravaged by these complaints as not to be able to muster a hundred effective bayonets after a few months' residence in a certain part of the country. The annual incineration of Rangoon therefore possessed a redeeming feature, and was certainly a "thing of beauty" while it lasted.

Late one evening, in the month of April, the garrison was roused from its wonted propriety by what appeared to be a very heavy discharge of artillery and musketry in the immediate neighbourhood, and the commanding officer was on the point of calling the troops to arms, when some one discovered the origin of the alarm—the yearly fire! The flames literally ran along the streets faster than the natives could run themselves—the reports being due to the bursting of sections of bamboo; and the scene resembled (I ask pardon for seeking my illustrations in such commonplace sources), a Benefit display of fireworks at the Crystal Palace, at the moment when the large set-piece is ignited. It burned itself out, simply because there was nothing else left to feed upon; nothing but charred remains, the outcome of a very short reign of terror.

History, sacred and profane, alludes to a bird, sacred to the dread Osiris, the All-seeing and Many-eyed, that was said to pay a periodical visit to the land of the Pharaohs. The most credited account concerning the bird is that, on burning itself, a similar creature sprang from its ashes, and, from its hiding-place in the surrounding tamarisk, continued to watch over the sacred burial-place. A very phœnix was Rangoon: it rose up on its own ashes rejuvenated and vigorous; no harrowing accounts ever reached us of loss of life or even serious injury; all went on as before, with increased energy, until new bamboos had supplied the place of old ones.

Equally singular were the circumstances attending the outbreak of the "monsoon," which burst upon us, less to our delight than to that of the vegetable and insect world. The change was startling. One day, the baked ground, as hard and bare as a rock, with only a stray blade of grass struggling for existence; creation groaning, exhausted, expectant. Then a change comes over its dream: there is a terrible and steady downpour; ere twenty-four hours have elapsed, the new blades of grass can be seen peeping out; there are innumerable insects on the wing, and millions of frogs are croaking in the marshes. The evening before I had passed a dried-up tank of large dimensions, the bottom of which was deeply fissured in every direction, and to all appearances as destitute of life as the Great Sahara. The next day it was full to the brim, and huge fish were leaping out of the water in evident delight at being released from their long and enforced captivity.

The rain had descended, the mud was softened, and its inmates, wriggling forth, took to their more natural element and mode of locomotion. Instances of dormant vitality we know to be common among seeds and insects; wheat found in an Egyptian mummy-case many centuries old has germinated freely; seeds of trees buried for ages have done the same, and those also of fruit found in a skeleton, that must have lain incarcerated since the beginning of the Christian era. The chrysalis stage of insects is too well known to need comment. But such a suspension of vitality in creatures like fish, whose organization demands continual aeration of the blood through gills, is somewhat strange, and runs considerable risk of being branded as a traveller's tale. I confess to having felt startled on my first acquaintance with these mud-fish. Many months of freedom could now be looked forward to; then again the daily decrease in depth; wriggling into the mud; diminution of vitality; and finally, loss of consciousness. Truly, a strange existence!

CHAPTER VI.

THE TEACHINGS OF BUDDHA.

*" For modes of faith let graceless zealots fight ;
He can't be wrong whose life is in the right."*

THE discussion of a national religion is always a delicate task, but, having so far considered only the physical and political aspect of the Burmese, I feel that I may no longer avoid giving some account of their conception of the universe and the Hereafter, matters with which, truth to tell, they were wont to trouble themselves less than any other Eastern nation with which I ever came in contact.

I shall endeavour to convey some idea of their attitude towards their great teacher, Buddha ; and I think that the reader will share my opinion that the absence of that fanaticism, so characteristic of the natives of Hindostan, is a blessing to rulers and ruled alike.

The " *Contemplative One*," after sacrificing all manner of brilliant worldly prospects, retiring in lieu thereof into remote places for the purpose of indulging in holy meditation, reached his eightieth year, and, having completed the necessary cycles of transmigration, passed away to " Complete Nirvana," the coveted annihilation and end of all things.

Next to him in the cycle came *Gautama*, to whom were dedicated the many pagodas and temples found all over the land.

Their images were of identical conception, no matter what their material; their attitude was invariably the same, sitting cross-legged, and contemplating the nether portion of their body, a pose suggestive of deep thought and unbounded indifference to the many allurements of this wicked world.

These images varied considerably in size, some measuring but a few inches, while others were of enormous dimensions, being occasionally hidden away in places where one would least expect to find them, the sole relics, it may be, of some old dwelling over which the jungle had reasserted a prior claim.

There prevails an idea, especially current among those who are ever ready to class under one and the same category every creed that differs in source and ceremonial from their own, that these were idols intended as a medium through which to address the Deity. This theory does not do infinite credit to the researches of those with whom it is in favour, since, in point of fact, the actual comprehension of a Supreme Being never having dawned on their minds, the Burmese are atheists in the true sense of the word.

No; this excessive multiplication of images took its origin from another motive, not a very creditable one, perhaps, but nevertheless forced upon them in a great measure by the despotic form of government under which they lived.

Regular taxation in proportion to wealth being unknown among them, the ruler of a province in want of supplies for his own or the public service, proceeded in a manner not quite unknown to the rulers of more civilized nations—that is to say, he first discovered the whereabouts of treasure by secret agency, and then set about extracting the same by the aid of an armed force.

Suspected individuals, having failed to succumb to the exigencies of torture, often paid the penalty of their real or imaginary wealth with their lives; and such continual insecurity necessarily drove them to other expedients.

In the reign of our first Edward it was found necessary to pass a statute forbidding landowners to place their property within "Sanctuary" of the Church without their king's consent; and the practice that occasioned the necessity for this enactment was in a way analogous to the motives that led to the erection of temples and images in Burmah. The images of Gautama were covered with gold and silver foil; and the natives were somewhat of experts in carpentry and metallurgy, having, like the Chinese, attained to a certain standard, at which point their fertility of resource ended.

Dedication to Gautama or to Buddha implied one and the same thing, in spite of the latter having ceased to exist here and hereafter, while the former was still undergoing transmigrations as tiger, crow, lizard, or mosquito. On the whole, therefore, the motive was of a worldly nature, and any idea that may have existed in their minds concerning the efficacy of such offerings to abbreviate the weary stages of transition was certainly illogical to a degree, considering that they acknowledged no Superior Being, through whose interposition any such relaxation could possibly be effected.

Their doctrine pointed clearly to a prescribed course through which all must pass according to their deeds; even the very best—those ascetics who had been crowned with all the virtues inculcated in Buddhism—must be born again and again, though under far more favourable circumstances than those whose life had been careless and indifferent. The absolutely wicked would be born again in one of the many hells situated in the centre of the earth, coming up, perchance, in the form of petroleum, to be tortured in another form through those terrible periods, the limits of which were assigned at billions of years. Billions! Let those think of it whose religion teaches of an eternity: of the two, the latter, as being undefined and imaginary, is less perplexing to the mind, if equally impossible to grasp.

The doctrine of transmigration is essentially an Eastern one. That remarkable people, the Egyptians, with their inbred polytheism—their divinities, Ptah, Osiris, Isis, Horus, and many others, not to mention a still greater number of "companion-gods,"—were confirmed believers in it. Hence arose the practice of embalming, the idea being, that the soul, having in a period of several thousands of years completed the wanderings assigned to it, might return to its original dwelling, to be absorbed in Osiris, the manifestation of Light.

The practice, which dates from very remote antiquity, is frequently alluded to in the Scriptures. Joseph commanded his servants to embalm his father; and he in his turn was similarly embalmed, having died at the very respectable age of one hundred and ten years, and placed in a sarcophagus.

One frequently hears the doctrine of transmigration attributed to Pythagoras; but we might with about as much reason credit the Pope with the invention of the Old Testament! The Philosopher merely imbibed the notion from the Egyptians, and, as it appeared in harmony with his own system, he carried it back to Europe and spread it among his converts.

In Hinduism too, a religion that recognizes three gods—Brahma, the Creator; Vishnu, the Preserver; and

Siva, the Destroyer—metempsychosis is paramount. An ordinary life being too brief a span for the completion of a mortal's allotted task, he had to be born again as often as necessary for the fulfilment of whatever remained for him to perform.

Not many years ago a severe epidemic broke out in a certain district of India, almost depopulating that part of the country, which the year following was subject to an extraordinary visitation of rats. The authorities having, as in duty bound, made arrangements for the speedy extermination of these pests, the Brahmans interposed in their behalf, on the plea that the souls of departed were thus revisiting their old haunts, guided thither by the force of association.

For the same reason a high-caste Brahman will neither kill anything himself, nor will he eat anything that has succumbed to a violent death, be it flesh, fish, or fowl. Life to him is sacred in all its many forms, for therein may reside the troubled spirit of a departed relative.

An old friend of mine, a Brahman of exceeding uprightness and more than ordinary intelligence, constantly upbraided me with the sinful cruelty of shooting and fishing. Out of my great respect for him, I bore his harangues with a patient shrug, worthy of Shylock, knowing full well that any attempt to argue the point would be worse than useless; for it would be easier to train an old oak, high-top bald with dry antiquity, as an espalier or cordon, than to influence such a one to the extent of "the twentieth part of one poor scruple," the more so, that he was consistently acting up to his own belief.

The children of Nature who hunted the buffalo in the prairies of the Far West do not appear to have entertained any serious idea of transmigration; they looked death boldly in the face, believing it to be a mere translation to happier hunting-grounds.

The Incas of Peru worshipped everything that appeared in the vault of heaven, including sun, moon, stars, lightning, and rainbow, and their worship was as devout as it was original.

The moon was regarded as the spouse of him from whom she derives her light; Venus was her attendant, and the remaining heavenly bodies ranked as inferior deities. But it was to the sun that their attention was principally directed; in his honour a temple was erected at the seat of government, wherein sat enthroned his image, on which his own rays impinged with great effect. It is scarcely to be wondered at that the idea of transmigration took such hold upon a considerable section of the human race, especially if one considers the climatic and physical conditions under which Eastern nations have existed throughout all ages.

We go out there full of life and spirits, and manage to derive some compensating pleasure out of riding, driving, sport, and sundry national games. To the native, however, life is "tedious as a twice-told tale;" essentially apathetic beyond a certain monotonous routine, he never ceases to wonder how we can find pleasure in such physical exercise; and death itself can have but few terrors for those who only endure existence in the hope of something better.

Who knows whether, were it not for more smiling conditions of existence, added to the aspirations of a higher faith, we too might not welcome the prospect of entering another state?

Buddha, unlike Mohammed, tasted the pleasures of this life for thirty years as only the son of a king and husband of a princess could; but the unrestrained gratification of his desires seem only to have added fuel to the fire that smouldered within him, for he rejected them all as totally unsatisfactory. Then followed the period of his retirement in the fastnesses of his native mountains, where he endeavoured to work out the origin and remedy of pain, sorrow, sickness, and all the evils flesh is heir to. Having arrived at satisfactory conclusions, he commenced to preach. At first his converts were few, but in time the rivulets united to form that mighty stream which covered the whole of India, Burmah, and China.

Mohammed, on the other hand, lived a hard and somewhat chequered life throughout, and was further advanced in life when the pseudo-revelation changed the current of his thoughts.

As in every other respect, the two religions differed greatly in the means employed to disseminate them; the teachings of the Light of Asia seemed to flow on throughout the length and breadth of the land as a great stream with unruffled surface, acquiring strength and durability by appealing to the fairer side of humanity; Mohammedanism resembled rather a mountain torrent bubbling and fretting at every turn, promulgated moreover amid all the attendant miseries of savage war.

The early life and bringing up of Buddha would naturally lead one to suppose that he was a highly educated man; yet, strange to say, no traces of his writings have been discovered, even supposing that he ever committed his thoughts to such an ordeal, in order that his followers might not forget them after he had passed away.

More worldly wise was Mohammed, who, either in his own handwriting or in that of an amanuensis, left behind him a copy of that wonderful compilation, the Koran, as well as the severe ritual, setting forth the number of prayers, the long, trying fasts, the extent of charity in money and produce, and the pilgrimages to the holy city of Mecca, with their attendant ceremonies, including the sevenfold circuit of the Black Stone.

The Anglo-Indian has daily opportunity of observing how faithfully these religious observances are carried out in the face of many obstacles, but his admiration will not be unmixed with relief at the comparatively slight hold this creed of fanaticism has taken on the natives of Hindostan.

The remissness of Buddha in not committing to writing his many and valuable teachings was amply atoned for by his followers; and, as in many other religions, the numeral 3 seems to predominate in the ordering of their rites.

"All good things," says the German, "are of that number;" and this superstition seems to have derived its origin from the doctrines of the world's creeds. We have the Trinity. The Egyptians divided their gods into three sets; thought, word, and deed formed the Peruvian triad; so, too, the flowery language of the East is exemplified by the pious Buddhist's "Triple Basket."

The fountain-head of every misfortune lies, according to the teachings of Buddha, in having been born into this world at all, in expressing which opinion the "Contemplative One" spoke, at all events, in direct defiance of all law where recent causes are always preferred to those more remote.

This unfortunate beginning necessitates a frequent repetition of the same process under different forms, animate or inanimate, the great aim of this life being to attain "Complete Nirvana," of which, however, only those seem to have the least chance who from the first embrace a religious and ascetic life.

The strict code of discipline left no loophole for the indulgence of that which is earthly in thought, word, or deed: terrible self-denial in food, raiment, and dwelling was incumbent; one meal a day, and that a gift; rags covered with a yellow cloth; the shade of a friendly tree—these constitute the sole conception of earthly luxury permitted to the good Buddhist. Sleep, too, must be indulged in, not extended at full length, but in a sitting posture; and systematic contemplation on the best remedies for worldly evils was to abstract the mind from its desires and affections.

The march of time has naturally brought with it many relaxations in this terrible code, and, as with most other nations, practice has fallen very short of theory.

It is no easy matter to picture the city of Benares, now the head-quarters of Brahminical bigotry, as the stronghold of Buddhism, yet relics are not wanting to point to this as the true order of succession. Somewhat singular, too, is the process by which this most ancient of religions was driven from the continent right and left, taking a last refuge at its extremities— the Himalayas on the one hand, Ceylon on the other. Thibet, Bhootan, and Nepaul are essentially Buddhist, and, along with two-thirds of China, it is, in spite of its having been ousted from India proper, still numerically superior to any other religion.

The medium through which it so successfully marched over the greater portion of the East appears to have been zealous, indefatigable missionary enterprise; one reason for its many victories was its non-aggressive character and its fundamental doctrine inculcating respect for other creeds. The absence of this forbearance among us, and among Western missionaries generally, may in part account for our own want of success in spreading Christianity in the East.

Moreover, their own religions have long since taken too firm a hold. An old and respected friend of mine, who had laboured in this direction for about five-and-thirty years, told me plainly the strongholds of the two great religions of India were, so far as the adult population was concerned, all but impregnable; the only prospect of a measure of success lies in those orphanages, the inmates of which are as yet subject to only the indirect influence of heredity and free from contact with their co-religionists; once they are back among their own people, preaching to stones would be about as effectual. Further, we are not to the manner born; besides which, our position in the land constitutes an impediment.

Another great and peaceful revolution effected by the teachings of Buddha was the overthrow of the rigid, unnatural system of caste. Whatever benefit this order of things may have been to us in India as a bar to combination, no other scheme has ever been devised better calculated to keep men asunder and clog the wheels of progress. It hampers all enterprise, causing the machinery of government and industry to creak along after the fashion of a native bullock-cart.

No such arrangement exists in Burmah, and, if only for this reason, its inhabitants will soon forge ahead of India. Years of meditation convinced Buddha of the lasting evils of such a system, and he therefore expunged it—another instance of the difference existing between the influence on matters temporal exerted by both these great religions.

In order to gauge with any accuracy the general effects of Buddha's doctrines in controlling such propensities to evil as his devotees may have possessed, some knowledge of their condition before the promulgation of such teachings would be indispensable; and I am further prevented from forming a judgment in the matter by the fact that my ignorance of their language, at the period of which I am writing, afforded me but scant opportunity of mixing with the inhabitants.

Moreover, we were then virtually at war with them. We had, it is true, fulminated a " Proclamation," annexing the country up to a certain point; but, *ipso facto*, beyond a few places along the river, we could not call an inch of territory our own. A guerilla warfare was maintained for some time, accompanied by reprisals and cruelties common to fighting in all countries and ages, no matter whether the combatants are barbarians or civilized. On the whole, however, I hardly think the Burmese displayed any special aptitude for inflicting torture, although a general idea somehow obtained currency that they were *facile princeps* in this respect. Most assuredly they never tarnished their nationality with such hideous and indelible stains as the natives of India brought on themselves during the whole ghastly course of the Mutiny, by unparalleled atrocities that sent a shudder through every land, branding them with infamy throughout all time. What more natural than that the Burmese, knowing from bitter experience their own inability to cope with us in the open field, and occupying every coign of vantage in their jungle fastnesses, should pounce down upon us when least expected?

We received more than one salutary lesson in this wise, and had to retreat under difficulties, often with loss; nevertheless, though the enemy were smarting under frequent repulses, no after acts of wanton cruelty could be brought home to them, such as are but too common when the civilized nations of Europe fly at each other's throats, mowing down human life as if it merely represented so many fields of standing corn ripe for the harvest.

Irrespective, then, of its many glaring faults, there cannot exist a shadow of a doubt as to the beneficial influence which Buddhism exercises over its votaries in many ways, and we can scarcely feel surprise that these should number nearly one-third of the human race.

The doctrine of metempsychosis, if it taught them nothing else, brought home to them a widespread respect for life in all its forms; they evinced considerable reluctance to subjecting a certain human parasite to the microscope for fear of injuring it; they would not beat a dog that had offended, because of some fancied resemblance between its bark and the voice of a departed friend. Absurd such extremes, no doubt, yet fraught with signal benefit to Buddhists in general, far more so indeed than any opposite condition.

Another very conspicuous feature in their daily life was the unselfishness inculcated by their religion. In India the representatives of the "lords of creation," both Hindu and Mohammedan, were exacting to a degree, first satisfying their own hunger, and then allowing wife and children to regale themselves with the "residue of the remainder," the former being generally chastised, often killed, if the food were not prepared exactly to her lord's liking, or ready the moment he returned home. Among the Burmese, however, father, mother, and children would share alike; and even if only one cigar were forthcoming, it would be passed round for every member of the family to take a few whiffs.

The moral code of Hinduism was at a far lower level than that of the other religion.

Almsgiving, to priests in the absence of beggars, was much more general in Burmah. As in every community, and under every form of religion, there were the good, bad, and indifferent. They were more unanimously guided by one light than any other nation I ever knew, and their religion, for all its exaggerated asceticism, partook more of the practical than that of many a professed Christian.

They could, it is true, boast a number of past-masters in the gentle art of appropriating other folks' goods, yet during the whole of my stay in their country I never lost a single article, though many of the dwellings in which I resided had not even a single door! Scarcely, however, had I returned to India when I missed a bag of rupees and my watch and chain. Other crimes *were* equally uncommon among them. I think my position enabled me to judge of this; and I cannot recall a single instance of necessity for *post-mortem* on a victim of violence or poison; whereas in India not a day passed without one, and their multiplicity rendered life a burden. Corpses, masses of corruption that had run the gauntlet of a hundred miles of hot sun, were brought at all times to one's private dwelling—one met them on the road—everywhere!

Nothing appeared to give such exquisite delight to some of our civil authorities as having plenty of dead bodies brought forth from every nook and corner to be examined and reported on, and if dead bodies were by some rare *mischance* not forthcoming, they would exhume a few bones, which were then decently shunted from pillar to post as evidence of a murder some score of years old!

This absence of outrage, agrarian or otherwise, speaks trumpet-tongued for the morality of the Burmese, their respect for religious observance, and the teachings of their priests. Such wholesale acts of murder as Thuggee and infanticide found no place in their ethics; nor does the senseless practice of Suttee seem ever to have occurred to them.

In many respects, therefore, the teachings of Buddha transcend Hinduism in no measured degree, being both more elevated and more practical, exalting instead of debasing the minds of those who profess them. So ingrained had become those evil practices in India that it took years of most stringent legislation to grapple with the hydra-headed monsters, Heredity and Fanaticism. Now, however, bands of organized Thugs are almost unknown; a Suttee will only occur rarely in some remote district, and infanticide will soon be a matter of history and tradition.

There are, however, Buddhists and Buddhists. Of all the nations embracing this religion the Chinese and Nepaulese seem most unmindful of its teachings, whilst in Thibet and Burmah the flame burned brighter than elsewhere. The Nepaulese, as I saw them for months together during the Mutiny—I allude to the men sent down by Jung Bahadur when the Mutiny was at its height—were a set of bloodthirsty savages, pig-headed and untrustworthy, brave indeed, as a pariah-dog might be when driven into a corner—a rabble which but for the energy and judgment of the English officers in command would at once have dissolved into thin air. They were quite free from any kind of principle, and had no idea of true religion; while the Bhootanese were if anything still lower in the scale.

Buddha enjoined on his followers to avoid abusive and indecent language, to become peace-makers, to endure privation, and show resignation in the face of calamity. Underlying the Burmese character, one could, as a rule, trace the influence of these teachings in their treatment of one another, more than in many a country professing a religion that points to a happier future. If faith and good works, irrespective of the medium, are capable of earning peace and happiness hereafter, then do the disciples of the "Contemplative One," who thought out and purified their religion, enjoy a brighter prospect than most other nations.

The doctrine of "Complete Nirvana" is, to our belief, the fatal blot, but it is at least preferable to the hereafter of the Mohammedan, where, under the auspices of a Supreme Being, the carnal appetites are only intensified.

The absence of that deadliest of all poisons, fanaticism, and the broad, modest respect which refuses to brand as heretical and damnable every other form of belief, also combine to lend a charm to Buddhism which one seeks in vain in many other religions; and the moral precepts scattered promiscuously throughout the Koran, and admirable so far as they go, are terribly neutralized by an unforgiving and intolerant spirit, that is ever breathing forth enmity in place of concord.

It is my belief that our missionaries will meet with greater success in the fair land watered by the Irrawaddy than along the banks of the mighty Ganges, where a century's labour has made but little lasting impression.

Nor is the failure surprising, when we consider our want of uniformity.

The Tabernacle of the Old Testament, appealing to the senses rather than to the intellect, made but little impression on the surrounding Gentiles, who proved far more susceptible to the simplicity inculcated in the New. And what wonder that the Asiatic sees nought but chaos in our Church, when we ourselves hear each clergyman interpreting the rubric according to his own views! When all are at loggerheads in ecclesiastical litigation, every variety of Church—high, low, broad, narrow, deep, shallow—which the mind of man can conceive, how is the missionary to succeed?

CHAPTER VII.

RIVER-LIFE UNDER DIFFICULTIES.

> "How many perils do enfold
> The righteous man to make him daily fall."

I ONCE had the temerity to volunteer my valuable services for an expedition which was fitting out for the purpose of reducing a rebel stronghold; and the answer to my application informed me in somewhat laconic terms that "due information would be given when they were required."

This was a trifle rude; but I had long since sacrificed my independence, and had to grin and bear it. Very shortly afterwards, however, they *were* wanted; and I was ordered to proceed without delay to Pegu, where I was to take charge of the garrison. The summons was accompanied by the pleasing intelligence that the river was infested with gangs of dacoits; and indeed the kindly warnings and exhortations to extreme wariness and energy were tantamount to an assurance that, if I fell into the hands of the enemy, my head would in all probability be sent to Ava as a trophy. Provided, however, that it were permitted to retain the position assigned to it by nature, I was to report myself at Pegu in the shortest possible time.

Early next morning I was sauntering along the muddy banks of the river in quest of a suitable conveyance; nor had I much difficulty in finding what I wanted, for, among their many accomplishments, the Burmese are very fair boat-builders, their craft, if not very ornamental, being at least large and roomy, with plenty of beam, and provided with thatched roofs as a protection against the fierce rays of a tropical sun. I soon concluded arrangements for one provided with sails as well as oars, and manned by a crew of four rowers and a steersman. Just as I had struck a very satisfactory bargain, I was saluted by a Madras native officer in command of four sepoys, who also had to join their regiment quartered at Pegu. They carried muskets and a goodly supply of ammunition; and I therefore thought fit to propose that they should accompany me, convinced that they would help me give a good account of any Burmese war-boats that might venture to molest us.

The offer was eagerly accepted; and I had every reason to be satisfied with my companion, who proved a very intelligent fellow, and was fortunately sufficiently master of the English language to enable me to dispense with that painful medley of distorted English, mongrel Hindustani and original Burmese by which I was in those days compelled to give expression to my thoughts when conversing with Asiatics.

It was customary at the time of which I am writing— and, for all I know to the contrary, may be so still—for the Bengalese to look down upon the Madras soldiers as a vastly inferior set of men, and especially to ridicule their helmets and general attire. Physically inferior they were without a doubt; but there was much in the way of compensation, notably their freedom from the unnatural trammels of caste; they were also more sociable, readily joining their officers in cricket and other games, and far more eager to acquire information.

The Bengal sepoy, on the other hand, was better set up and more imposing-looking, and there his qualifications ended: drill and other duties over, he became a somewhat sensual recluse, with no thought for anything save eating and drinking, and weighed down with sheer grief if he infringed the rigid line laid down by his own sect.

Beyond the ordinary and unvarying routine of everyday life, his mind was a blank; and it was no easy matter to avoid the mere shadow of offence with men so ready to impute their own sinister designs to others. Subterfuge and cunning occupied the place of intelligence; and when the veil was at last thrown aside, they appeared in their true character, repulsive and forbidding. Even then we were slow to believe it; and officers pinned their faith in their integrity, until the men turned round and shot them down without compunction.

The sun was well up, too much so indeed to be exactly pleasant, when we stood by the boat next morning impatient to be off; but our eagerness was to all appearances not shared by the Burmese, who seemed to have lost their heads, their courage oozing away as the time for departure approached, assailed no doubt by visions of decapitation, which would assuredly be their lot if captured in the act of conveying the enemy.

We were twelve, all told: under the thatch, which covered the middle of the boat, sat the native officer and myself, the sepoys and my servant; the steersman squatted on a raised platform astern, and the rowers sat for'ard.

I have mentioned my servant, and must devote a few

words to so important a personage. This admirable Bengalee, who *out of his own country* was bearer, cook, waiter, cleaner and tailor all rolled into one, seldom or never gave me occasion to find fault with him, either during the two years he remained in my service in Burmah, or when he afterwards rejoined me on my return to Bengal.

But perfection is no plant of earthly growth, and the poor fellow had one great drawback, certainly no fault of his own, and that was intense ugliness. So repellent indeed was he, that he absolutely struck terror to the hearts of certain charming young ladies at a large up-country station where there was much dining out. He was of abnormal height, and of unusually dark complexion; from his long, gaunt face shone very prominent, staring eyes; and he had a silent yet determined way of moving about, as if his master were the only person of consequence present, and ought to be attended to first.

I, of course, was quite used to his unprepossessing appearance and singular ways; not so the others, and I was eventually requested to discontinue bringing him as my table attendant.

The tide of public opinion ran so strong against him, that I very reluctantly had to send this excellent factotum away, though I felt thoroughly ashamed of my weakness in yielding to the braying of *vox populi*, dictated as a rule by some ignorant prejudice and not by a proper sense of the fitness of things.

The boat at length got under weigh, the mainsail was hoisted, and we made for the mouth of the river, at which point it divides into two branches, the Irrawaddy proper and the Pegu branch.

Here occurred disaster number one, a sudden and

violent gust blowing us high and dry on a sandbank. It was impossible to move the heavy boat with so few hands, so we called to our aid all the patience in our virtuous natures and waited amid howling wind and drenching rain, until the rising tide once more set us afloat.

We had not proceeded far on our way up the river before the sun gave signs of setting, and darkness was upon us. I left to the Burmese the solution of the difficulty that now presented itself, viz. where to lay to for the night, and they soon entered a creek covered in by thick foliage, which indeed, besides almost concealing the entrance, completely shut out the sky. But it contained an enemy not provided for in my despatches: the mosquitoes, evidently enraged at our unwarrantable intrusion, came forth in myriads, filling the air around with their hideous buzzing.

Nature and habit enabled the pachydermatous sepoys and aborigines to treat the onslaught with indifference; but my own irritation became ere long unbearable, and I ordered the boat into midstream, where we anchored for the night midway between two vast forests.

In one other place only, and that the notorious Panglang creek, have I experienced any approach to these in number and ferocity.

Their furious attack even disturbed my rest, provided though I was with curtains; while the sufferings of over a hundred European soldiers, ranged along the lower deck of our cargo boat, were displayed next morning in unequivocal signs. The language used throughout that trying night was more forcible than polite, though considerably more justified than the foul language one constantly hears at home from a certain class of people whom a heredity, as strong as that of drink or gout, has taught to embellish every sentence of their conversation with irrelevant oaths.

On this occasion I believe even the "Contemplative One" would have indulged in expressive language, at the risk of having to undergo a few more transmigrations, extending perhaps over a trifling billion of years.

Besides being free from the attacks of the mosquitoes, of which only a few stragglers continued to harass us, it was far more pleasant away from the trees, which shut out the little breeze there was; and, to my way of thinking at least, much safer, as the Burmese are adepts at stealing noiselessly through their own jungles, and we might have easily been boarded and cut down in cold blood.

As soon as the anchor held, and the boat pointed bow up stream, the all-important process of cooking commenced, and I was soon served with a curried fowl, an omelette, and a bottle of beer. The natives of Eastern lands can cook as no other race knows how; their curries and omelettes are unequalled at any restaurant in Paris, and they will improvise a kitchen of the simplest materials and under the most trying circumstances.

In camp, under the leafy canopy of a mango tree, I have often sat down to a dinner consisting of soup, fish, entrées, joints, game and pastry, all served *secundum artem*.

Things are sadly otherwise at home; if the kitchen range gets temporarily out of order—a very common occurrence—the cook becomes as irritable as a bear with a sore head, and even the simplest substitute for a meal is served to the accompaniment of *parliamentary* language.

Dinner over, I retired with my pipe to the stern to ruminate. After the excitement of the day came the inevitable reaction, and I certainly felt to all intents and purposes alone in the world.

Hitherto I had belonged to a comfortable mess, enjoying plenty of company and diversion, and surrounded by all the pomp and circumstance of war; now I was on an unexplored river, with unknown dangers at every turn. Amid these novel surroundings my thoughts naturally took a wide range, annihilating distance and dwelling upon the old, familiar faces at home. Anon the roar of a wild beast would recall me to my present position; and in one of the painful silences that followed—the *animals* in the boat had fed and were now buried in happy oblivion—I felt sure that another boat, much larger than our own, was rapidly approaching. To make assurance doubly sure, I dipped the blade of a paddle under water, and with the handle to my ear, distinctly heard the enemy advancing and already close at hand. As it was now past eleven, they had evidently calculated on finding us all asleep, and only with the utmost expedition did I succeed in arousing the guard in time.

By the time our arms were in readiness they were upon us: and, covering the gentleman at the helm, I informed him politely in his own language that any further advance on the part of his friends would compel me to deprive them of his own valuable services.

An ominous silence on their part convinced me that they were determined to board us, and indeed though my instructions concerning the prompt use of cartridge and bayonet would have made a considerable gap in their boat, the odds would still have been fearfully against us. This trial of strength was, however not to be; the boat steadily fell back, and the rapid current soon carried it out of sight.

We now breathed more freely, though some acquaintance with the native manner of conducting warfare caused me to station sentries fore and aft. For a time, our imagination supplied all manner of strange sounds, and at about one the native officer begged me to lie down and rest, promising that he and his men would be on the *qui vive*, and arouse me if necessary. I was at first reluctant to follow his advice, as the idea of having my throat cut while asleep and waking up a dead man, as the Irishman said, was not a pleasant one; and it was really out of deference to the officer's feelings that I at length assumed the horizontal, fully armed, and without the least intention of sleeping; for a refusal on my part would have implied unequivocal distrust of him and his men.

In spite of myself, however, I fell into a sound sleep, from which I awoke only when the sun was high in the heavens.

The native officer expressed a hope that the sleep had refreshed me, and then detailed to me all that had transpired since I had lost consciousness. Shortly after the commencement of his watch his attention was attracted by a fire some way up the right bank, round which a number of natives appeared to be dancing.

This was evidently a ruse to put us off the scent; for no sooner had the embers died out, than the hostile boat again approached, but, on being challenged, fell back as before. He had therefore refrained from waking me, and had evidently kept everything on board as quiet as possible, that I might not be disturbed by Burmese exclamations, never notorious for melody. It was thoughtful to a degree; and I did not fail to report all circumstances on arrival.

The enemy had evidently hoped to steal a march on us, finding us napping and consequently achieving their object without risk to their precious selves; strange to say, their plans were frustrated by so trivial a chance as my resolve to indulge in another pipe before turning in. The fire on shore was only an ingenious and favourite native *ruse de guerre* intended to restore us to a false state of security; in the creek we should undoubtedly have been massacred, so that the mosquitoes, reprobates though they were, unintentionally did us a good turn. After somewhat restricted ablutions, performed under considerable difficulties, and followed by a hearty breakfast, I resumed my seat in the stern of the boat, and, under the friendly cover of a large umbrella, proceeded to inspect the banks past which we slowly glided.

On either side stretched a vast forest of trees, festooned with creepers and thickly populated by various species of monkeys; the females, with their young clinging to them, remained in the background, but the males came out to the ends of the branches that overhung the water, evidently very angry at our approach, to judge from the manner in which they grinned and spat at us. They are timid, nervous creatures wherever met with, and interesting only when wrought up to a high pitch of anger, in which state they are charming and more engaging indeed than any other animal.

I was on one occasion called in to attend one that a friend had made hopelessly drunk. It was a somewhat cruel joke, but not without its ludicrous aspect. I put my patient to bed, where with its head on the pillow he looked painfully human. Next morning I found him awake, lying quite still; and in reply to my inquiry, which I made from sheer force of habit, he raised one hand to his head; and, out of regard for his general resemblance to my own species, I prescribed a brandy and soda, which actually had the desired effect.

Now and again a splash ahead would reveal an alligator finding it in his discretion safer at the bottom—such fear does man inspire among created things, many of which, could they but know their own strength, would soon lower his pride.

Birds possessed of gaudy plumage and discordant voices were very plentiful: there was the kingfisher perched on an overhanging bough with one eye on the water and his head on one side; and the burnished flycatcher darted to and fro in search of food.

My observations were rudely interrupted by a puff of smoke from the jungle, followed by another and another.

We were in fact being made a target of, which was the more awkward that the river narrowed considerably at this point from the fact of its flowing through a range of low hills.

These efforts, whether made by our friends of the previous night or by an independent party, were unsuccessful, though a kind of bullet did now and then bury itself in the thatch of the boat; we decided that to return their fire would be an imprudent waste of ammunition, as the party doubtless shifted their position after firing each shot.

We therefore steered straight up the centre of the river; and as some safeguard against treachery I held my revolver close to the steersman's head, and placed two sepoys with loaded muskets over the rowers, with instructions to shoot any one who attempted to jump overboard.

Proceeding in silence, interrupted only by the faint report of firearms from the bank, we soon reached a broader part of the river, where we once more anchored in midstream, and I instituted regular sentry duty, as the enemy were still unflagging in their attentions.

The persevering way in which they hovered about us pointed to some special reason; at one time I fancied "loot" was the object, and that, seeing soldiers on board, they had come to the conclusion that we must be escorting bags of rupees wherewith to pay the troops occupying Pegu. Or perhaps they thought that a single European, proceeding with a guard up country, must be some important personage worth a heavy ransom; even killing such an official might in some way benefit their cause, besides leading to some substantial reward.

In the immediate neighbourhood of Pegu I do not remember a single flag or pagoda, and certainly no trace of a village.

Birds, reptiles, and similar creatures seemed to be in undisputed possession; and as the mail-boats were seldom molested, and commissariat stores usually arrived intact, I suppose the authorities thought any periodical patrolling of the Pegu river quite unnecessary. On my report, however, an armed boat was sent down, but without encountering any marauding party, so the affair was allowed to blow over. Towards the evening of the next day we reached our destination, and were one and all heartily glad of it.

The prospect was nevertheless far from inviting. With the exception of a span of raised road, and a very inadequate apology for a town, the whole country side resembled an endless waste of water, broken only by patches of trees and shrubs.

The road, which was about a mile long, terminated at the foot of a flight of steps that led up to a large pagoda, on the terrace of which, some thirty feet above the surrounding level, the troops were located, and would have to remain during the remaining few months until the monsoon was at an end.

There was, at any rate, no immediate fear that lack of water would be included in the many straits to which we might ere long be put.

Ascending the steps—and they were legion, giving me a far better idea of infinity than any professor of mathematics had ever succeeded in demonstrating—I found myself on a level platform extending all round the pagoda proper, at the edge of which stood the European and native barracks, that accommodated the detachments from various regiments of which the garrison was composed.

There were samples from Bengal and Madras, including some of the 1st Madras Fusiliers, the finest men I ever set eyes on. Cabin'd, cribbed, confined as they were in this limited space, all looked well, contented, even happy, though I was at a loss to imagine how they managed to pass such long days with so few duties to perform, and such slender resources, in the way of books and other amusements, at their command. The secret of their health lay, without doubt, in their being unable to obtain more than the authorized allowance of "grog."

Some there were too who, a few years later, took an active part in suppressing the Mutiny, being especially conspicuous in the operations that centred around the theatre of the most important engagements of the whole movement, Benares and Lucknow. I need not dwell on their exploits, for they are written in imperishable letters throughout the chronicles of that mighty upheaval. My intercourse with them was marred by one unfortunate and unlooked-for circumstance, over which I prefer to draw a veil, for the person concerned succumbed after performing miracles of valour; and then and ever since I regretted my inability to be near him before it was too late.

After having reported my arrival, and mentioned our adventures *en route*, I was conducted to the abode I was to occupy, nothing more or less than a huge *pongyee* house, large enough to accommodate half a dozen. It was constructed of teak, supported by massive pillars, and substantially roofed; moreover, it was open at the back, where it abutted on the pagoda, and innocent of doors.

The flooring, composed of split bamboo, was rather more than two feet from the ground, and was covered with mats of the same material.

But for this raised flooring I should, when the floodgates of the upper regions opened upon us, most probably have lost all my available furniture, which, though scarcely worth insuring, certainly sufficed for my modest requirements, comprising, as it did, a camp bed, table, and chair; two bullock trunks, a brass washing basin and stand, and a strip of carpet.

My new lodging was not by any means as snug as my old quarters in the Rangoon stockade; nor was my "factotum" slow to perceive the difference, though with that practical common sense that went so far to atone for his afore-mentioned ugliness, he at once set to work to make matters as straight as possible. In the first place he swept the place out, above and below, the vigorous application of a *vis a tergo*, in the shape of a birch, giving sundry frogs and scorpions summary notice to quit their old homes on the ground-floor.

H

Then, having next dislodged from the interstices of the upper storey a vast accumulation of dust, ants, and spiders, he arranged my furniture as his own judgment approved. Most of all I missed the verandah, to which I had always been accustomed, a place where, in sunshine or rain, one could always obtain some sort of exercise and enjoy the beauties of nature. Here they were all hidden from view, though I could hardly bemoan the want of ventilation, since the wind searched out every nook and cranny of the house, blowing at times so hard as to create no little difficulty in the matter of keeping one's lamps alight.

A breeze was, however, generally more welcome than not, for the direct rays of the sun, and reflected heat from the pagoda, induced a temperature very trying to Europeans in general, new arrivals in particular. A hot mist, the result of evaporation of the surrounding water, stretched as far as the eye could reach in every direction. The average rainfall during the monsoon was, as far as I remember, some 120 inches; and whenever Jupiter Pluvius checked the flood, the clouds would roll away, the sun shine forth in all his might, and even the crows would pant in comparative silence.

As the sights of the place could be disposed of in a quarter of an hour, consisting of barracks above and water below, and as it was moreover impossible to move a step beyond the terrace, life soon narrowed down to the routine of daily duties, occupying the early morning and evening, and leaving the day to be disposed of with such resources as individuals possessed in themselves. To those destitute of such, life must have been as slow as a twice-told tale; day after day, week after week, month after month, the same ordeal, the same familiar faces, identical surroundings, and nothing to do; everyone glad when the rain fell, equally pleased when the sun shone; anxious to rise, still more so to go to bed. Yet in spite of this almost intolerable "*nuy*" —as I once heard a soldier pronounce it—I never had charge of a healthier garrison. They were, it is true, cut off *in toto* from all sources of dissipation; but, even allowing for this, I was unable to account for the unusual immunity from illness, the more so that even among the native population it was equally noticeable.

Indeed, a few cases of snake-bites and fever, as well as an occasional accident, yielded all the professional work which fell to my lot; I felt, in fact, almost ashamed to accept my pay, but it was so generously pressed upon me every month by the paymaster that I had not the courage to refuse it for fear of giving offence; and my conscience was, after all, somewhat quieted by the recollection of all I had to endure in the shape of climatic hardship and personal inconvenience from every kind of tormentor, insect and reptile, which in this place converged to a focus. Crows and kites found it a most agreeable *rendezvous;* they swarmed around from "rosy morn to dewy eve," the former eternally jabbering and quarrelling over the remains of defunct animal life and the *débris* of many a repast.

Impudent, arrant thieves as they were, not unfrequently advancing boldly inside the barracks and other dwellings, we should have suffered without such admirable scavengers, insatiable, and endowed with singular intelligence, cunning, and general aptitude for the position assigned to them by nature.

Pariah-dogs would also steal into the place by some mysterious path, also useful scavengers, but rewarded, I fear, with more kicks than caresses.

In Burmah, as in India, they are only half domesticated, showing the same aptitude for education as elsewhere. They are as omnivorous as the jackal; nothing comes amiss to them, animal or vegetable, dead or alive. The jackal is, if I remember aright, not met with on the Burmah side of the Arracan hills. It may be the country is distasteful to them from the luxuriance of its vegetation; anyhow, their absence is a blessing to mankind, were it only on account of the manner in which they make night hideous with their weird cries, to say nothing of their predatory proclivities and offensive smell.

Another matter of vital importance to all desirous of enjoying a good night's rest—upon which more depends in the tropics, where the excessive heat so thoroughly exhausts the whole system, than at home—was, as I soon had occasion to learn, constant attention to the entirety of one's mosquito-curtains, ever so small a hole being fatal to one's repose.

These blood-sucking savages were greatly in evidence at Pegu—as where in the East are they not?—and of a fine, vigorous breed, gifted with healthy appetites, and evincing a decided preference for white flesh, wherein they resemble their pelagic prototype, the shark.

Most to be dreaded was the speckled variety, which, besides being more active and persevering, buzzed more loudly, and secreted a more irritating poison; a brace of them under the same canopy were not to be brought to book except after a long and tedious chase, involving a deal of tongue-banging and the employment of expressive adjectives, for which it is to be hoped every allowance will be made here and hereafter.

Whatever purpose the mosquito may have been intended to serve in nature's economy, other than that of tormentor-in-chief to mankind, has not yet been revealed; but for this post at least no one can deny its especial aptitude.

In spite of a prevalent idea to the contrary, it would indeed be difficult to exaggerate the discomforts of living in the East, even under favourable conditions; but when the adjuncts essential to even comparative comfort are from force of circumstances unobtainable, existence is more easily imagined than described. And those people give a very loose rein to their imagination who are wont to include a carriage and punkah in the category of luxuries: as well might an Anglo-Indian condemn the effeminacy of using fires and warm clothing during a severe winter in England.

Self-denial is a virtue that should be practised wherever occasion offers, but it is far easier to do so at home than abroad. Those that have never visited our Eastern possessions are too fond of decrying the luxuries of the Europeans that reside there; and this readiness to throw stones at their less fortunate brothers and sisters is particularly out of place in a nation so notoriously luxurious and extravagant, that it eats, I really believe, more than any other in Europe, and annually drinks sufficient to float the allied fleets of the world!

In the Pegu garrison, whatever our hereditary national tendencies might be, we could only procure what the gods, or rather the commissariat, sent us; and not the veriest ascetic could have lamented either the abundance, variety, or quality of our fare.

For the four months during which I was cooped up there the daily ration consisted of 1 lb. meat (including bone!), 1 lb. bread (including sand!), some tea, sugar, and salt, and a wineglassful of rum—the whole costing Rs. 15 *per mensem*, or one shilling a day.

The beef was doubtless furnished by buffaloes that had rendered many years' hard work to their rightful owners; the bread would have been tolerable, had it not been so gritty as to wear away one's teeth: the Commissariat Sergeant was one day very gratified by my complimenting him on the excellence of his bread, but his countenance fell many degrees when I begged that he would serve me the sandy part of it separately, so that I might add, as they say in the cookery book, "according to taste."

But there was from this time forth a marked improvement in the bread; and the other articles were not bad, though I had certainly tasted better tea, and had doubtless used sugar that left less residue at the bottom of the cup.

The condition of the surrounding country rendered it next to impossible to tap its resources, and our individual attempts to procure fowls and eggs met with no success whatever. The aforementioned commodities had accordingly to do duty for a considerable period; and it was during the trying time when necessity compelled us to make the best of them, that I especially regretted never having dived into the art and mystery of cooking, which I regard as conducing more than any other to length of years, domestic happiness, and a steady, unruffled stream of good temper and forbearance with everything and everybody. My "factotum" certainly did his best, but that did not include miracles.

Beef alone admitted only of being roast or boiled, and the changes were accordingly rung on these economical methods of cooking. To rum in any shape I was never very partial, although, when good and indulged in judiciously, I believe it to be a most wholesome beverage. Made into punch with various adjuncts, it may commend itself; but the only one procurable here was water, largely impregnated with organic matter. All who neglected to boil and filter it incurred a very troublesome form of ringworm, which broke out all over the body, especially on the thighs and abdomen.

That troublesome worm the "Dracunculus" was also very common, and I should not like to venture on a statement of how many dozens of yards of them I have wound round various substances.

Towards the end of the rains, an appalling case of that singular disease Beri-beri occurred in a Madras Sepoy, though I cannot say whether the water was in this instance to blame.

I swallowed the daily allowance of rum religiously as a corrective to the water, generally reserving it for the post-prandial pipe, a combination that assisted the mind's eye in viewing matters in general through a roseate lens.

On very damp nights, when the rain was still coming down in its might, I found it salutary to keep a large wood fire burning on an uncovered spot at the other end of my residence; the smoke drove away insects, the heat dried the saturated atmosphere and damp clothes, while the flames brightened the gloomy surroundings.

Over this conflagration I would silently smoke my pipe and husband my meagre allowance of rum and water, and this was frequently the most pleasant hour of the twenty-four, as, keeping well to windward, neither flames nor smoke incommoded me in the least.

Among the many insect pests, whose view of the beauties of the fire differed in all probability from my own, were those extremely disgusting creatures, yclept "Flying Bugs," which are of a greenish colour, about the size of a lady-bird; and which, on the slightest provocation, emit their horrible effluvia. They come forth of an evening only: the musk rat is bad enough, and to be avoided; the Flying Bug is ten times worse, and to be dreaded!

To keep these visitors at bay, my "factotum" used to hold a large umbrella over me at meals; many of them would nevertheless alight on my tablecloth and would even occasionally invade my plate; nay, I even remember a specimen between my teeth, and shall never forget the fœtid taste or the sickness that resulted.

Not fifty yards from my abode were the barracks of the 1st Madras Fusiliers. On night, as the sentry was pacing up and down, an animal suddenly sprang over the low parapet close to him; it was a tiger, and on his coming to the charge, it disappeared as suddenly as it had come. They had been reported prowling around the cattle, for the rains were nearly over, and dry land was beginning to appear.

The circumstance caused a sensation at the time, and became a nine days' wonder in the garrison, after which it was forgotten.

Some little time afterwards I awoke in the night—a very unusual proceeding on my part—and beheld two great, fiery eyes glaring at me out of the darkness, and apparently belonging to something within a few feet of my mosquito curtains. In an instant the idea flashed on me that this was *the* tiger, and terror so prostrated me, that I could only lie still, scarcely daring to breathe, turning hot and cold, and looking in a fascinated helplessness straight into those cruel orbs, while I marvelled even in my agony at their changing colours.

It occurred to me that the mosquito curtains were bothering him; otherwise, why should he keep staring at me thus?

A thousand things flashed through my brain, and the events of my young life marshalled themselves before me in rapid succession. Perhaps my thoughts, varied as they were, did not take many seconds of time, but to me it appeared an eternity: and yet the tiger never moved!

At last the suspense became intolerable; and, having at length resolved to end it one way or the other, I stealthily grasped my sword, and with sudden energy drove it into the curtain and into a soft body, which disappeared with a fearful yell—a pariah-dog! He and his companions had to their advantage discovered the whereabouts of my food, and it was the sound of the lid falling back on the now empty chest that had awakened me; and to this day I never could conjecture why one of the troop preferred watching me in that way and giving me such a fright.

Henceforth I bore the race no very friendly feeling, and lost no opportunity of retaliating.

To keep them clear of my sacred precincts, I employed a native bow of peculiar construction, termed a "Golail" and bullets of well-baked clay; and I soon became a sufficiently accurate shot to convince them of the desirability of giving my quarters a wide berth.

I carefully replaced the lid on the empty provision chest, without telling my "factotum" a word of the night's events; but on calling for breakfast, fully aware that not a crumb had escaped the burglary, I watched his face narrowly and was glad!

Utter bewilderment, fright, anger and despair were

all portrayed there; he managed to brew some tea, and
I had to be satisfied with that and a pipe—fortunately
my tobacco had been stowed away elsewhere, otherwise
I verily believe that they would have eaten that as well,
and probably felt none the worse for it!

As the waters receded, native dwellings sprang up
around as if by magic, and Burmese came from—goodness knows where! They divined our wants, and, like
every other nation on the face of the globe, were not
averse to supplying them at a good profit. Hitherto,
my expenditure had figured at the modest amount of
Rs. 25 a month, 15 for rations and 10 for my servant,
while the balance was accumulating. Two pound ten
shillings was not excessive for a month's living and
attendance, while quarters were free.

A new arrival brought to the station some beer and
other delicacies, and the morning after I had dined
with him, I awoke a wiser and a better man, for, truth
to tell, the sameness of diet was beginning to tell on all
of us: man may not require a variety of stimulants,
but the stimulus of variety is at all times essential to
his well-being.

We were also able to extend our sphere of exercise;
at first along the main and only road to the river; and
then, with extreme caution, in other directions.

This was an intense relief after having been cooped
up so many months in such limited quarters; indeed
we were in some respects worse off than Noah and his
family when they left the ark.

But though there was no miraculous intervention in
our behalf, we were wonderfully protected from native
hostility from without; what would have told fearfully
against us was an epidemic of any sort, such as cholera,
dysentery or typhoid; and that single case of Beri-beri,

so acute and so rapidly fatal, afforded me great anxiety for many days afterwards.

The sufferer was pitiable to behold; every secretion of the body was in abeyance, and there was a total suppression of water and comatose. I was preparing a dry bath of heated air, by means of very hot bricks that were to be placed under a chair on which the patient was to sit, enveloped in blankets. But time was not afforded to try this, the only plan that occurred to me.

When he died, he was unable either to articulate or swallow; the latter process would in any case have been of slight use, since there was not a drug in the whole of the Pharmacopœia that could have saved him.

There was indeed a species of "Mudar," a plant with succulent leaves, that fringed the wells, and the juice expressed from it had a very beneficial effect upon the aforementioned ringworm: the complaint and its remedy were thus strangely in juxtaposition, one inside the well and the other outside.

Supposing, however, that Beri-beri was induced through the same channel, one could scarcely expect to find its antidote there also; and even if it were there, it would have to be administered at the outset before the disease had sufficiently declared itself to admit of diagnosis.

In cholera, intermittent and yellow fever, together with many other diseases of an epidemic and endemic nature, I have for many years believed that the true remedy will be found in germicides administered, not through the digestive functions, but hypodermically direct into the system, so that its actual contact with the germs shall insure their destruction, at the cost of some suffering, maybe not without risk, yet the only possible remedy. I advocated it in the East in respect of cholera, but in the service one was never free to act, except under the auspices of a host of inspectors, whose chief talent lay in the art of dishing up piles of statistics, sufficiently appalling to confuse any government.

Life was beginning to wear a very different aspect, for we were elated at the approaching prospect of shooting in the jungles that were teeming with large and small game; and moreover the weather would greatly improve in our favour.

Alas! certain detachments of European troops were ordered to the front, and I had to accompany them. Such is military life, especially during a campaign; and there was nothing left but to pack up and obey.

The men and officers were equally jubilant at the idea of proceeding to the headquarters of their regiment, and enjoying the good things that were invariably to be found there.

A new place is moreover always attractive in prospect, whatever its reality may prove; all fields look green in the distance, a happy provision for mankind in general.

Here, at any rate, was a chance of disturbing the mental cobwebs which had accumulated during our enforced isolation, and an opportunity of seeing what might prove a brighter side of life. All was at once transformed to bustle and activity; and the boats inspected and portioned out might be seen a few days later floating down stream with their living freights.

A day or two previous to our departure, an officer, who had just arrived, asked if he might have my quarters. He hailed from the Madras Presidency, and proved a very jolly companion. His bed was placed parallel to my own, though some little space intervened, an arrangement that enabled me the better to observe the habit that had acquired irresistible influence over him—

he was an inveterate smoker. He invariably affected Trichinopoly cheroots, things of a gigantic size with a hollow reed down the middle, a specimen of which I remembered having indulged in on the Hooghly, when hard up for tobacco, and I also remembered that the consumption of this delicate weed had made me so giddy that I could hardly reach my cabin.

Now, amongst this officer's baggage stood a large square package, done up in "ganny," and looking for all the world like a bale of cotton. He informed me that this held 10,000 *Trichys*, "the number I generally carry about with me, you know!"

He smoked all day long, and even at nights there was an eternal globe of fire glowing through his curtains— he evidently was not destined to be prematurely cremated.

CHAPTER VIII.

UNDER ORDERS.

"He is a soldier, fit to stand by Cæsar,
And give direction."
SHAKESPEARE.

Facile est descensus! It was one thing to be pulled against a strong stream; quite another to have it in our favour. It was one thing to ascend the river, a solitary European in the company of many natives, but very different to be one of a fleet going down with some two hundred Europeans fully armed, men of training and renown, who had won many a hard-contested fight in the face of fearful odds.

I do not suppose that any regiment had seen more active service than the old 1st Bengal Fusiliers, or had been more instrumental in conquering and defending our vast Asiatic possessions.

In physique they could not on the whole compare with their brother regiment on the Madras side. The reason was obvious; the constant gaps occurring in their well-tried ranks had to be filled by an annual supply of young recruits, while the Madras contingent were, from their position, deprived of the opportunities of seeing such service till the Mutiny broke out, when they demonstrated unmistakably that their fighting qualities were only lying dormant, and waiting for an opportunity to come to the fore.

With either regiment you might go anywhere and accomplish anything that lay within the power of man; and, though several decades now lie buried with the past, I doubt not but they are still the same, only called by different names.

We had approached Pegu under difficulties, creeping along in a nervous, spasmodic manner, and on the look-out for unknown dangers at every turn; we left it at such a pace, that even the monkeys looked askance at us, all their former anger now changed to sheer amazement.

If my memory serves me right, we reached Rangoon the same evening, and were transferred to a river-steamer and flat, the latter being a cargo-boat. I beheld the old stockade, and some of the familiar faces, for the last time.

When I next landed there, eighteen months afterwards, not a vestige remained; the whole place having been transformed to suit the European style of living. The only episode that remains to recall this landing to my mind was, strangely enough, my being introduced to a European lady. I had long concluded that all Europeans were of my own sex, so that on the occasion of this *rencontre* I was as bashful and tongue-tied as a youth in love. Since then, when I have been more constantly thrown into their society, my tongue has gradually loosened and my blushes have—alas!—grown imperceptible; but all this has not been accomplished in a day, nor without a considerable amount of inward perturbation.

This reintroduction to a specimen of the fairer portion of creation, though of an ephemeral nature, doubtless had a salutary effect on me; but, however much I may have desired to improve our acquaintance, inclination had to succumb to duty, and on the morrow the paddle-wheels were in motion, and the steamer forged ahead, while the flat, attached by a stout hawser, followed merrily in its wake.

Rangoon gradually faded from view; we were ploughing the main artery of the Irrawaddy, and our worthy navigator took a short cut, which may have saved time, but was in the end far from conducive to the comfort of the men.

Sunset came upon us in a creek notorious for its elephantine and ravenous mosquitoes, for when that fiery orb sank in the western sky, the captain had no choice but to anchor.

Navigation of a river required the utmost caution even by day; by night any attempt in that direction would have been foolhardy.

I have already given a faint idea of the sufferings endured by the men the whole of that livelong night. I have already apologized for the tropical temperature of their language, and I shall not dwell any longer on so painful an experience.

Leaving this place of evil reputation the following morning, we once more entered the main stream and pursued the even tenor of our way. Some unusually large alligators were basking in the sun along the muddy banks of the river's many outlets; and so nearly did their own colour correspond with that of their surroundings, that it was often impossible to distinguish them, until, on being awakened by the thud of the paddle-wheels, they would look up and then crawl or tumble into the water. Now and again, a rifle was brought to bear on them; but the bullets would simply glide off their impenetrable hides, and they crawled leisurely down to the water as soon as they had had enough of such amusement.

Years afterwards, when floating down a river, I shot one that was lying asleep on a sandbank. Beyond once opening its mouth, it never moved; but on landing and approaching cautiously, we discovered that it was quite dead. That shot was, in the mysterious phraseology of sportsmen, a "fluke"!

We soon passed the scene of the disaster that had, only a few months before, caused such a sensation in Burmah and Calcutta, bringing on the devoted heads of certain parties one of Lord Dalhousie's stinging rebukes.

Curiously enough, this check to our otherwise triumphant progress occurred in the same place (and under very similar circumstances) as that of 1825. Mismanagement, divided authority and imperfect knowledge of the place and its resources, one and all combined, led to the failure.

The "butcher's bill" was a heavy one, and our hospitals at Rangoon were crowded with wounded men. As I was probing the wound of a soldier who had been struck in the thigh, there rolled into my hand a gingal ball the size of a small orange. It was of iron, beaten into circular form and covered with facets; an ugly missile, capable of causing a very dangerous, jagged wound.

Fortunately for my patient, it had well nigh spent itself, otherwise it must have shattered the whole thigh. In another case, a bullet entering the elbow of the right arm, came out at the left. He was in the act of loading when hit, and the bullet had travelled the whole way under the skin, which subsequently mortified, leaving an extensive surface that was only healed with the greatest difficulty.

Instead, therefore, of viewing the scene from a cargo

boat, and surviving to delight the reader with these interesting reflections, my bones might have been bleaching in that very jungle, for it was actually for this expedition that my services were declined in an abrupt manner that has already received recognition in a previous chapter.

Not far above the place with such a chequered military history, we encountered a boat proceeding down river with unusual speed, and could only just gather a bare outline of the news it was conveying—viz. the assassination of a person holding a high position—when it continued its course with the same energy as before.

Circumstances of a peculiar nature must have attended a tragedy of this kind, for, as I have already pointed out, crimes of such turpitude rarely disfigured the Burmese character in the days of yore.

They were singularly free from the foul breath of that "green-eyed monster," jealousy, the mainspring of two-thirds of the long and appalling list of crimes with which the natives of India are branded, and furnished with abundant food for litigation.

Climate is no doubt a powerful factor; but this does not account for such wide differences in the character of two neighbouring nations, the reason for which must be sought rather in the degree in which they act up to the moral code laid down for them by Buddha.

On a par with the rest of this teaching, the distance between the sexes was strained to its utmost extent, an exaggeration that amounted to absurdity, if not crime, for to attain "complete Nirvana" a man must not even look at the opposite sex, not even, in theory, at his own mother if she were drowning. He might throw her a log, if at hand, but no more. The ties of matrimony cannot, one would imagine, be very strong among a nation, of which the men think nothing of staking their wives and children on a wager, while the wives acquiesce in it as a perfectly reputable proceeding!

The appearance presented by the banks between which we were now advancing, was by no means as wild and undisturbed by the hand of man as the Pegu branch; villages and cultivated patches met the eye rather frequently, though of so inconsiderable an extent as to imply that the country was but sparsely populated. It was up the smaller tributary streams that their dwellings nestled, beyond the immediate influence of a river subject to sudden floods. They were built on piles as an additional security, and even then, communication could at times only be kept up by means of boats.

Not an agreeable mode of living, according to our notions, but then the Burmese had never known any other, and besides, being to all intents and purposes amphibious, they were endowed by nature with temperaments of the Mark Tapley order, and consequently happy under almost any circumstances. Very weird was the sound of their strange voices, as they passed us dexterously paddling their canoes, and chanting one of their barbaric songs.

They would stop and look at us as we steamed past, as would also the women and children peeping from behind the trees, wondering whether we were really children of this earth, and doubtless frightened by the noise of the paddles. Many of them probably recalled the incidents of the first Burmese war; the manner in which we fought and the weapons we made use of accounting for the rapidity with which they yielded all the important places to an organization well fitted, as they could see, to carry all before it. Now and then by carefully planned ambushes in the depths of their jungles they might score an occasional advantage, but any open encounter invariably ended in their confusion.

Temples, poles bearing all manner of flags, and images of Gautama, cross-legged and contemplative as usual, and certainly the reverse of prepossessing, met the eye wherever villages existed, and in many places where they did not.

Some of the temples and Pon-gyee houses were exceedingly elegant in their design.

Without any remarkable adventure, we arrived one evening at Prome, where we anchored, without, however, landing. It was unquestionably situated in the prettiest part of the river, which here narrowed between a range of low hills clad in verdure.

The Pagoda, some little way inland, stood out in bold relief on rising ground, while the numerous Pon-gyee houses, scattered here and there, lent an additional charm to the scene. As the sun blazed against the Pagoda next morning, we were off again, having but a short distance to traverse before forging the last link in the chain by reporting ourselves at that important frontier station, Theyetmyo.

The reunion of a regiment, that has been for some time scattered in detachments over a large country, resembles that of a large family under similar conditions; and human nature, bad as it may be, undeniably scored on the credit side in such a meeting. There is generally no lack of gaps, whereby such proceedings are duly leavened with sadness, and there may be raw recruits, uninfluenced as yet by the *esprit de corps* which animates the older hands.

On this occasion the absentees returned intact, which

was not only a piece of good fortune, but reflected great credit on the officers in command; in a bad climate and under every disadvantage, such a satisfactory result could not have been attained without constant supervision, attention to important details, and a thorough knowledge of the conditions of a soldier's life, and how to handle a body of men discreetly. It is to be hoped that they obtained the praise due to them. It is not always so in mundane affairs. Among notable instances of neglect in this particular that occur to me, I may mention a couple of cases in the Mutiny that appeared to me especially flagrant.

A clergyman, for instance, who bore the heat and burden of the day, was present at all the operations in and around Cawnpore, scrupulously read the burial service under a heavy fire, and nursed gallant Peel in his own quarters at imminent risk to himself. All he obtained for this heroic conduct was a scant notice in the Gazette, not even a decoration or cross.

On another occasion, a handful of officers responded to the call and charged some guns, when the Goorkhas had refused to advance: the thanks which they received were hardly worth the paper they were written on.

The welcome was cordial on all sides; all hands vied in their eagerness to carry the baggage from the boat to the barracks, and there was no mistaking the expression of honest satisfaction which lighted up their faces. The men celebrated the event after their own fashion, and the scanty means at their disposal; the officers in theirs by a dinner which, if not aldermanic, was at least creditable to caterer and cook in such an out-of-the-way place.

I was honoured with an invitation, and went with the captain of the steamer, in whose company I had to return to Prome the following morning. There is no rest, they say, for some people. Having delivered over my charge, I had no longer any immediate responsibility, and should be a free man for about a day. The pleasure of the evening was further enhanced by my unexpectedly meeting an old schoolfellow, one of the officers of the regiment. Although we had not met for upwards of a dozen years, recognition was mutual, indeed his face was not easily to be forgotten. A mournful kind of beauty ran through his family in a very marked degree; and on one occasion during the Mutiny, when riding into a station, I recognized standing by a gun, a brother of his, with whom I was also at school. The former I still encounter occasionally where men most do congregate to watch our game of games; his brother is at rest.

One of the saddest features of a "retrospect" consists in the thinning of the ranks of old comrades. Year by year they fall away, leaving one feeling very old and isolated, and new friends are but poor compensation for those of one's youth, around whom cling so many pleasant memories. I well remember the day that my old friend went into action by my side: the bullets came in showers; men were falling fast, so indeed were the leaves, which gathered thick about us like those in Vallambrosa. We were five hundred against ten thousand, but, as our men refused to advance, a hasty retreat back into the entrenchment was our only alternative. . . . . . .

The party was certainly kept in full swing until a late hour; and we had much to relate of past and present, for there was no knowing when we might meet again. The regiment would in time return to India, a larger country than those at home are generally given to suppose; and there again we did encounter one another, and, curiously enough, both were once more on the war-path.

At last, we broke up; and, bidding our entertainers adieu, the captain and myself made our way back to the steamer, where I slept the sleep of the weary.

Had I been my own master, I should have elected to remain for a few days at Theyetmyo, in order to look around; but I was under orders, and literally, as well as metaphorically, the captain was in the same boat as myself, more work having been cut out for both of us by those who pulled the wires.

Landing late one afternoon and re-embarking soon after daybreak, enabled one to form but a hazy idea of the place. I remember a very brief walk, a mess-room and—the reader will forgive me any details of what occurred after dinner! It was an important station, as it guarded the line which separated our acquired territory from that of the King of Ava, the legitimate owner of the whole.

I noticed, however, that the position was judiciously chosen; and was doubtless impregnable while protected by the 1st Bengal Fusiliers who, if attacked, would have given a good account of themselves. The men were also more healthy on the whole than those of other stations, where disease usually gave the doctor more work than either sword or bullet.

Our operations had so far been confined to the banks of the rivers; of the interior, its mighty jungles and mineral resources, we knew little or nothing. We merely annexed the lower half of the country, rich indeed, but from all accounts inferior to the upper part.

Most men, weatherwise in political meteorology, prophesied that the course of events would compel us to steal the whole loaf; but the time arrived considerably later than they had anticipated.

The Mutiny, disturbances on the Indian frontiers, European complications and the stealthy encroachments of Russia kept us otherwise well employed; an advantage, inasmuch as it enabled us to consolidate the territory which we had already acquired, before impetuously rushing further afield.

When the occasion did arrive, the succession of events clearly demonstrated the difficulty of subduing the more warlike and energetic races further north, at bay in the heart of a country immeasurably more adapted to their peculiar mode of warfare; and the annals of that campaign reveal many obstacles in the shape of trying marches and loss, irrespective of disease, but they also teach how perseverance, supported by ample resources, conquered in the long run.

With this last achievement in furtherance of our already colossal mercantile development, it looks as if, as far as Asia is concerned, we had at length arrived at the end of our tether; and well might we echo Alexander's complaint, that there are no more worlds left to conquer.

With the vast empire of China, which bounds our possessions on the east, we are scarcely likely to meddle; looking at the northern frontier, neither Nepaul nor Bhootan would be particularly desirable acquisitions; and as for Thibet, we shall, if wise, leave that inhospitable region alone, except under the utmost provocation. Our western frontier has certainly caused sufficient anxiety, and in the event of European complications is likely to cause more. Not very long ago, we had a golden opportunity of rendering it unassailable; but just then another party took up the reins of

Government in this country, a party pledged to reverse the policy of its predecessors. It fulfilled its promise with a vengeance; so much so, indeed, that its advent was by many considered synonymous with Russia's opportunity.

Our eastern frontiers having at length received their geographical limitation, insatiable John Bull is now gaining ground in the neighbouring continent, and it is an unfortunate omen for the new departure, that at the very outset its horizon was darkened by accusations, which, whether true or false, must dim the halo that at first surrounded that well-intentioned expedition to relieve a party who, it appears, would much rather have been left alone. . . . . . .

In spite of the late hour at which I turned in, I was up on deck at an early hour next morning. With the indispensable cup of tea and the most enjoyable pipe of the day, the captain and myself paced the deck as the vessel travelled down the river at a great pace, passing objects almost as soon as they came in sight. I should have liked more of this river life, which always appeared to me the most enjoyable way of travelling in a hot climate. By day, the movement created a breeze; at night, which was much cooler than on land, one was considerably less tormented by mosquitoes.

Early hours, so impressed upon us in my younger days by the advice contained in a well-known couplet, were also the rule to the advantage of every one, and they were certainly conducive to health, if not in every case to wealth and wisdom. A speciality of our river steamers used to be the excellence of the food supplied on board; you might sit down without an appetite, but the Malay cooks would provoke one: in the serving up of fish they were particularly successful, though unfortunately their own species lack flavour, while we spoil our own delicious harvest of the sea by our lamentable ignorance of cookery. A Malay would do more with the sole of one's boot than an English cook with one from the Doggerbank; and would make it more palatable and digestible.

When travelling by steamer on duty, the sum of Rs. 5 per diem was deducted from one's pay under the name of "table money;" and, as it included everything, it could not be termed excessive. In the matter of liquor, the system naturally admitted of great abuse, though in all my river trips I never saw more than one instance of advantage being taken of it.

Long ere this, Government has probably taken a leaf out of the book of the P. & O., reducing passage-money, and charging wine, &c., separately.

And now, having arrived alongside the jetty at Prome, it only remained for me to go ashore and report myself. No; another duty had first to be performed, one seldom or never of an agreeable nature; and that was taking leave of the captain, a very good fellow, who had studied our comfort in every way and was a favourite all along the line.

It proved only a temporary farewell, for I often met him again in his cruises, smoking with him the pipe of peace and enjoying a certain dish which he knew how to prepare *secundum artem*.

CHAPTER IX.

PROME.

> "A Daniel come to judgment! yea, a Daniel!
> Oh wise young judge, how I do honour thee!"

UNINVITING as may have been the immediate surroundings of the last place, few stations could vie with Prome in all that was picturesque. Situated on the left bank of the river, it consisted of a limited and undulating tract of country, covered with fine trees, from the branches of which hung beautiful creepers in graceful festoons; shrubs and undergrowths also grew thickly among the timber. The Burmese must, in selecting the spot, have had an eye to that which nature had already rendered beautiful; they then improved upon it according to the canons of native art—not by any means for the benefit of "οἱ πόλλοι," but as a sylvan retreat, wherein priest and monks could lead a purely isolated and ascetic life, away from the busy haunts of men, with every facility for contemplation and with as few hindrances as possible on the main road to "Nirvana." Judging from the size and number of the Pon-gyee houses, one would imagine that the religious fraternity must have mustered there in great numbers, ere the spoiler turned them out and appropriated their sacred dwelling to his own sacrilegious uses. All is fair in war; these elegant edifices of teak, built on piles along either side of the main road, and now converted into residences and mess-houses, had, but a few years since, presented a picture that would have evoked ecstasies from an artist. There, shaded by the luxurious foliage of the tamarind, dwelt the original occupants, some reading, others sitting cross-legged in emulation of their master, a few, maybe, imparting to the young the doctrines of their wondrous religion.

Then, everything suggested peace and harmony; now, alas! the bugle is for ever resounding with its periodical "Puddings and pies for officers' wives;" whereat the officers would assemble alone, for their wives—poor "grass-widows!"—were far away.

Facing the river to the right were blocks of hastily constructed dwellings for all sorts and conditions of men, necessary adjuncts to a large force, which had to be lodged, fed and clothed; and some way behind these came the "Sepoy lines." To the left, well intrenched and guarded, lay the Commissariat Stores, on which so much depends when once the dogs of war are let loose. All men, irrespective of race or colour, fight, as did Napoleon's soldiers, "on their stomachs;" but it is the European element which so taxes the hard-worked officials of the Commissariat department; they must have their daily rations of meat, bread, porter, tea, sugar and condiments, besides every kind of comfort, when lying sick or wounded. And when I assert that the Indian Commissariat department was second to none in the world for efficiency, organization and uprightness, I know no one can contradict me. Presiding over this essential adjunct at Prome was a man who, to the regret of all who knew him, died in India some years afterwards, and we shall perhaps never look on his like again.

The Burmese quarter of the town was still further to the left, occupying more level ground and of considerable extent. Many of the native buildings were on a grander scale than those usually met with, bamboo being discarded in lieu of teak.

In the midst of them we naturally constructed a prison, near which soon sprang up that emblem of civilization, the gallows; but I am happy to put it on record that, during my tenure of office in a medical capacity, it was never once used. Neither—to the credit of the Burmese, be it said—were there many candidates for the gaol, though I never shall forget the amazement of the few at such an unintelligible mode of punishment.

Of all the people I ever came across, I should consider the Burmese the least capable of bearing such restraint; they were so independent, so fond of freedom, air and exercise. With our egotistic proclivities and insular pride, we are but too prone to pounce down upon a conquered country and force upon them there and then our own laws and notions of the fitness of things, utterly regardless of the material with which we have to deal, and ignoring the impossibility of moulding it all at once to our own complicated judicial system.

We make no allowance for the influence of centuries of heredity; we overlook the fact that their notions of right and wrong are based upon a totally different code of ethics from our own.

That faithful servant, who made away with his father's murderer in obedience to the laws and faith of the tribe among whom he was born and bred, should have merely been dismissed from the service, without being in addition deported to the Andamans; and it would have been better for India in general, and an exalted personage in particular, had his sentence been thus simplified.

We lose sight of the fact that we are aliens ourselves, and only in possession of these countries by might, and not by right; our strength is that of a giant, and as such we use it. One of the most pitiable sights I ever saw was the incarceration of these few Burmese.

Our system was to blame and not the Assistant-Commissioner, than whom not a kinder or more humane man existed.

With the welfare of the people at heart, he resided among them in the centre of the town; and the very fact of his being able to do so in safety so soon after our conquest speaks volumes for native principles and his own moderation. Many a time and oft did I wend my way through the streets of an evening to keep him company, and return at night, without a sign of molestation.

The opposite side of the river, which was at this point narrower and deeper, was also hilly and laid out in plantations of custard-apples, the fruit of which did justice to the care and skill lavished upon them. Those in India were very inferior to them, as much so perhaps as is a crab-apple to a Ripston-pippin! After the rainy season, and as soon as it was sufficiently dry to admit of the operation, the undergrowth in and about them was set on fire, and a pretty sight it presented at night, as the zig-zag lines of flame ran up the hills in every direction.

I can quite understand how this annual celebration enriched the soil, directly through the distribution of carbon and potash, and indirectly from its increased exposure to the sun and atmosphere; but what passes my comprehension is how the trees themselves escaped injury.

Either the rapidity with which the flames advanced prevented any real danger accruing to them; or else the cultivators themselves must have devised some expedient whereby the trees were rendered fire-proof. They could be seen superintending the operation, regulating the direction of the flames, and beating out any that ascended too high with long bamboos. The soil on these hills was no doubt peculiarly adapted for this fruit, a fact which the inhabitants probably discovered by having seen some originally there in a wild state.

In spite of their laziness, they were no mean cultivators, and, as I saw on an occasion hereafter to be related, endowed with considerable ingenuity. That the soil of these hills fulfilled the requirements of the fruit in question in a unique degree, I gathered from the fact that I never came across it elsewhere. I should much like to assign a scientific reason, based on an analysis of the soil and the geological formation of the hills; but I regret to say that my knowledge in this branch of science was, in those days at all events, extremely elementary and unpractical. I had soon special reason to lament my ignorance in this respect, for I was to traverse a hitherto unknown tract of country, where nature had been exceedingly lavish of her gifts, animal, vegetable and mineral. Advanced age brings in its train to the majority of mankind varying degrees of regret for neglected opportunities, the inevitable longing after that which "might have been."

Chosen no doubt from the facilities it afforded, as well as for its strategical position, the military eye may nevertheless have been attracted to Prome by the sense of the picturesque; though, as it turned out, these superficial allurements concealed such deadly enemies as dysentery and an intractable form of intermittent fever, which played especial havoc with the European troops. And, contrary to all calculation, the higher they were quartered, the more severely did they suffer. Some European infantry, for instance, located in barracks half-way up the hill, was reduced at one time to a state of almost inefficiency; while the artillery men further inland, and in more open ground, were much less affected. The former arrived in its full strength, but in a few months could scarcely muster a quarter of their number of effective bayonets. As I passed their quarters on my morning "constitutional," it looked as if the men were mustering for parade in their dressing-gowns, and convalescents filled every verandah. But the garrison was not in very great danger, as besides the above, two regiments of native infantry and one of cavalry were quartered there; a force in itself amply sufficient to cope with anything the Burmese could bring against us. Nor was it at all likely that they would beard the lion in his den, for, as experience had already taught us, their fighting was as a rule confined to remote spots in the heart of the jungle, a species of warfare of the most trying and unsatisfactory nature. A heavy responsibility rested at this time on the officers in command, who found it difficult to steer between the Scylla of severity and the Charybdis of leniency; and their difficulties were no wise lessened by the recent publication of the proclamation annexing the country, in spite of the significant fact that in reality we held little more than the actual banks of the river, the interior being virtually a *terra incognita*, where collisions were still the order of the day. As might be expected, a nice point arose out of this somewhat premature notification, with reference to the treatment of spies taken in our camp. A detachment in a difficult position, away from further assistance and threatened by armed bands, captured one in their midst. He was tried by a drum-head court-martial, sentenced and shot, according to the usages of war. But, said the authorities, we were at peace, and therefore the punishment was illegal! But we were only so on paper! War was still going on, even if it were in a desultory fashion; and for the preservation of the party it was deemed expedient to employ energetic and deterrent measures. Who was the best judge of the situation, the officer on the spot, or one thousands of miles away? To have kept the man a prisoner would have been no easy matter in such a situation, besides entailing a guard and thereby weakening a force that was already numerically small. Time and circumstances considered, it was a mistake to descend to such hair-splitting, as it tended to weaken the authority of the officers, besides causing them much unnecessary dissatisfaction. It was in fact one of those many cases in which theory and practice cannot be reconciled.

Soon after landing, I joined the battery of artillery on the other side of the hills. They assigned to me a large bungalow perched on a hillock, composed of three rooms communicating with each other and surrounded by a verandah. It was simply palatial in contrast with some of my recent abodes, making me feel a person of some consequence.

My stock of furniture was certainly somewhat limited, but I had all that was necessary, and in such a country the absence of anything superfluous was a decided advantage, tending as it did to limit the powers of concealment of various nuisances, such as rats, snakes and insects.

I could watch the rats with the utmost *nonchalance* as they chased each other along my bamboos; and many a snake forfeited his life through his inability to conceal himself. One afternoon I observed a very large one coiled up in the very centre of my bed, and, justly incensed at such unwarrantable intrusion, I grasped a long-bladed Burmese sword and advanced to to do battle. But in spite of my extreme caution, the bamboo flooring creaked, and the reptile decamped, not, however, before I had cut him in two. Snakes enter houses as a rule in pursuit of the rats and frogs which harbour there; in this instance, however, the intrusion seemed to have for its sole object the luxury of occupying my bed—a temptation to which he yielded with unlooked-for results.

Others I frequently killed when capturing a frog, which in such a case utters a series of sounds resembling the cries of a flogged child.

The solitary position of my abode was a matter of complete indifference to me, as I was generally out till late, and dined every evening at the mess, besides which, I always had writing to do when at home, and consequently preferred being undisturbed.

The mess fare was simple; but even had it been much more so, compensation would have been afforded by the society one met there. From the commanding officer downward, one and all were a refined, intellectual set of men, among whom I spent a most agreeable time, the pleasurable recollection of which is marred only by the afterthought of how many perished soon after in the Mutiny.

"Heroic Willoughby," of Delhi fame, was there,—all, all were good men and true!

As my sphere of duties widened to embrace the civil department also, the place grew upon me, and I hoped to remain there for a long time. Looking back, I often wish it had been so decreed! Men who had resided for some time in India thought differently, they longed for the time when their regiments should be ordered back.

And their wish was soon to be gratified: they returned just in time to get entangled in the outbreak, in which the majority of my old comrades were shot down by the men they trusted.

I was caught in the same trap, but escaped by the skin of my teeth. Circumstances unfortunately compelled me to remain on for many years; but I place it on record that from that time forward I loathed the country and the altered mode of Government, and I maintain, without much fear of contradiction, that under John Company's *Raj*, Europeans and natives were far happier than they have ever been since, or ever will be.

At Prome there certainly was a dearth of those amusements to which the majority of officers had been accustomed; but this was the case at most Burmese stations. The band and the mess were all that remained. There was very little sport; and libraries and billiard-tables were inadmissible, as part and parcel of campaigning equipage; the ladies too—where were they?

In its palmy days of yore, before the great convulsion, India was celebrated for its sociability, for the brotherly feelings that knit together Europeans of every denomination, and for the deference shown them by the population at large.

In every walk of life there is the hard lesson of how to take the good and bad together; and there is some justification of the way in which the officers yearned after their accustomed dances, picnics and hunting, in the fact that history has proved, in the most unequivocal manner, that the man who shines in the drawing-room and field makes the best officer under any conditions. He possesses more self-reliance, clearer judgment, and greater fertility of resource, not to speak of better-tuned nerves, in an emergency, than the more modern bookworm, whose mind has too often been developed at the expense of his body.

If the human machinery is to work efficiently, bodily and mental training must go hand in hand, and this is especially necessary in the case of the soldier. The pendulum with us is always swinging to extremes, and the present tendency is to train the one, and leave the other to look after itself.

The old Company may have erred in the opposite direction, by permitting young fellows to enter their service before, indeed, their education was sufficiently advanced; yet, what able men they produced!

The Mutiny arose from no fault of theirs, but rather from the evils of interference from home, by which the door of appeal was opened too wide, weakening that authority so essential to commanders, especially in the East. The leaven rapidly permeated throughout the mass, and the Sepoys, recognizing their advantage, improved upon it, as Asiatics know how.

The "annexation of Oude" and the "greased cartridge" episode occurred opportunely, and served as handles.

In judicial matters we were exacting; but in military matters we were far too lenient, the reason of this being presumably that the supreme command was vested in officers imperfectly acquainted with the Asiatic character, these new acquisitions coming periodically fresh from home, and consequently tinctured with much of the maudlin sentiment that thrives there in certain quarters.

In India generally, Europeans were but little given to pedestrian exercise, partly because the youngest subaltern could afford to indulge in a horse or pony, partly because the country was so very uninteresting, hundreds of miles of dead level road, lined on either side with the useful and ubiquitous mango, and acres of cultivation without a break, by way of relieving the depressing monotony.

Riding put a totally different complexion on the matter; the animals, unaccustomed to inequalities, were well suited to the roads; the exhilarating exercise covered a multitude of shortcomings, while hunting obscured them *in toto*.

At Prome, however, there was more by way of encouragement to pedestrians; well worth traversing on foot were the many interesting roads, turning here and bending there; now ascending a greasy hill, anon dipping into a valley, and following up a meandering stream, flanked with stately trees and flowering shrubs.

On all sides, the fly-catchers with their burnished plumage flashing in the sun, while various other birds in gaudy livery flitted from tree to tree; woodpeckers ran round them, tapping here and there with their hammer-shaped bills in quest of hidden treasures, while the agile movements of the squirrel lent additional charm to the scene. One walk was in special favour, leading, as it did, along the banks of the river, and then sweeping inland, enclosing with two others a huge space, in which lay our entire force. Its breadth and culverts were evidence of its military design.

The life in Burmah may have been irksome to many, but none could complain of its expense. What with no house rent, a necessarily curtailed mess, and various subscriptions in abeyance, military tailors realized many an outstanding debt.

Extended credit, and proportionately protective prices had placed purveyor and recipient on the horns of a dilemma, from which this campaign released them.

It must certainly have been an anxious time for the man of business; and as he ran his eye down the list of casualties, one must sympathize with him, as much as is possible in the case of traders that make those who meet their liabilities pay for those who do not. I was young at that time, and had only advanced a few paces on the independent road of life; and the yarns unfolded afforded me an insight into the recesses of human nature.

War, whether waged in a just cause or the reverse, is always a lamentable occurrence, but this campaign afforded another illustration of the adage relating to an "ill wind." To save money in such a situation reflected no credit on any man, simply because there existed no loophole for extravagance of any kind. It was a case of necessity rather than choice.

As soon as the river had contracted once again into its ordinary bed, which it does very soon after the rains are over, I obtained a day's leave of absence, in order to pay a visit to a famous haunt of wild-fowl. Such at least was its reputation, and for once in the course of her long life, Dame Rumour had spoken correctly.

Something like an hour's journey by boat brought me to a perfect El Dorado of geese and ducks. When we had reached the extensive "jheel," or swamp, where they most did congregate, one of my men procured me a small native boy, who was delighted at the prospect of paddling me about in his own canoe. I had soon taken up my position in the bow with gun and ammunition—those were the days of powder-flask, shot-belt and wads—and we forthwith raised the alarm, the immense numbers of fowls fairly blotting out the bright sky for several moments.

I discharged both barrels into the flock, and, ere I could look round, my amphibious little guide was in the water, retrieving the dead and wounded, which were all ordinary ducks and geese in excellent condition. As this was a very likely place for an alligator, I felt extremely nervous on the boy's account—the only drawback to a very pleasant and exciting day; but as he seemed rather to enjoy it than otherwise, I tried to persuade myself that the danger was one of my own creating. He enjoyed both the fun and the "tip" I gave him, for it was not every day he had the chance of earning a rupee.

Ere many weeks had rolled by, the kaleidoscope of military affairs was again shaken, and, to my infinite regret, the battery was ordered elsewhere.

My country house had therefore to be vacated; and I believe that even the colony of rats, lizards, frogs and mosquitoes, with which I had shared it, regretted my departure. The snakes, upon whom I always waged unrelenting war, were doubtless mightily pleased. As for the others, as long as they kept their place, I lived, and let live. Their name certainly was—legion!

Whatever may have been my regret at the sudden

and unexpected turn in the tide of affairs, very little leisure was permitted for the purpose of brooding over the stern decrees of fickle fortune.

Military life consists in being here to-day, there to-morrow; and is indeed a nomadic existence, only relieved by its eminent respectability.

"Move on," is the everlasting dictum of War Office and policeman; and one has, during the active years of one's life, but few opportunities of settling down in the midst of one's few household gods. This constant moving under orders is apt to cling to men, even after their retirement from the service; and this accounts for the reputation enjoyed by Anglo-Indians as the most restless of mortals.

On first returning home, they pitch their tents in "Asia Minor" (known to some as Bayswater); thence they move on through Bath, Cheltenham, and Leamington, until their circuit of the island is put a stop to by a last fatal illness. This wandering proclivity is further encouraged by the absence of ties to any particular spot; for the Anglo-Indian, returning after years of service in the Far East, is ever thrown into a train of melancholy associations by the reiterated question: "The friends of my youth, where are they?"

CHAPTER X.

A SECRET EXPEDITION.

"He deserves small trust,
Who is not privy councillor to himself."

ONE evening when at dinner, I received an official letter, which ordered me to proceed on the following day to a spot some miles down the river, and on the opposite bank. My luggage was not to exceed a specified weight, and further instructions would await me on arrival. I was moreover to consider the communication of a confidential character, which pointed clearly to some enterprise only to be revealed to those actually concerned, and not by any means intended as food for station gossip.

I accordingly dropped down the river the following afternoon with my old attendant, any possible difficulty in discovering the place having been surmounted by their placing a look-out there to show that I was expected. But for the unmistakably official character of the communication which had summoned me hither, the proceedings resembled a ruse to entrap me.

Nor did the place serve to allay such a suspicion; on landing I saw nothing but trees and shrubs, and the smoke from a fire some little way inland.

The look-out now assumed the character of guide, and politely asked me to follow him to the camp, at which we soon arrived. Nestled among trees at the base of the hills was a considerable force of European and Native Infantry and Irregular Cavalry, while guns and gunners were conspicuous by their absence. That intelligent and useful pachyderm—the elephant—also mustered strong, those present being strong and of large size, evidently carefully selected for the occasion.

This formidable array of colossal mammals were picketed apart; had they but been cognisant of their own strength, they might have nipped the expedition in the bud.

This largest and most sagacious of animals is also the most docile and obedient, gifted with a good memory, affectionate in return for considerate treatment, but never failing to resent an injury.

Perhaps his most apparent characteristic is extreme restlessness; viewed at any time, either his whole body is swaying to and fro, or else one of its members; the large ears flapping, the trunk fidgeting, or the feet being raised alternately from the ground. He is wonderfully observant of all that is going on around, for his eye, though small to outward appearances, is very strong of vision, its disproportionate minuteness being a beautiful adaptation of a means to an end, since, were it larger or less protected, it would be liable to constant injury in the tangled vegetation of the jungle. Many folks are unaware of the somewhat singular fact that twice the circumference of any elephant's foot, measured on the ground, gives the exact measurement of his height. I once gave practical demonstration of this curious fact to the manager of a menagerie, and his astonishment was certainly great.

The total absence of wheeled conveyances in itself told a tale, implying an excursion into a wild and unexplored country devoid of roads, for some specific purpose known only to those in authority, while the importance of the enterprise was to be gathered from the fact of its being led by the Chief Commissioner himself. His intimate knowledge of the people and their language, to say nothing of his many other eminent qualifications, fitted him for the post; and, moreover, whatever he undertook, he was in the habit of performing thoroughly. He was in fact our Commander-in-Chief. There were, besides, two officers belonging to the European detachment and a quartermaster with the natives.

I shrewdly suspected that my summons to attend was an afterthought at the last moment, the original intention being to employ only a native "medicine man." I was confirmed in my suspicion by the fact that everything was ready for a move, even to an armoury of medicines and appliances. When and how this force of men and elephants had assembled there, was best known to themselves; at Prome, few if any suspected it, so adroitly had everything been managed; as for myself, I had not the faintest idea of what was going on, until the scene already described burst upon me.

That evening was a very pleasant one; my welcome was cordial, and we chatted during and after dinner, though not even a passing allusion threw any light upon the object or destination of the expedition.

This was my first march, and I was therefore deeply interested in all the preliminary details, including several readjustments of weights.

As I moved to my allotted quarters, my eyes fell upon a very pretty scene, the first of its kind that had ever come under my notice.

The night was fine and clear, and the silvery moonbeams dancing on the river close at hand, brought out in bold relief the whiteness of the tents under which reposed so many soldiers. Lower down appeared the horses and elephants, tethered *secundum artem*, the former comparatively still, the latter still busy with their arboreal food, and evincing signs of that characteristic perpetual motion to which allusion has already been made.

The camp fires were dying away, yet ever and anon a puff of wind would fan one into flame, which lit up the sleeping forms enveloped in thick blankets. Besides warming the surrounding air, the fires emitted large volumes of smoke, to the detriment of mosquitoes and other equally unwelcome intruders.

The profound stillness in which the whole scene was wrapped was broken only by the ripple of the river or the occasional splash of a fish.

So absorbed was I in the scene before me, that I was, until addressed, unaware that any other man was near me. It proved to be my assistant, a native of much intelligence, who ultimately showed himself a trustworthy man, always ready to assist in his own or any other department.

After a brief conversation with him, from which I gathered several important details relating to the package and transport of our available stock of medicines, I called my valet and turned in, my last words being those of the poet, "Call me early!"

This injunction proved unnecessary, for I awoke of my own accord a great deal too soon, ere the darkness had fled. Soon, however, we heard the sound of hammering at tent-pegs, and we knew that our first day's march was about to commence. By the time we were dressed and discussing some hot tea and toast under a tree, the first faint streaks of dawn appeared in the east, and the force moved inland.

With the advanced guard, consisting of some troopers, rode our Burmese guides: close on these followed the Commissioner and officers, accompanied by a few more Burmese, men of some standing, as was evident by their dress and bearing.

Behind marched the bulk of the infantry; then the elephants laden with camp-baggage, while the rear was brought up by the remainder of the infantry and troopers.

Roads, properly so-called, there were none; here and there we came upon some kind of tract, but it never lasted any time; notwithstanding, but few halts occurred, and these were chiefly owing to signals from the scouts, who fancied they descried movements ahead.

The country was undulating and covered with low trees and shrubs, many of which bore bright coloured fruits or berries, which we admired, but let alone, knowing from experience that things fair to look at in those lands are oftentimes dangerous to eat.

In the declivities we crossed several *quondam* water-courses, which now contained but a few small pools. Some little apprehension was at first entertained as to a sufficient supply of water, and the length of the marches had to be regulated by what we came across of this very essential commodity. For the bipeds a moderate supply would suffice, but the horses, and more especially the elephants, required a large allowance, and the anxiety was chiefly on their account.

From the nature of the country, the column was necessarily attenuated, forming an imposing sight when viewed from an eminence, as it moved leisurely across country. The dips and rises in the ground made it appear as if broken at intervals. It is an old-established custom, when on the march, to call a halt when about half the distance has been accomplished; the men are then allowed a good quarter of an hour, during which they fall out and refresh themselves with cold tea or water, which they carry for the purpose in bottles cased in leather and slung over their shoulders. Very short black pipes also come to the front on these occasions.

Officers perform somewhat similar manœuvres; and in times of peace, arrangements are made for enjoying such luxuries as hot tea and coffee.

At the end of the day's march the Europeans and natives soon pitched the tents; the process of cooking made rapid progress under the skilful hands of the natives appointed for the purpose; the elephants, relieved of their loads, went a short distance into the jungle, where boughs were lopped off certain trees for their consumption.

After we had refreshed ourselves with a bath and a good meal, we sat outside our tents chatting, and presently turned in, having first repacked many things ready for an early start next morning.

With the exception of some birds in the surrounding trees, the country seemed devoid of living things, bipedal or otherwise. The animals had doubtless been scared by the unaccustomed noises inseparable from the march of such a force. There was not a sign of a village in any direction, our route had evidently been most carefully considered beforehand, and we were steering clear of all frequented places, with a view to effecting a surprise.

In this way we crept stealthily along. As march succeeded march, the character of the country varied, our surroundings becoming daily wilder and more picturesque.

The jungle grew taller and thicker, numerous and extensive clumps of bamboo reared their graceful heads high in the air; trees became more abundant, of immense size and venerable with age, while creepers with thick skins and large leaves ramified in every direction to such an extent as to render many parts inaccessible, save on the back of an elephant.

After the first day's march, game literally swarmed. Of a morning, the clear, shrill note of that handsome and delicate bird, the jungle-fowl, resounded on every side, and when able to use the elephants, we shot large numbers of them with a fair sprinkling of partridges. Deer were plentiful, as also tigers and bears.

During a halt, one of the Europeans engaged in pitching the tents happened to see a pair of eyes peeping from a thicket close at hand, and, aiming a blow with a mallet, he succeeded in felling a small deer, which had evidently been too paralyzed to effect its escape. As an addition to our table, venison was not to be despised; at the same time the Eastern produce is very inferior to our own, which may be said of the game generally, with the exception of the jungle-fowl. This bird combines elegant plumage with a piquant flavour rarely met with in Asiatic birds, yet only when hung the proper time. It is a very shy bird, frequenting those spots where the undergrowth is thickest, and running for some distance when alarmed, eventually rising a short way from the ground, and flying along with cries of alarm.

Situated as we now were, the chance of a shot rarely occurred, though later on we made amends. Neither, as subsequent events clearly proved, was it wise to enter those thickly wooded parts *on foot* in search of game.

I was taught a lesson which eventually cured me, but will reserve an account of it for the proper place.

Instead of marching direct on our quarry, whatever that might be, it soon became evident that we were describing a circuitous route, not only for the aforementioned reasons, but also to avoid a deep and rapid river, which would have brought us to a standstill. On we plodded, therefore, through wilder country, coming one day upon a few houses strongly pallisaded, but to all appearances long since deserted. It was indeed difficult to conceive what could have induced a few families to migrate to such a place in the heart of a jungle swarming with wild beasts, which must have carried off their children and cattle even during the day.

This may have led to their departure; if chosen for retirement from oppression, or for the purpose of contemplating amid nature in her primæval condition, the selection showed admirable judgment. The residential portion of these dwellings must have been twenty feet or more from the ground and the pallisade, which included a circle twelve or fifteen feet in diameter, and contained only one door.

It was a great relief to find that the settlement had been uninhabited for some time; otherwise, had the residents simply fled at our approach, there was no calculating how far the news of our proximity might not have preceded us. Still greater caution would then have been necessary, for the Burmese, with their knowledge of the topography of the country, might have opened on us all the inconveniences of a guerilla warfare.

So far, fortune had favoured the brave Commissioner whose fertile mind had conceived and organized the undertaking. If he entertained any misgivings as to the ultimate success of the expedition, they never appeared on the surface, for he was bright, cheerful and sanguine throughout.

We were far away from any kind of help; few indeed were aware of the expedition; and being himself the ruler of the country, there was no one to whom he could report progress. He was, moreover, dependent on the integrity of those who were guiding him through a country hitherto untrodden by Europeans, destitute of roads and bristling with almost insurmountable difficulties. He was mainly depending on secrecy and a circuitous flank movement.

On the other hand, he doubtless placed considerable reliance on his thorough knowledge of the Burmese character. Yet, in spite of this, how could he be sure that intelligence would not by some means or other be conveyed to the party in revolt? We have reason to know how rapidly events and proceedings are communicated in the East; how they travel through the length and breadth of lands that know not the telegraph; and if anything like a determined opposition had been offered along the line of march, we should have suffered great losses, until retreat would have probably been still more disastrous than any advance. Thus the Commissioner was unquestionably taking upon himself a heavy responsibility and courting unusual risks, from motives best known to himself. We could only enjoy a satisfactory peep here and there, and indulge in conjectures; but ere long, the curtain was to be raised and the whole scene viewed at a glance. It was a bold conception, and ably carried out by a master mind!

Hitherto it had not been my good fortune to come across a teak forest, but we now skirted one. Judging from the regularity of the spaces between the trees, it looked as if the process of thinning had been employed, and the survivors were of large size, great height and immense value.

As this was the season at which they shed their large rough leaves, the interior of the forest was lighted up, otherwise it must have been as dark as Erebus. In one place, a bear was seen shuffling along as fast as he could travel, evidently dismayed at our intrusion, and too far off to have a shot at, even had we been so minded.

There was then a craze for teak-wood, and, as the forests were indiscriminately and ruthlessly felled in this and subsequent years till irreparable mischief ensued, this one probably shared the fate of the rest. Subsequently our Government realized the gravity of the situation, and appointed a forest conservancy, which, considering the mischief was already done and the teak requires about eighty years to arrive at maturity, was rather worse than locking the stable-door after the steed has been stolen.

Defoliated as they were, the sight was nevertheless a grand one, and more than realized my expectations. This tree has been introduced in various parts of the East, but nowhere does it thrive as in Burmah, the soil and climate suiting it equally well.

The largest bamboos too that I ever came across were in this country, and I have cut specimens some nine inches in diameter. The rough leaves of the one and the glossy surface of the other contain a large proportion of silica.

No wood approaches teak for ship-building purposes, as it is easily worked, durable and insect-proof. Most of our old East-Indiamen were composed of it, outliving even those constructed of oak.

Since entering the "Iron Age" of ships, the demand has greatly decreased; but this wood is still employed almost exclusively for the purpose of decking vessels of any size and importance.

I believe the P. and O. used formerly to send their vessels to Bombay, where they were decked with teak under the superintendence of Chinese carpenters, who understood that particular branch better even than ourselves.

I shall have occasion to return to the subject of the Teak trade in a subsequent chapter.

Leaving this forest on the left, a few days' march brought us to the fringe of a sparsely inhabited country, and we came suddenly upon its one village.

So far from being afraid of us, men, women and children approached the camp, squatted down, and surveyed us with ludicrous curiosity, seemingly forgetting all else. They merely sat there, looking first at one thing, then at another; admiring the tents, but amazed beyond measure at the whiteness of our hands and faces.

My canvas having been erected, I retired to have a wash, and, nude to the hips, I was soon enjoying a lather. Finding the atmosphere very stuffy, I told my servant to throw back one side of the canvas, thereby admitting what breeze there was.

He did so; when, what was my surprise on finding myself face to face with some twenty natives of both sexes squatting around my tent. On beholding me, their tongues were loosened, and they uttered exclamations indicative of wonder and delight.

My first impulse was to have the opening closed again; but it was a very hot day, and after all, if my ablutions afforded them satisfaction, there was no harm done. Inwardly I was convulsed with laughter, which

I managed, however, to control with the aid of my towel and soap.

They watched me dress and brush my hair with the same interest, and were unfeignedly sorry when the operation was concluded, and I stood before them clothed and severe. Then it was that they beckoned my servant, to whom they imparted their strong desire to possess some of that wonderful stuff, which would make them white also.

He gave them a cake of soap which they examined with extreme curiosity, and departed. During the rest of the day, applications for soap, coming chiefly from the women, were numerous.

The account I gave of the scene at breakfast evoked much merriment.

CHAPTER XI.

FURTHER DETAILS.

> "Oh solitude! where are thy charms
> That sages have seen in thy face?
> Better dwell in the midst of alarms,
> Than reign in this horrible place."

PRESIDING at the table was the Commissioner, who, with the rest, appreciated the ludicrous position in which I had been placed. I do not think that he was altogether pleased at having come across the people at all; but it now only remained to look the matter boldly in the face, and, as far as possible, to prevent the news from spreading. In this I think he was successful, for the march was continued without any attempt at opposition, and, as matters turned out, we eventually arrived at our destination without having to strike a blow.

At the best of times, even under cover, the natives lack cohesion; in the open they are nowhere, being too heavily handicapped by want of discipline, indifferent weapons, and inherent apathy and ignorance.

It is more difficult to assign any adequate reason for their poor show of fighting qualities when strongly entrenched; the few who had ever faced and survived disciplined troops and English guns probably exaggerated their own prowess, and consequently, too, the number and strength of the enemy.

The theory of fighting appears to constitute in the eyes of the Burmese a very amusing game: it was their delight to build a great stockade, arm it with what weapons they could muster, and fancy themselves secure from even the most daring of intruders. Untaught, too, by numerous reverses, it was also their fancy that an enemy invariably attacks in front, so that any flank movement completely disorganized them, all their strength having been concentrated on the front of their building. Had we, for example, attacked the Rangoon Pagoda—the key of the whole position—from the front, our troops would to a certainty have been frightfully punished; but we moved under cover of the jungle to the east side, where we were least expected, and its defenders ignominiously fled without anything more than the faintest show of resistance.

The result of coming in contact with such peaceful, well-behaved natives inspired greater confidence into our party; and while scarce a shot had been fired hitherto at any kind of game, partly owing to the nature of the surroundings, and partly because we thought it might be distasteful to our worthy chief, no objection whatever was now raised to a little shooting, and it was in this wise that I encountered my first tiger in his native haunts and majestic beauty.

We were encamped in a large open space by the side of a somewhat broad but shallow stream, which furnished men and animals with the best and most abundant supply of water that we had come across since our departure. Nor did its advantages end here, for, besides to some extent protecting one side of the camp, its rippling music was very refreshing to our ears as we rested during the heat of the day.

As the result of a conversation, in which sport was

the leading topic, it was agreed that four of us should go in a body and see what we could make of the jungle-fowl, which had, as usual, been crowing away that morning all along the line of march.

Accordingly, towards sunset we sallied forth, the two officers belonging to the European detachment and their orderlies, the officer in command of the Sepoys, and myself, with a Burmese lad to carry my ammunition.

A few minutes' walk brought us to the jungle, which we at once entered, on the *qui vive* for whatever small game might turn up, the idea of encountering anything larger having, strange to say, never occurred to any of us. We were soon threading our way through an exceedingly pretty part of the jungle, amid gigantic trees with gnarled trunks, festooned with creepers, and inlaid with delicately-tinted and waxy-looking orchids, that peeped out everywhere from a profusion of spotless green leaves. These beautiful flowers, which always appear to me to be gifted with more expression than perhaps any other, seemed to warn us of dangers lurking within that tangled mass of vegetation, the haunts of the cruel python and other formidable creatures. There is much to be said in favour of the orchid, in spite of its lowly position in the vegetable kingdom as a parasite, or, to let it down more easily, an epiphyte. It is, in point of fact, a veritable robber, though not to the extent generally supposed; for, though it derives its sustenance from the tree on which it grows, yet this is extracted from the effete bark, and not from the juices. In this respect, therefore, orchids are more sinned against than sinning; sinners or no sinners, they are worthy of adoration, whether abroad in their sylvan haunts or as exotics at home. Exquisite in themselves, they show how, on so frugal a diet, they can rival any of our favourites, on which animal and other manures have been lavishly expended.

The forest now resounded with the report of double-barrelled firearms, and jungle-fowl were falling on all sides. Reloading, I followed, as I thought, in the track of the others, but their reports sounded further and further away as I advanced, and at length died away completely. Now and again I hailed them by name, but I might just as well have searched for a needle in a haystack as my companions in such a labyrinth, so I soon followed an independent course. That we had scattered was not to be wondered at—indeed, unavoidable; twisting about and facing every point of the compass in order to avoid trees and to steer clear of patches of thorny, low-growing jungle, both for their own sake and for the sake of what they might harbour, anything like keeping in touch was impossible. I found myself, therefore, alone, but for my little ammunition-bearer, who kept as close to me as he could, bounding forward whenever I fired, and every bit as interested in the proceedings as I was myself.

I had been creeping along cautiously for some time, looking to right and left and listening attentively, when it suddenly dawned upon me that it was time to get back to the camp. I accordingly did so with every feeling of confidence, but a few attempts convinced me of the fact that I was lost.

In my perplexity I took my boy into confidence, but, either owing to my imperfect knowledge of the language or his timidity, he proved but a Job's comforter. Nor was there any help to be derived from the position of the declining sun, as it was completely hidden from view by the thick foliage overhead and everywhere around; so I proceeded at random, all interest in the excursion having vanished, and my every thought centred on how to get clear of the forest.

Having performed the operation of "right-about-face," I must surely be making progress; and it is astonishing how, under such circumstances, a straw seems sufficient to clutch at. I was still fresh, which was something; a trifle warm perhaps, and well disposed towards a pint of the *dimidium dimidiumque* of the ancients had such been available, but, in default of nectar, I sought another comforter, that had often helped me to pull myself together and look an unpleasant situation in the face. My companion looked as if he would liked to have followed my example, but I had not even a cheroot to offer him.

Barely ten minutes after this the jungle terminated abruptly, and we came upon a green sward of considerable extent, and fringed with trees and undergrowth. It almost resembled an artificial clearing, inasmuch as not even a shrub intercepted its continuity; and I was on the point of crossing it when a terrific roar on my right sent all the blood back to my heart, and a magnificent tiger trotted into the enclosure. I was too taken aback to move; my pipe dropped from my mouth on to a stump, scattering its lighted contents over my feet. The tiger was a grand specimen—graceful, sleek, and beautifully marked, but for the moment his beauty concerned me far less than my own slight chances of escape. My thoughts involuntarily wandered for an instant to that farce in which the pariah-dog enacted a leading *rôle*—what a contrast to this awful reality! and I was just resolving to pour the contents of both barrels into his face, in the hope of blinding him, when he snarled at me and disappeared, lashing his tail.

This was a great relief, for the perspiration was

streaming down my face, and my teeth were clenched as in death. I recovered my pipe, and looked round for my boy. He was gone, and my calls received no answer. I would have signalled to him by firing, but the young absentee was in possession of both powder and shot, leaving me with only two charges to depend on in case of further emergencies. I was therefore compelled to proceed alone, coming to the conclusion that he had bolted on hearing the tiger roar, and had either made off to his own village or else succumbed to fear, or to *something worse*, the bare possibility of which I dared not contemplate.

Absolutely alone! Lost in a tropical forest, with night coming on apace, and no ammunition other than the two charges of small shot already in my gun. This was truly an enviable position, especially as the forest was known to be swarming with wild beasts, such as I had just encountered. I shouted once more for my boy, and plunged again into the thicket at haphazard, and in a state bordering on desperation. Anxiety and fear quickened my steps; my eyes seemed to penetrate further than usual, and my ears detected the faintest sound. I was startled by the snapping of a twig under foot, while the cry of a jungle bird terrified me. How I wished they were all defunct, or that I had never attempted to molest them in their hidden retreats.

In addition to my gun, I carried a stout branch, which I hurled at every suggestive clump likely to harbour any kind of animal. I realized to its full the couplet of the poet—

> " As in the night imagining some fear ;
> How easy is a bush supposed a bear :"

in my case a tiger. Hope was ebbing fast, so I scanned

the trees around, with a view to taking up my position in one of them for the night.

Even then I should not be beyond the reach of tigers, snakes, and black ants; while, if I fell asleep, I might have occasion to prove the literal truth of the words: *Periculosior casus ab alto!*

The outlook, both above and below, was certainly as bad as bad could be, and I felt sick with anxiety, and so weary with suspense that I almost wished the end would come and leave me at rest.

It was, however, decreed otherwise, and to my intense satisfaction the trees became further apart and the undergrowth less dense, and—oh, joy!—a familiar sound smote my ear, and I once more stood on the brink of a stream.

This was a relief in many ways. First and foremost, I lay my gun down, tucked up my sleeves, and drank greedily, for I was both hot and thirsty; and then I once more lighted my pocket companion and considered my position. Though matters had decidedly improved, I was still on the horns of a dilemma. We were encamped, it is true, on the banks of just such a stream as this; but, even if this were the identical one, ought I to follow its course up stream or down? The pleasing thought also occurred to me that animals are wont to make for the water to slake their thirst during the first watches of the night, but this troubled me far less than the choice of direction.

The ultimate result of my calculations was a decision in favour of moving with the stream; so I advanced with extreme caution, looking on all sides whenever I was following one of the many bends of its tortuous course.

Once, a large moving object loomed some way ahead,

leaving the water's edge and striking inland; it was probably a tiger, but the increasing darkness rendered identification impossible; and my attempts to ascertain the nature of its footprints when I shortly afterwards crossed its path were equally fruitless.

Save for the rippling of the stream perfect silence reigned around, a few stars twinkled overhead, and the dark line of the forest looked more gloomy than I had ever yet seen it. Doubtless my feelings painted the surroundings in unusually gloomy colours.

It was now half-past-six by my watch; and on making the next bend, I saw a light not very far ahead. It might of course belong to a party of the rebels out reconnoitring, in which event I should be between two fires. Stooping down and gliding inland from cover to cover, I approached cautiously; while, as I neared the place, other fires came in sight, and figures flitted past them. I crept closer and closer, resting for a few seconds behind each convenient bush; the figures were in the "shadowed livery of the burnished sun," though taller and slighter than the average Burmese. Still more cautious, and bent almost double, I traversed the remaining distance, soon making out every detail of the camp I had quitted the same afternoon. Not sorry to stand upright once more, I sauntered gaily into the place, whistling a tune, answered the challenge and proceeded straight to my tent.

The others were just sitting down to dinner, at which I soon joined them; after which, in return for their consideration in allowing me to enjoy the meal undisturbed by questions, I gave them a full account of my adventures, and was heartily congratulated on my narrow escape.

Comparing notes with my fellow-sportsmen, I found

that the whole party had scattered, returning separately, but in good time. Captain H.—the "long one," as we called him—had also encountered a large tiger asleep, and was just pushing a bullet down over the shot, when the animal awoke, snarled at him, and walked unconcernedly away. Considering how these animals rest during the day and prowl about in the evening, there was every reason to suppose that his tiger and mine were identical; if so, its experiences that day, encountering no less than three white faces—the captain's, his orderly's, and my own—were indeed probably without precedent.

That night, I slept soundly; and we started early next morning, for time was precious. Not long after the commencement of this march, we came upon a herd of wild elephants, which at once fled, making the jungle appear as if agitated by a strong wind.

It was just as well from our point of view that they did not attempt to fraternize with our tame ones. As a rule they are timid creatures; but the Rogue is an exception, and a very ugly customer to deal with, moving at a pace far beyond anything that could be expected of his size and awkwardness, and making the forest resound with his trumpeting.

Soon after this encounter, the camp was thrown into an unusual state of excitement. The Commissioner was cool and collected as usual, but news of an important and possibly disagreeable nature had evidently just reached him.

At any rate, a number of padded elephants, heavily laden with armed Europeans and Sepoys, were at once ordered to the front, and went off in hot haste. Without being aware of it at the time, we were within a day's march of a large stockade, the capture of which was the main object of the Expedition. For a few hours the camp was plunged in profound silence; the remaining troops being kept under cover, ready at a moment's notice for any emergency.

And so we remained until the shadows of the trees began to lengthen considerably, when one of the troopers galloped up with a despatch, from which it appeared that, as our force appeared in sight, the Burmese had fled for their lives, leaving only a few decrepid old men and women, some pariah-dogs, and a number of cooking utensils. Thus was extracted this thorn from the Commissioner's side without a shot having been fired. He out-Cæsar'd Cæsar, for he came and conquered without even seeing! Those who were not needed to garrison the place returned to camp that evening, while other elephants went with provisions, &c., for the new occupants.

From this it would appear that the Burmese were totally ignorant of our approach until we were within a day's march of their stronghold, and then in all probability only by the merest accident.

Some woodcutter in the vicinity may have spied us out that morning and, seeing so many laden elephants and armed men, conveyed a very exaggerated report of our strength. On the backs of these pachyderms must be large guns; at all events he fancied he saw them, and reported them.

He must any way have piled on the agony, else the enemy would scarcely have evacuated a position already strong by nature, and rendered still more so by art, without striking so much as a blow.

Such conduct indeed could only be accounted for on the supposition that they imagined us in possession of large cannon; the range and power of our guns may have been known to some of them, and, having already profited by the lessons of hard experience, they were by no means anxious for further instruction.

The evacuation was described as one of the most disorderly, precipitate, *sauve qui peut* affairs which it is possible to imagine. They melted away on the principle of "The devil take the hindmost," and they certainly left very little for his satanic majesty.

Some allowance must, however, be made for their behaviour. To their intense bewilderment they were about to be attacked in the rear, a direction from which they least expected it; and, while still cogitating over the unwelcome intelligence, they suddenly behold a herd of elephants bearing down upon their stockade as fast as they could be urged along, each teeming with redcoats armed *cap-à-pie*. A belt of forest moreover hid our force till close at hand, when its sudden appearance created a "panic."

All doubt and uncertainty were now at an end, and the sole remaining impediment to the peace of the province had now been removed by a bold strategy, in which were displayed some of the finest qualities of the human mind—true courage, self-reliance, ability to act on one's own convictions, and far-seeing perspicuity.

And yet our Commissioner was still anxious. The finale must have rushed upon him so hurriedly and unexpectedly; the relief from a state of tension to one of an opposite nature was also too abrupt, and the reaction gave him sleepless nights, during which he doubtless reviewed the momentous proceedings of the past three weeks. Extremes meet and produce like effects; and a sudden, unexpected stroke of good fortune will sometimes unhinge us more than an unlooked-for disaster.

All this was mere conjecture on my part, for, as I

have already mentioned, he never allowed his own troubles to be shared by others.

Another important qualification that characterized him was an instinctive knowledge of the exact moment at which to strike the decisive blow. It goes without saying that he must have employed trustworthy spies who, in the garb of mendicants or some other guise, succeeded in gaining admission into the stockade, heard all that was going on, and reported that afternoon the state of consternation in which the inmates were at the time. Nevertheless, had the enemy but delayed a day longer, there might have been some awkward resistance.

All round, then, the future Sir Arthur Phayre displayed the highest qualities, not only of Governor in a civil capacity, but also of General, *au fait* in the military branch as well.

CHAPTER XII.

"EL DORADO."

"Lovely indeed the mimic works of art,
But Nature's work far lovelier."

THE march was resumed next morning under the most favourable auspices, though still in the same methodical order; for although we were no longer in continual fear of molestation, it was nevertheless incumbent on those in command to make assurance doubly sure.

News arrived *en route* that "all was well" in the stockade, and that there were no signs of any gathering in the immediate neighbourhood. While traversing one of the last fringes of forest, our ears were struck with a peculiar droning sound, which seemed to come from our right. We were puzzled as to whence such a sound could proceed; it became louder as we advanced, and as we emerged from the forest, the cause of the disturbance met our astonished gaze.

At the bottom of the valley ran a broad and tortuous river. Rather to the left lay the stockade on what at first sight appeared to be an island, though a closer inspection showed that it was connected by a short, narrow neck with the mainland.

The land, which was under cultivation up to a certain point on either side of the river, was being irrigated by enormous wheels, curiously constructed of bamboo, much after the fashion of paddle-wheels; and the exquisite balance of the axles, combined with the action of the water, went as near as possible to "perpetual motion."

As these huge wheels revolved, the bamboo cylinders poured a continuous stream, the flow of which was regulated by floats, into a trough on either side, joined by a third, through which it was conveyed to the fields. There were a number of these wheels on either side the river, and by means of a dam, the water was turned in any required direction, with a force proportioned to its breadth. Altogether, I never saw anything more ingenious.

Beyond the cultivation on the opposite side, the country presented a still more hilly appearance, and was covered with trees of immense size and considerable variety. It was a picture of wealth and fertility, as charming a view as could well be imagined; and when the camp was pitched near the stockade, man and beast gladly looked forward to a few days' rest amid such enchanting surroundings.

Owing to the proclamation issued by the Commissioner, the agricultural population soon gained confidence and returned to their various occupations, seemingly only too glad to be allowed to do so.

Buying and selling became the order of the day, bazaars were opened, and before forty-eight hours had elapsed, a friendly feeling animated both parties, resulting in mutual confidence. Burmese men, women and children moved about as if nothing had happened, a little curious, maybe, and occasionally squatting near the camp, attracted more by the European soldiers than anything else.

These constituted in their eyes the greatest attraction; and the lady portion in especial regarded them with unconcealed admiration. Oh, the sameness of human nature! We all know the dangerous interest that these uniforms will inspire at home, from the domestic upwards; and here was the same magnetic attraction far away from civilization among the most unsophisticated of races.

On the day of arrival, many started off at once to inspect the stockade; but I curbed my curiosity until the sun was down in the west, when I knew I could proceed with greater comfort.

The entrance was well guarded, though open to all except the Burmese.

As I have already pointed out, the greater portion of its circumference was protected by the river, which it consequently commanded above, below, and across.

No wonder, then, that its original tenants thought themselves secure against the invader, until the unwelcome news suddenly burst upon them that we had outmanœuvred them!

In accordance with their customary mode of military engineering, the face of the stockade presented a curved line of stout timbers driven into the earth at an angle, and almost touching one another.

Behind, the natural level had been considerably raised, with a view to putting it above the influence of any abnormal flood.

The inner circumference was lined with wooden and bamboo houses, around which lay a pile of half cooked food and *débris*, just as the fugitives had left them.

A gang of men were, however, soon at work clearing a place and preparing suitable quarters for a permanent garrison.

When I had inspected all this to my own satisfaction, I made my way to the bamboo bridge which spanned the river a short distance below.

In spite of the alarming manner in which it creaked and swayed, it was very strong, though, by the very nature of the material of which it was constructed, adapted only to very light traffic. In the middle of the stream the water was deep, but so clear that one could distinguish every pebble on its gravelly bed. The sight of numbers of large fish darting hither and thither at once aroused my Waltonian proclivities, and I recollect that some of us tried our hands at the art with considerable success, though I have unfortunately no record of the size or species of the fish.

Most of my notes, together with everything else, perished a few years later in that wretched and disastrous Mutiny; could I but have foreseen it, I should have elected to remain in this El Dorado, and turned Buddhist!

An opening at the middle of this bridge afforded a glorious place for a dive, and, as far as we could ascertain, there were no alligators about, the water was too clear for these loathsome amphibians, which—being of the dirt, dirty!—delight in the solitude of a muddy river bedded with slime and ooze.

From this bridge, which was a favourite *rendezvous* of an evening, the view above was exceedingly grand, especially as the rays of the setting sun streamed along the valley in a gorgeous blaze, the like of which—and that only on a very small scale—I have only seen at Govilon on the Usk.

The dangers attending any expedition into the jungle afoot having been impressed upon the party in general and myself in particular, we determined to rove in search of that delicate chanticleer once more, but perched this journey on the backs of elephants. We made up the same party as before, each with an elephant; but this was a different affair, inasmuch as a quartet of these animals, advancing in line with stolid indifference to any obstacle smaller than a large tree, routed out the game wholesale.

I noticed that the jungle-fowl, partridges and hares swarmed especially near the edge of the forest, and concluded that they had, with a creditable eye to the main chance, taken up their abode as near as possible to the surrounding fields of paddy and other grain.

As there were eight barrels between us, the fusillade was continuous and the havoc considerable; what it would have been with breech-loaders I know not; but these were comparatively primitive days, and the delay consequent upon the process of reloading afforded the birds some respite.

Nor did every shot take effect, for the undergrowth was thick and the birds were strong and active; besides which, with the driver immediately in front, it was no easy matter for any one like myself, unaccustomed to firing from the back of an elephant in motion, to shoot in an oblique direction. Still, we managed between us to keep the larder well stocked during our stay there, though I fear I was more prominent as a consumer than otherwise.

A cold bird for breakfast was very appetizing; at lunch not to be despised; and not lacking customers when roasted for dinner.

These excursions were certainly most enjoyable; but there is no rose without its thorn, and none know the invariable truth of this better than those who have resided in the East.

In this particular locality grew a rampant creeper, fascinating to behold, but woe betide the unlucky individual who chanced to shake the plant while passing underneath it.

Hanging from various points among the surrounding trees, among which it twists and turns, may be seen large racemes of Papillionaceous purple blossoms, harmless, except for their unpleasant smell. At a latter stage, however, when they have podded, the outer surface becomes covered with fine, brittle hairs, which shower down whenever the creeper is agitated. Should they lodge on the naked skin, the irritation becomes maddening in the course of a few minutes, increasing as one scratches. It is the *Mucuna pruens* of botanists; in popular phraseology, cowage or Cow-itch. Strange to say, on this occasion three out of the four elephants steered clear of this undesirable " thing of beauty;" the fourth did *not*, and its occupant, Captain H——, the short one this time—received a dose on the nape of his neck which caused him to struggle as if he would pull his head off his shoulders.

He would without a doubt have inflicted serious injury on his neck, had not a native suggested a remedy: if an apothecary's shop had been available, we might have found something less disagreeable and equally oleaginous, the quality on which its efficacy mainly depended. In lieu thereof, we proceeded to a village where cows were kept, and the remedy was applied.

The natives have great faith in it here as in many parts of India. Formerly, it was considered an excellent vermifuge, and was administered incorporated with treacle, honey or syrup. How the rest of us escaped the same annoyance was a wonder!

The other drawback to the pleasures of this kind of

sport was the tiring movement, half jolting, half lounging, of the elephant.

Given the choice under ordinary conditions, I had rather walk ten miles than ride an elephant over two; bad as he is, however, the motion of a camel is a thousand times worse. There may be camels and camels, but agonizing are the best.

The stockade having been swept and garnished for the reception of the men detailed for this especial garrison duty, and friendly relations having been established with the natives, the elephants conveyed our equipage over a ford, and the pedestrians crossed the bamboo bridge, to a point on the other side of the river, where the camp would remain a few days preparatory to our final departure. This was a diplomatic test of how our friends would fare when we had marched off altogether.

The surroundings were still more wild and picturesque, the hills were also more broken, often almost perpendicular, and covered with very fine timber.

One glen in particular was extremely interesting from the number of images of Gautama perched on every available rock, it was evidently a place of resort for the pious aspirants to the true Nirvana, where they could contemplate in the midst of primæval nature, and far from the madding crowd. At the same time, I never saw a more likely-looking spot for a tiger; which would, for a true disciple of Buddha, constitute rather an advantage than otherwise, affording a good chance of another transmigration!

There were also a few temples, and excavations, which led—goodness knows where! Buddhists have at all times shown a preference for underground temples, as well as a special aptitude for constructing them.

A huge tree might be seen here and there, or rather

its configuration in *white ash*. For some purpose or other—most probably cooking—a fire had been lighted at its base, spreading to the tree and rapidly consuming the decayed wood. The fire would thus smoulder on, until trunk and branches were consumed and the ash fell *in situ*.

There were other prostrate trunks so completely petrified as to be hard as adamant; and the steps leading up to one of the temples were carved out of the fossilized remains of trees. Here, then, there evidently existed a highly fossiliferous stratum; and it was a source of deep regret to the Commissioner and myself that time and opportunity did not admit of further exploration in that interesting locality.

It was interesting to see how silica or iron pyrites can particle by particle permeate through the interstices of animal and vegetable tissues, thoroughly reproducing and replacing their lineaments to the minutest particular. A transverse section of one of these trunks would present the same appearance as wood—pith, medullary rays and concentric circles, and from the last named one could obtain a fair estimate of its age.

Once organized, endowed with sap and a circulation, giving out oxygen and absorbing carbonic acid, and performing a number of other functions, it became, under special conditions, nothing but a mould for the deposit of inorganic material, which permeated its structure by some almost inexplicable molecular attraction.

Constant wear had so told on these steps, that they were slippery to a degree; and, armed as we were with heavy boots, great caution was necessary when descending them.

Being moreover numerous and very steep, a fall would

have resulted in broken bones. The natives could run up and down them barefooted like so many cats; and were inwardly amused, no doubt, at our awkwardness, though far too polite to betray such unseemly exuberance in the presence of the "Lord-High-Chief-Commissioner!"

A most unusual combination of excellent soil and climate, assisted by so perfect and unique a system of irrigation, stamped the valley as a place of productiveness out of the common.

In those days, the country at large enjoyed a considerable reputation for tobacco, which, when cured, was remarkable for its dark colour and somewhat rank flavour.

I preferred it, however, to what "Trichys" were made of; though I only smoked the cigars when better were unavailable. The price was sufficiently tempting to decoy many, and to the officers of the ship in which I went out, I forwarded several thousand of them at the apparently improbable cost of a rupee a hundred.

It would be idle to add that the price rose rapidly soon after our occupation of the country, as everything invariably does in those places that we merely frequent!

In 1852, Pegu ponies cost Rs. 30; in 1858, Rs. 300 were asked and given. The fact is, both were novelties; and what Englishman will not pay a ruinous price for a novelty! I am of opinion that tobacco was not indigenous to Burmah, for the history of that important plant points rather to a western origin and a gradual spread eastward; while, with the single exception of the Manilla, it deteriorates the further we advance in the latter direction.

A Manilla is, I confess, a choice article; but compared with the genuine Havannah, the difference is as great as that between a Stilton and a Dutch cheese. Climate and curing are certainly important factors; but, even in perfection, they cannot compensate for certain qualities in the soil, found only in the west.

Nevertheless, this valley yielded at any rate the best to be had in a country where men, women and children, who cannot get tobacco, smoke an article composed of very fine chopped wood wrapped in a leaf.

Of grain, the principal was rice, a larger and coarser variety than that found in India or at Akyab; but we had no opportunity of seeing it in the fields, as it had long been cut, and they were irrigating for other crops.

It is the crop of which the Scripture saith, "Cast thy bread on the waters, and it shall be found after many days." The ploughman, with his primitive scarifier and his pair of buffaloes, stirs the mud, while the sower flings the seed broadcast in his wake. Ere long a green film is perceptible at the surface; next come the blades and clusters of flowers on single stalks; finally, the water dries up and the crop ripens.

With the exception of the plantain, or banana as it is called in this country, the season for fruit was not. This exception, however, was sufficiently luscious to make the appetite grow by what it fed on. It is a fruit that nature has provided with a whole list of recommendations; it is obtainable all the year round, as the young shoots spring up of themselves from the rhizomes, causing the plantation to spread independently; it may be eaten at any time and with anything; is both cheap and nourishing; and, last but not least, as soon as the skin has been removed and the downy layer scraped off, there are no stones, cores, or pips.

Any one who has once made a lunch of bread, butter, cheese, beer and *plantains*, will, I guarantee, repeat the experiment; only the *correct* way of eating the fruit is after the downy covering has been removed, a process which, while it involves a little additional trouble, results in a very appreciable difference.

As the longest day must come to an end, so did our sojourn in "El Dorado" draw to a close, for affairs had settled down sooner than was expected, and out of regard for economy, it was considered unnecessary to keep the troops out any longer.

The native contingent was to garrison the place, and in that respect I wished I had, for a few months at least, been part and parcel of the same. But, alas! the "white face" cannot change his skin, whatever he may do as regards his spots.

Once more, then, we made a move in a north-easterly direction this time to Theyetmeyo, where the camp was to break up *in toto*.

We now marched through a more elevated tract of country, neither so undulating nor so wild as on the other side of "Jordan," and more thickly populated as we approached the Irrawadi.

This march was, compared with what had preceded, naturally a tame affair, as we were no longer on the tiptoe of expectation. We had moreover entered the "promised land," and after having tasted of its delights, we were going back to the ordinary duties of life.

Marching for six weeks without a specific object is apt to grow wearisome; the abnormally early hour of rising in semi-darkness; the noise of tent-peg hammering, and the sudden collapse of the tents; and the hideous noises made by any camels that happen to be present—all these conditions are extremely trying. As a beast of burden, the camel is a very useful creature, and there his qualifications end. In disposition he is a veritable savage, the process of lading him requires extreme caution, for with the slightest provocation, or without it, he will crane his lanky neck and endeavour to bite, treating any one he can lay hold of much as a terrier does a rat. Failing to bite, he utters the most dismal sounds imaginable, proceeding apparently from his very bowels; he kneels down under protest, and only after much tugging at his nose; and rises with such a jerk and grunt, that any articles not properly lashed on are hurled into space. The two periods, therefore, of loading and unloading these amiable creatures are extremely trying; while for riding, where the choice lies between a camel and a donkey, I should, unless I were in a desperate hurry, unhesitatingly choose the latter.

This time we shook hands with the officers of the frontier garrison from the land side, and were as hospitably entertained as before.

They had heard of our proceedings by means of the organized runners instituted for the purpose; from this quarter alone could succour have reached us in case of need. They too must have made a detour, though but a short one; and after all, a demonstration in front would probably have sufficed, for the Burmese, finding themselves between two fires, would have decamped in a stampede.

With but periodical instalments of news to vary the monotony of life from day to day, the details of our expedition proved very acceptable, and were devoured with special eagerness by those in whose veins flowed the love of sport.

Indeed, from what I afterwards heard, leaves of absence were since spent *not far* from the recently acquired "El Dorado"! Then indeed the reign of peace enjoyed by animals and birds in that hitherto favoured region must have come to an abrupt end. A force greater than their own invaded their solitudes, once so free from our insatiable propensity to take life in all its lower forms.

By this time the game has in all probability been scared far away; and it may, for all I know, be safe to have a picnic where once the tiger had his lair, or one may wander without even the chance of a shot through tracts where the shy fowl once strutted in numbers, consequential and pugnacious as usual.

Maybe too, bungalows and barracks now dot its original outskirts, where balls and picnics are of frequent occurrence, while shooting and hunting are the order of the day.

I should certainly, for the sake of comparison, like to see the place as it now is; a military band, playing perchance at one end of the stockade, would certainly sound divinely in that valley.

Alas! if I were only a Buddhist, I might be cheered by the hope of visiting that earthly paradise in another form.

The camp broke up shortly afterwards, and I returned to Prome with our chief and a few others. We had described a considerable circle during the past month; little more than a month, and it seemed more like a year.

In connection with that march, now nearly forty years ago, a somewhat singular coincidence occurred to me in the summer of 1889 at that paradise of cricketers, Lord's. While I was conversing at the refreshment bar with an acquaintance, the subject of Burmah cropped up, and I happened to refer in detail to this particular expedition. "So well do I remember it," I was saying, "that I could mention the names of the officers concerned, though I have not come across one of them since."

I then proceeded to fulfil this undertaking, and had just named the one who remained behind in charge of the garrison, when a voice behind me exclaimed, "I am that individual."

We had probably met many times before in that enclosure, maybe sat near one another; but seven-and-twenty years tend to alter *men ;* and unless that keynote had been struck, no recognition would have ensued, as in the following spring he joined the majority. He was a regular attendant at Lord's, and had, he told me, occupied the same seat for many successive seasons; the following year I looked for him in vain—his place knew him no more!

He was a keen sportsman and a first-rate shot, and nothing pleased him better than being left behind at Mendoon, the real name of my "El Dorado."

CHAPTER XIII.

CLOUDY WEATHER.

" Diseases, desperate grown,
By desperate appliance are relieved,
Or not at all."

" Angry looks can do no good,
And blows are dealt in blindness ;
Words are better understood
If spoken but in kindness."

THUS far, the tide of prosperity had been flowing without a check ; we had visited many scenes, encountered dangers and surmounted difficulties, when a sudden and unexpected ebb set in.

I had quite made up my mind to remain in the country on the principle that a bird in the hand is worth two in the bush ; besides which I was a little incredulous as to the oft-repeated and over-estimated advantages of India, and by no means eager to partake of its imaginary delights. Calcutta was odious, and Rangoon, in comparison, a paradise ; while, besides enjoying excellent health, I was saving a goodly number of rupees, and making many friends. Hitherto the gates of Burmah had been closed to ladies, for whom " No Thoroughfare" had been the stern decree; but all this must ere long be cancelled, and then what an influx there would be of grass widows and perhaps too unmarried belles, tempted to try their fortunes in fresh woods and pastures new!

For some time to come, the comforts and pleasures might be inferior to those of Indian stations, but then there would be the reunion of loving hearts, that could find bliss in a cottage, even where the roses and honeysuckle were not.

The other day I came across a little book, "The Queen of Flowers," which the author dedicated to his wife, and my thoughts were carried back to the date at which it was written, the days ere chivalry had fled and men had contracted the bad habit of talking disparagingly of the gentler sex. Now, in the height of their selfishness, they shut themselves up in their clubs, where they pore over the papers, criticize passers-by, and enjoy the fat of the land!

With us at that period, civilization was only at its budding stage, but nowhere perhaps did the plant make more brilliant progress than here, under the fostering hand of its Chief Commissioner, who paved the way for the prosperity which was to follow.

Some there were who vilified the land in no measured terms, but only such as missed certain comforts to which they had been accustomed. The leaven is working among the rising generation, who, unless pampered with all manner of luxuries that we were unacquainted with in my young days, profess to find life scarely worth the living.

Not choice, but dire necessity compelled me to quit a country so pregnant with future advantages. I was standing one morning by the bedside of a patient, when a shiver passing through me warned me that the fever of the place had at length taken hold of my system.

I was in for a very stiff attack of the quotidian or

daily variety, so intense indeed that it defied such supposed antidotes as arsenic or quinine.

The "bacilli" must have originated from a strong and determined race of microbes, for the "cold, hot, and sweating" stages were unusually protracted, and unaffected by quinine in 30-gram doses, which nearly blew the roof of my skull off, and certainly paralyzed my organs of digestion.

After a fair fight, medicine succumbed to microbes, and I had to beat a retreat.

A river trip failing to have the desired effect, I determined to try the sea. I was accordingly carried on board a steamer early one morning and placed in an easy chair under an awning, where I reclined, totally indifferent to all around, and perfectly willing to be heaved overboard. My appetite had completely vanished, and for several days I had eaten only oranges, solid food having been utterly distasteful and tobacco equally so.

The bell struck for breakfast, and the captain tried to coax me down into the cuddy, but without success. Towards evening, however, I suddenly felt hungry, the first time for many days past, and I actually managed to get through a good round meal, followed by a quiet smoke on deck.

The voyage lasted a week, at the end of which time all traces of the fever had completely vanished. The snake was, however, only scotched; for the next twenty-five years it periodically raised its head feebly, always of course when least wanted or expected; generally when I was going to bed, and once even at the most awkward and critical period of an accouchement.

This intermittent recurrence continued until I left

the East for good and all, when it expired in a singular fashion. I had been suffering for some time past from the most painful boils, all of which had vanished, save one on my leg. Some ten days after my arrival in Europe, and while still in Germany, I was seized one morning with a most acute pain in the region of the abdomen, followed by an attack of the *old Burmah fever*, from which I lay insensible for three days. On coming round, my attention was at once drawn to a spot on my leg which felt icy cold, and I found that the boil had mortified and was black as a coal. It came out with a charcoal poultice, leaving a circular, deep excavation, which only healed after many weeks.

One of the numerous eccentricities of this disease is to lie dormant in the system for many years; in my own case the "bacilli" appear to have concentrated themselves in the boil, and, after having killed it, must either have died themselves, or come bodily away with the tissues, for I have, during the past twelve years, never suffered the least approach to ague.

The specific germ of this disease will, without a doubt, soon be isolated either in this country or onthe Continent: there is a current idea that the mantle of medical discovery has descended upon our friends across the water to our own exclusion; an idea against which such names as Harvey and Jenner alone cry trumpet-tongued.

At the same time some nicety will be requisite to distinguish between those producing quotidian, tertian, quartan and more irregular forms; how it comes to pass that these germs can be in abeyance for many years, and then return to life and activity, is so far a hard nut to crack.

Heat, moisture and vegetation are a combination

that produce the most virulent germs, hence the dangers attending the period in the East when the rains are drying up.

Two of the three chief causes used also to operate with disastrous effect in the days before the Lincolnshire fens were drained.

Just as in all countries we can estimate the character of any soil from its natural vegetation, so in India, the appearance of its inhabitants is a sure indication of the healthiness of a district. A leaden complexion, for example, betokens an enlarged spleen, due to constantly recurring attacks of ague, and where this is on the increase, the locality is an unhealthy one.

Unpleasant as such an experience unquestionably is, one can scarcely help being struck by the strange symptoms produced by the circulation of this poison through the system; shivering, accompanied by icy coldness and an insatiable craving for everything warm, inside and out, is succeeded by violent perspiration, and a similar and opposite longing for everything cold. The worst of it is, too, that the germs, nowise routed by this outpour, live to fight another day!

The entire phenomenon is due to a specific impression on the nervous centre, or what is popularly called the spinal marrow, the brain remaining as a general rule uninfluenced. The cellular, spongy spleen, acts as a reservoir into which the blood can flow, when driven by certain emotions from the surface; but for this, the stream would probably overwhelm what our distinguished lecturer used to call the tripod of life, viz. the heart, lungs and brain.

From repeated attacks, the spleen will lose its elasticity, becoming enlarged to such an extent as to occupy the principal portion of the cavity in which it resides, and withal so exceedingly brittle, that a push or even a deep sigh will cause it to rupture, resulting in almost instantaneous death.

The germs are also guilty of other eccentricities, of which perhaps the most remarkable is inducing an attack one day in a pregnant woman and the next in her unborn child.

It is therefore impossible to overrate the importance of the discovery of specific germs, for it must lead to a more rational treatment of many diseases, a mode by which they can be acted on direct, instead of through that long-suffering organ, the stomach.

In one disease of Asiatic origin we know that the functions of that organ are so completely in abeyance that any medicine administered through it is either unabsorbed or rejected.

Altogether, it will be a happy period for suffering humanity when some process is brought to light by which hypodermic injection of a germicide produces immediate contact.

Such a discovery will doubtless take time; but then Rome was not built in a day, and the marvellous contributions of Jenner, Harvey, Simpson, and Lister were the result of years of patient study and untiring research. And what a result! Think of the millions that have been saved by vaccination from a loathsome disease, of the floods of pain that have been averted by the use of anæsthetics; of the manner in which atmospheric germs have been kept at bay, while the surgeon searches for a deep-seated aneurism or performs an amputation! Pasteur's inoculation for that harrowing disease, rabies, is progressing slowly but surely; and the discovery of Koch—based on the presence of "bacilli" as the *fons et origo malorum*—will probably lead to results of which we can at present scarcely form an idea.

In India cholera is endemic and devastating; in this country we have scrofula, struma or tubercle. Neither respects persons, attacking rich and poor alike, the latter being particularly subject to tubercle for reasons which need no explanation in these days, when education stalks through the length and breadth of the land, dragging pianos, science, and art in its train.

We may therefore hope that the cure of "intermittents" will be performed on the same model; then will the alkaloid of cinchona descend from the position of anti-periodic and febrifuge to the level of a valuable tonic.

Just as the gardener must thoroughly fumigate his greenhouses with tobacco in order to rid his plants of aphides, so must these "bacilli" be attacked early and thoroughly, and then I feel sure that sea voyages would be attended with better results.

I am aware that one swallow does not make a summer; but, taking into consideration the palpable improvement mentioned above, only one deduction could fairly be made as to the beneficial effects of sea air.

The average time spent by me in any one place during the two years I had been in Burmah was about four months; the next three years this increased to seven; and the year afterwards it fell to a week.

A rolling stone may gather moss, but is almost sure to drop it again; in my second nomadic stage, a clear sweep was made of all that I had accumulated, and, by this time, the surface had probably become too slippery for any to cling to.

But it is not my intention to enter into the particulars

of the next three years, for my book has already swollen like a mountain stream, and I have more to relate about the part of our dominions I was now leaving. The curtain falls; and, after the manner of the dramatic author, I must ask the reader to imagine an interval of nearly four years before it rises again upon the land of Gautama the contemplative.

And, as the audience are looking round the house, I may as well finish this chapter by forging a few connecting links.

Those mean "bacilli," mixing with my pure blood, hurled me from a happy position and forced me to encounter not only cloudy weather, but a hurricane of angry passions dark as Erebus. The first cloud was comparatively no larger than a man's hand; but it rapidly spread, soon blotting out the azure vault of heaven.

Instead of returning when my leave had expired, I was persuaded in some unaccountable manner—still perhaps under some subtle influence of the fever—to join a regiment, with which I marched for six weeks through a country the monotony of which is not to be described.

Having obtained "Privilege leave" for a month, I should have a fortnight for looking about, leaving a week for the journey either way.

Instead of carrying this programme into force, I found myself—oh, irony of fate!—marching in a diametrically opposite direction. The destination had been depicted in glowing colours, and I found it commonplace, not to be compared with Rangoon or Prome.

Two years afterwards the sky cleared again for a period of six weeks, after which it became darker than ever; for no sooner had I settled down in a comfortable manner with a young wife, than the Mutiny burst upon us in all its fury, scattering everything to the four winds, ourselves included.

It is well known that during a campaign soldiers of every denomination keep in good health; whereas the hospitals fill soon after peace is proclaimed.

In the one case they are kept from flagging by activity and excitement, hope of distinction, and "seeking the bubble reputation even in the cannon's mouth;" but, when the "dogs of war" have been chained up again, their spirit barometer falls suddenly and low. I have noticed the same with our principal trees during and after a heavy storm.

The Mutiny formed no exception to the rule; climate, weather, and every kind of hardship were forgotten, as Europeans marched with impunity under the most trying conditions to a conflict tinctured on both sides with the worst elements of human nature.

Having witnessed some of the worst episodes of the Mutiny—the sudden shooting down of trusting officers; arson, massacre, and pillage; blowing from guns, beheadings, and such like cheerful proceedings—and, having marched with camp for many months from pillar to post, the reaction necessitated a thorough change; and, as a return home was impossible, I decided upon a trip round the Bay of Bengal, which brought me once again in contact with Burmah.

Before bringing this chapter to a close I wish to allude to a painful subject, which is, however, of too much interest to all connected with the East to be omitted.

Wise people at home are pleased to find fault with the order of matrimony as applicable to officers abroad, and their arguments would carry more weight with them were they directed to the anxiety entailed in supporting children at home.

That ordeal is unquestionably its principal sting, not from a pecuniary standpoint, but from the sad record of the treatment they endure when their parents are far away and helpless to shield them.

Confining myself to personal experiences, I have found relations far ahead of any others for sheer cruelty. One of them, herself a mother, surpassed the rest in her artistic brutality. I have to lay at her door the fate of my eldest son and the early death of two sweet daughters. She was well paid, but turned and stung us as soon as our backs were turned. With such a dearly-bought experience I turned to the stranger. The age of advertising "Happy homes for children, whose parents were going abroad," was then in its infancy, and not yet raised to a fine art as now-a-days.

We tried one; and a short trial sufficed. However, what we failed to find at home we met with abroad. It is, I know, the fashion to say everything bad about foreigners, but all I can say is, that, whatever be their faults, their sense of duty is at least equal to their greed for gain, which is more than can be said for many at home.

Marriage, therefore, to nine-tenths of the European population in the East is shadowed o'er with this dark and lowering cloud.

Many of our periodicals teem with advertisements anent the "happy home," in which all the advantages of a thorough moral and intellectual training, combined with much motherly kindness and fatherly discipline, are set forth in glowing terms. Specious as are these insertions, the places themselves prove on inspection still more so—charming people, salubrious locality, and most desirable surroundings.

The scenery has been well got up, and the inimitable acting is worthy of a better cause. The inconsolable widow, so passionately fond of children, so anxious to drown her thoughts in occupation, and resolved never to marry again, is to be shunned like a cobra.

One of these, whom I have reason to remember, produced excellent testimonials, and took a house by the sea, where she entertained the parents sumptuously before their departure, winning their regard and the affections of the little ones; and as soon as father and mother were gone, a complete change came o'er the spirit of her dream. The children were utterly neglected, and, but for the interposition of a friend, heaven knows what would have become of them!

This growing thirst for the *care* of children hailing from the East has its mainspring doubtless in that universal regulator of thoughts and actions, money: the parents pay well and punctually, generally too in advance; and as some thousands of miles intervene between them and their offspring, the *care-takers* have the whip-hand all round.

Their strength is that of a giant, and as such I have ever found them use it. The amount of direct and indirect cruelty practised upon their helpless charges is simply appalling. The despised Hindoo despatches a female infant for whom he can anticipate no dowry; the enlightened European sacrifices male and female alike for reasons still less valid. Infanticide is extensively carried on in this country under the euphonious and rural *alias* of "Baby Farming," a process by which infants are permitted to die by inches—the result of starvation and neglect, whereas the more merciful Oriental has his suffocated almost before full birth.

Indian legislation has almost stamped out the evil by vigorous and well-timed measures, while the machinery employed to effect the same purpose at home falls very short of the desired end. Ask those genuine philanthropists who pass their time amid the poor quarters of our over-populated towns and villages, what goes on *sub rosa*, aggravated by the modern facilities for insurance, which more than covers the simple funeral (expenses).

Periodical fits of indignation likewise surge up at home against the line of conduct adopted by the Indian Government with regard to the continuance of the opium-traffic. There is something sublime in the public disregard of far greater evils at our own door; though any well-informed physiologist can demonstrate that excessive smoking of opium is less deleterious in its effects than excessive consumption of alcohol.

The former exalts the imagination to a region of blissful dreams, where it can revel in all that is bright, and even the succeeding depression is not accompanied by any injury to either brain or stomach.

Alcohol, on the other hand, irritates the nervous centres permanently. A very large slice of our home revenue is flavoured with alcohol and tobacco; and our Indian Government also derives much support from opium. But there is a mighty difference: the Chinese are supplied from India with a pure, unadulterated article. What *is* unadulterated in modern England? Echo answers.

Without further delving into the abyssmal and prolific mine of our misdoings and shortcomings, I think I have succeeded in directing the reader's attention to the subject of the treatment of our young ones that we are compelled to leave to the tender mercies of relations, friends, and strangers.

Children from the East require even greater care than those born at home; and there ought therefore to be some safeguard, some compulsory registration and reliable inspection.

My own experience may perhaps be an exceptional one—I hope and trust that it is so—but if such things can be done in the green tree, what may not occur in the dry! It is time we bestirred ourselves to legislate, for something is rotten in the state of Denmark!

CHAPTER XIV.

"LEAVE OF ABSENCE."

*"There is a divinity that shapes our ends,
Rough hew them how we will."*

THE selection of the route narrowed itself to that of "Hobson's choice"; for the embers of the Mutiny were still smouldering in various quarters, where the roads were consequently unsafe. I was therefore compelled to reach the sea by river, and was the more ready to adopt this course as an old friend and his wife were going as far as Moulmein.

My antipathy to the country was by this time as deep-rooted as the lilac crocus in autumn, and has never since relaxed its hold. I felt I must leave it at any cost, while the thought of ever returning weighed upon me like a day- and night-mare.

The India of the past was irretrievably blotted out by the Mutiny; henceforth no dependence could be placed on anything; there was no safe anchorage, all was adrift.

The pack was always being shuffled; pay, rank, nomenclature, uniform and precedence were distributed *seriatim*, each deal being declared a false one.

Of that huge pudding, made up of England's possessions, our Indian Empire certainly contains some of the plums; and young men are naturally not backward at competing for them. What is to be the end of all this feverish competition I do not care to think, for these are congested days, and, for want of a comprehensive scheme of emigration, we at home are striving to make a pint hold a quart.

With extended emigration, smaller holdings at home, and a tariff more equitable to our own producers and less so to foreigners, something might possibly be done to allay the sufferings of mankind.

It was refreshing to hear the sound of the paddle-wheels, and to find ourselves moving rapidly with the Gangetic stream, which was, as usual, flowing swiftly past before the end of the monsoon. We needed this help, for there were several hundred miles between us and the sea, which we could traverse only by day.

Pleasant as was the sensation of leaving the country, we were not a merry party by any means; some were leaving behind those who had been very dear to them, while others were hard and fast in the dread clutches of disease; and the prospects of nearly all were utterly ruined.

Lower down, we had to run the gauntlet of a stronghold still in the hands of the rebels, who might fire into us; and the consequences of a round shot striking the ship might be undeniably unpleasant. But we steamed past "danger point" at a great pace, without a sign of molestation, never dreaming in our fancied security that a far greater danger was lurking near us, in the shape of a plot to destroy the vessel, fostered by treason on board, which was only frustrated by the captain's promptness.

The next day brought us alongside the jetty of what I remembered as one of our liveliest stations; in the old days it contained a European regiment and several native ones. I took the opportunity of going ashore; turning to the right along the main road, I approached the European quarters on the one side and the bungalows on the other; but all was forlorn and forsaken, a sad contrast to the gay scene of eighteen months ago.

The scene was depressing in the extreme, and carried my thoughts back to the many old friends who had recently gone to their account. I was only too glad to get on board again; and my thoughts, as I sat there on deck, were not of a rosy hue.

The events of the past two years seemed as a dream; perpetually on the move by land and water, exposed to all manner of dangers; once a prisoner, deprived alike of luxuries and necessaries—all this was enough to make one recoil. But the rope which bound me to the country was a strong one, and the only way I could see of cutting it would have been a leap from the frying-pan into the fire.

Moreover, I was infinitely poorer than when I first came to the country. With the exception of a scanty wardrobe, everything I possessed — house, furniture, books, plate—had been ruthlessly swept away in the Mutiny; and there were souvenirs of the past which no money could replace.

Nothing of moment occurred till we were nearing the end of our journey; when the aforementioned plot to run the vessel ashore at a very dangerous spot came to the knowledge of the captain, who immediately took the helm himself, after the steersman proper had been duly placed in irons. He afterwards confessed, and was handed over to the civil authorities.

If anything was wanting to complete the prevalent gloom, it was furnished by the death of a passenger shortly before reaching Calcutta. In the very early hours of the next morning, my friend and myself saw him consigned to that capacious repository, mother earth.

When the rising sun had dispersed the heavy pall of vapours, the City of Palaces was bad enough in those days; but words would fail to describe the sickening effluvia that prevailed in the early morning. Years after, I recognized the same at Naples!

On this occasion—I believe I have already mentioned the episode—I got a double dose of it, for I mistook the hour, and consequently arrived much too soon.

The *rendezvous* was in the immediate vicinity of that filthy river, the Hooghly, on whose turbid bosom floated various carcases in every stage of decomposition; crows perched on the putrid remains of defunct Hindoos, digging their beaks into the more tender corners; while some of the bodies became entangled in ships' cables, and not a few were washed ashore on to the black ooze that covered the banks. But for the intervention of tobacco, I should have been poisoned. Courtesy has compelled me to give Calcutta its popular title; but the "City of Sepulchres" would have been far more appropriate.

The somewhat ambitious plan which I now had in view was to visit the various places of interest on the eastern side of the Bay of Bengal as low as Singapore; then to cross to Ceylon, and thence to Madras and the far-famed Neilgherry Hills, and, lastly, back to—purgatory! Man can, however, but propose; and I was doomed to accomplish not more than one-third of the distance. The ebb had evidently set against me, and seemed inclined to have a long innings. It is hard work pulling against it year after year; the eternal fitness of things seems deranged; and but for the hope which "springs eternal," how many more would give up the struggle!

But even here the wind was somewhat tempered to the fleeced human animal, for I started in ignorance, and a measure of compensation was vouchsafed me, as much, I suppose, as I deserved.

Well-remembered places hove in sight as we steamed down the river at a rapid pace and once more imbibed a draught of sea-air. The bay, although quieting down after the storms of the monsoon, was still much too lively for indifferent sailors, few of whom put in any appearance on deck, and fewer still at the festive cuddy.

The first port we touched at was Akyab, celebrated for its capacious harbour and extensive rice-fields. Backed as it is by hills of considerable altitude, which were clothed at this season in their richest verdure, the approach to the port was exceedingly picturesque, and the effects of the alternating lights were particularly beautiful as the clouds passed across the sun, and a hill enveloped in the gloomiest shade would of a sudden burst into a splendour of emerald green. Further down, the hills abutted on the sea, which broke against them with great force, displaying thereby a line of foam of terrible import to any vessel that should be unfortunate enough to get stranded there.

The harbour, which would contain several European fleets combined, is approached by a deep, yet narrow entrance between two perpendicular rocks, necessitating cautious steering by steam, and still more careful handling of a vessel under canvas. This passed, it suddenly expands into a sort of lake; on a very small scale, Lulworth Cove on the Dorset coast, between Bournemouth and Weymouth, somewhat reminds me of it.

The bungalows, each surrounded by its garden, were arranged from the rock along the shore, and the plantations were at the zenith of their beauty. There were but few vessels riding in the harbour, which would, however, ere long, be crowded by the vessels that convey thousands of tons of rice to all parts of the world.

Some of the residents showed us over the place as far as that part of the promontory known as "Scandal Point," from its being the spot most in favour with the residents, who would assemble there of an evening to enjoy the breeze and a cigar, and gossip about things in general. They seemed for the most part bright and cheerful; and in spite of their isolation, their existence amid such surroundings, with good shooting in the neighbourhood and good fishing in the harbour, must have been tolerable.

Passing Kyouk-Phyao and several other places, we came to a small island not far from the mainland, inside which our adventurous captain had a mind to take the vessel. Although this was not the orthodox course, and attended, moreover, by considerable risk, we had unlimited faith in our navigator, and were consequently pleased with the idea.

The venture proved more arduous than he had anticipated, necessitating the utmost caution and constant heaving of the lead. The water was so clear that I could in many places see the rocks and seaweed, among which great fish were darting in the utmost consternation at the appearance of such a leviathan.

In consequence of the many inevitable turns and twists, our progress was of the slowest. In some places we were almost close enough to have leapt ashore, if so minded; and to any one watching from the bows, and

o

forgetting the pranks played by refraction, it seemed as if we must strike the rocks every moment. The island, which presented but a tangled mass of vegetation, the abode of birds above and reptiles below, was undeniably pretty; not sufficiently so, however, to risk a steamer, and we were not sorry when we once more emerged into deep water.

The idea of thus going out of our way and courting danger emanated from the captain, a man of great determination and courage, who, being fearless at sea himself, never bestowed much consideration in this respect upon the "landlubbers" entrusted to his care, though his kindness and attention in everything else were unequalled.

This reliance on his own judgment was unbounded, too much so indeed to the shipowners' way of thinking; and for the many years during which he commanded certain sailing-vessels in which speed was essential, he maintained the reputation of being the most "carrying on" man in the service; but the cost of wear and tear of spars and other paraphernalia must have been enormous.

Some time after leaving the island we steamed up the Irrawaddy, and I again beheld the town of Rangoon, which, since the time when I had landed there fresh from England six years previously, had grown beyond all recognition. An embankment had sprung up along the face of the river, behind which were substantial buildings of all kinds—residences, banks, warehouses, every sign, in short, of brisk trade and increasing prosperity.

I at once went ashore, anxious to see if anything remained of the old stockade and the old quarters; alas! a severe epidemic of cholera was at its height, and we were not permitted to penetrate further than the frontage of the river.

I had, however, the unexpected pleasure of shaking hands with the Commissioner, and should have dined with him, but for the fear of carrying infection on board. He was but little altered; the same winning smile and the same drawn pale face as of yore.

Sitting on deck that evening and listening to the ripple of the water as it flowed by us, I could not help wondering how it would have fared with me, but for that fever, which drove me from the country. I should without a doubt have possessed a long array of figures denoting rupees at my banker's, whereas I could now muster but my pay; I should also have been spared the losses and miseries of the mutiny, and separation from a wife, but two months after marriage, on whose account I had to borrow money, that I might keep her comfortably at home until the country had settled down again. In all probability I should even now have been busy in the very place I was now gazing on in the pale light of a fitful moon, and should at any rate have been in a position to retire many years before I actually did, from a land in which I could no longer take the slightest interest. The light had become feeble in the extreme; and a mocking fate has ever laughed at my frantic efforts to make it flare up again. One by one, I am laying my darlings in the cold earth; had I remained, a mound of earth would have sufficed to cover my own remains; and, as far as this life is concerned, that might have been for the best!

The event of that dire scourge augured unfavourably for the sanitary arrangements of the place, or for the result of interfering with a virgin soil hitherto covered with vegetation. During my two years of knocking about in the country, I had to deal with plenty of fever and dysentery, but not a single case of cholera ever came under my notice, either in natives—Burmese, Madrassees, Punjaubees, or any other —ees—or among the Europeans. The Burmese left sanitation to nature ; but then they were unquestionably stronger than any other race that ever came within my experience; enjoying singular freedom from deformities, blemishes and malignant growths, and more than the average immunity from contagious diseases, at all events until the conquerors mixed with them.

Not very long ago, we had to grapple with these hydra-headed monsters; but before we could do more than scotch the snake, the Act was repealed. The medical profession stood aghast at such puerile sentimentality being allowed to guide our legislation, in which we are ever apt to "strain at gnats and swallow camels."

But they raised their voices in vain ; and the dire results attending such a course are even yet undescribable.

Except for the landing of a few passengers, a fairly strict quarantine was maintained, and we steamed away early the following morning, bound for Moulmein, an important station some way up the Salween, almost due east of Rangoon, and across the Gulf of Martaban.

I had calculated on transferring myself at this point to another steamer trading to Penang and Singapore ; and was therefore glad that we arrived a few days before her date of departure, as I should thereby be enabled to see something of the place in the interval. In due course we reached the mouth of the river, indicated by a lighthouse perched on a rock to starboard. From some peculiar conformation of the land, its waters are navigable for vessels of large burden at any season of the year, while its mouth is free from anything in the shape of a bar. Though deep, it is very narrow; and its water was wonderfully clear for that of a tropical river at the close of the monsoon, when thousands of tons of earth are generally being carried to the sea.

I mused over the likeliest reason for this exception, and was not long in thinking of the teak forests, with which the country is covered.

The rainfall averages rather more than 120 inches in these latitudes, and even this sheet of water cannot wash down the soil in any appreciable quantity, for the leaves break its fall, and the earth is bound together by countless roots.

When we were about halfway between the mouth of the Salween and Moulmein, we made out the smoke of a steamer coming down at a considerable pace. The captain, having scanned the approaching craft with his glass, coolly informed me that it was the boat by which I intended to reach Singapore. I rushed below to gather up my traps; and by the time I was once more on deck, we were abreast of the new comer; an active interchange of signals was going on, and the boat in which I was to be conveyed was about to be lowered. Then ensued an ominous silence, on which the captain came to me with the pleasing information that she was bound for Calcutta "for repairs"! A tale is told of a criminal being led to execution and meeting an unattractive female on the way to the gallows. He is offered life and liberty, on condition that he marries her at once; but one look at her face is enough, and the wretched man, covering his face with his hands, implores his gaoler to "drive on!" and get the worst over.

No; I had safely turned my back on Calcutta, and I was not minded to return there just yet. Still, it was a blow from which I recoiled; and, thanking the captain for his trouble, I retired to chew the cud of this last stroke of ill-luck.

Stranded, I told myself, and not one-fourth of the intended trip accomplished! The relentless ebb tide was evidently running dead against me, implacable at any price.

Thanks to the elasticity of my nature, I did not long remain in low spirits; what had happened was beyond my control, but as brooding would not mend matters one iota, I resolved to make the best I could of this unexpected *contretemps*. No doubt I entered the "Cave of Despair," sat down there and discharged a large quantity of pent-up steam; but I blew it off quickly, and not, as some prefer, in tiny intermittent jets. There are in fact periods in the lives of most of us, when the use of a safety valve becomes absolutely necessary; and I soon cooled down to the resolution, that my only course would be to start afresh and try the Western coast, since the Eastern had proved so treacherous and unreliable. The vessel would remain a week or ten days, sufficient, if properly utilized, for hunting down all the "lions" of the place.

My one difficulty, which had reference to a shakedown, was soon solved by my friend, who promised to get me an invitation, at all events until I could find suitable quarters.

And now I came out of the cave altogether. He was as good as his word, and I soon received an invitation, which was—need I add?—accepted. Englishmen, who never visited the India of yore, are unacquainted with the true meaning of the word "hospitality." The very fact of being able to entertain a traveller with the best the house could produce, seemed to afford positive, undisguised pleasure. There was a heartiness about it unknown at home, where, what with the coldness of our climate and the still greater frigidity of our natures, the practice is not to accept hospitality unless in a position to return it.

Around the fascinating custom in the East, that blessed alike the giver and the recipient, there still lingers a halo of light in my recollection, standing out in bold relief from the wreck which was soon to follow.

The rapid spread of railroads, main trunks and ramifications, naturally lessened the opportunities for exercising such kindly sympathy, for the increase of hotels and refreshment rooms was simultaneous.

I once occupied a bungalow close to the main road, and travellers pulled up at it as a matter of course, as readily indeed as if there had been a signboard over the door. The sheep and poultry, too, may have lent the scene the additional charm of domesticity; for, besides having charge of the Gynee (small oxen) Clubs, I had pigs, fowls, ducks and geese of my own, and cultivated moreover every foot of land around my house.

After a short row, followed by a still shorter drive, I found myself installed in a very comfortable house; and as my advent was unexpected, I had to be shunted to a corner, a very comfortable one, however, on which my hostess had evidently expended an amount of taste and ingenuity. Two things only interfered with my night's rest; the one consisting in a large and repulsive lizard crawling round my pillow.

It was quite harmless, no doubt, but it was the extraordinary size of the creature—it resembled a young alligator—that attracted my attention, and made me hope that it too would go to rest as soon as the light was out.

The other drawback to sleep was the absence of the thud of the steamer; and the perfect stillness reigning around positively kept me awake—such creatures are we of habit.

CHAPTER XV.

MOULMEIN.

"Gutta cavat lapidem non vi, sed sæpe cadendo."

THE capital of the Tenasserim provinces is situated on the left bank of the river, about half a day's steaming from its mouth. It is, if anything, even more picturesque than Prome; and, at that period, civilization had made considerable strides, calculated to enhance its beauty, in the shape of good roads and tasteful houses. The site on which it was built was of an undulating character, with imposing hills in the background, between which intervened a swampy belt, inundated during the monsoon, and under cultivation when the waters had subsided.

From motives of convenience and salubrity, the native and European residences were built parallel to the river, in a line extending over several miles.

Once again my eye rested on houses built on piles, and they appeared so familiar, that I could scarcely realize the fact of having for the past four years been associated with any other. The European houses boasted roomy verandahs, protected from the prevailing glare by luxuriant creepers.

Teak and bamboo entered largely into their composition, while the roofs were covered with "shingles," or flat, thin boards cut into fixed sizes and laid on after the manner of tiles. They resisted water wonderfully, but whenever it poured—it never *rained!*—the noise was such as to drown all attempts at conversation: Perchance a shower would descend in the middle of a meal, and the hush would then be as great as if a punkah had suddenly given way in the hot season, or a steamer with heated bearings had suddenly come to a standstill in the Red Sea.

In the native quarters too, the houses were more substantially built than anything I had seen elsewhere, and the excellent sanitation was a bright feather in the cap of the Commissioner, as well as those under him, who had to deal not only with Burmese, but with a medley of Chinese, Malays, Karens, Shans and Madrasees, who had settled in the place and were conspicuous by their industry.

Of these, I found the Chinese by far the most amusing; and it was a right down pleasure to ransack their shops for curios. They certainly appeared to me a unique race, what with their strange physiognomy, style of dress, their independence and way of rendering English.

The cream of our intercourse lay in the process of bargaining, wherein they displayed much temper, which I fear I encouraged rather than otherwise.

By way of a set-off, however, I found to my dismay, when I came to pack, that I had accumulated more china than I knew how to dispose of. And I may here mention, by way of warning to others, that ere long it was all "lost, stolen, strayed or broken." Such a collection in my possession at this time would be exceedingly valuable, for every item was of its kind genuine, and not the rubbish which passes muster nowadays.

A considerable number of Chinese, attracted to Moulmein by the shipbuilding carried on at the docks, had settled down as carpenters, in which capacity they have earned golden opinions in every quarter of the globe.

Even in exile, away from the Flowery Land, the Celestial clings to his pig, that white, sleek, well-bred animal, which has so improved our own stock. M. Huc was among the first to enlighten us with regard to the inhabitants of China and Tartary; and some of his remarks about the Chinese border on the marvellous; as, for instance, their expertness at telling the time of day or night by the appearance of a cat's eyes, and their method of preventing a donkey braying by tying a weight to his tail.

And these are not mere travellers' tales.

At midnight, a cat's eye is at its fullest stage of dilatation, gradually contracting till midday, when it represents no more than a longitudinal slit.

By patient observation—and who can beat the Chinese for patience?—the stage of dilatation or contraction constitutes a very fair index; not perhaps for those who are dependent on trains, but for all daily purposes in less sophisticated lands than our own.

It was also demonstrated to M. Huc's entire satisfaction, that in order to bray, a donkey must have his head, ears and tail erect, so that if the last named be kept down by a heavy weight, he has not a bray in his composition.

During one of my evening walks, I met a Chinese funeral procession; the coffin, as customary, was large and ponderous, and the unfortunate bearers seemed to stagger under the load. All the followers were busy throwing pieces of tissue paper into the air, which were carried here and there by the wind. Greatly perplexed as to the meaning of this strange proceeding, I made inquiries, and found that their object was to cheat the devil, the papers being imaginary bank notes, for which his satanic majesty had, they believed, a great weakness; while he was engaged in collecting them, the body could be buried in safety, and, once in the earth, he had no power over it.

They passed me on their way back, rejoicing exceedingly at the success of their stratagem, laughing and joking, as if they had been assisting at a wedding rather than an interment.

Besides being good carpenters, they were *facile principes* as leather-workers; and once a Chinaman has encased your feet, you will be reluctant to employ any other nationality, be it even a Frenchman, though he comes second best.

Having said this, I have said all the good for John Chinaman that I can—the rest is simply nowhere!

He is steeped in independence, being very unpunctual, and exceedingly brusque into the bargain. Keeping you waiting until it suits him to bestir himself, he will come forward with, "What you want?" "Boots mended," is the rejoinder. "Very good; I mend." "When ready?" you ask—remember, he can only understand his own kind of English. "You come next week," is his ultimatum. You go next week, and the boots have not been touched. "How is this?"—"Oh! I too busy; you come another time." "But when, you old thief?"—"Next week I make ready," and he vanishes into the back premises. For artistic and systematic thieving, too, he has gained a world-wide renown; while as for his other virtues—well, "all men are liars," and Chinamen form no exception to the general rule.

And now I must give some little account of the

wonderful vegetation, which eminently characterizes this part of our possessions.

The most conspicuous among indigenous trees is unquestionably the Jack-fruit, of which several may be seen in every garden, along the roadside, and shading the houses, in which latter capacity it is not to be beaten, for the thick, green, glossy leaves are very numerous. As an article of food, it ranks somewhat less highly, for a European needs some moral courage to approach the fruit, for a reason to which I have already alluded; though a native esteems it as honey in the comb, and will gorge to repletion on it, and then have a little more —if it is to be had!

Standing isolated, it is certainly more striking in appearance than when growing in the jungles; and one is particularly attracted by its curious tendency to grow fruit on the trunk.

The elongated mahogany-coloured seeds are, when roasted, palatable and nutritious; while its wood, which is much sought after for special purposes, takes a high place for durability.

Not nearly so common, but surpassing it beyond all range of comparison, is that crowning triumph of the vegetable kingdom, the *Amherstia Nobilis*.

This glorious plant, than which even a poet's imagination could conceive nothing more beautiful of its kind, is of the Papillonaceous order, a trifle too symmetrical perhaps to be artistic; it grows to the height of about thirty feet, and on the dense mass of light green, pinnate foliage rest large racemes of bluish-purple flowers in great profusion.

Following closely on its heels is the *Poinsiana Regia*, a native of Madagascar, naturalized in some parts of India, but not met with here. The *Amherstia* is, however, indigenous to these parts, flourishing in a limited area.

I do not think the specimens introduced by a friend of mine into the Calcutta Botanical Gardens thrived particularly well, neither am I aware whether it is to be found among our exotics at home. In a lofty glass house, with a high temperature, saturated atmosphere, and rich, loamy soil, it might flourish. The finest specimen I ever beheld was in the Commissioner's ground.

Several seeds of its near rival germinated in my own greenhouse in Herefordshire, but the heat was insufficient to carry them through the winter, though the gardener at Moor Park, to whom I gave some seeds, kept them in a flourishing condition for several years.

Various kinds of acacias and mimosas perfumed the air and delighted the eye; and the beauty of many a garden was considerably enhanced by well-kept clumps of the graceful bamboo and the elegant plantain. The display of floral wealth was also considerable, but there is a limit to my memory.

Those were the days in which whole forests of teak were cut down with a recklessness impossible to understand under any administration; no thought was taken of the future, which must take care of itself. Forests, instead of being thinned, were absolutely cleared on a principle of penny wise, pound foolish, which characterizes those of our own agriculturists, who refuse to replace worn-out fruit trees, because they themselves may not live to see them grow up and bear. Considering all that their forefathers did for them, such wanton selfishness is a little surprising—even in men! Day after day, huge rafts of teak, in charge of a Burmese crew, were floated down the river to the timber-yard. This had been going on ever since the monsoon set in, at which time this river, to the depth of which I have already alluded, is subject to sudden rises of twenty feet and more. One of the sights of the place was to watch the elephants at work stacking these ponderous pieces of timber; and, knowing from habit exactly what was required of them, they certainly set about it in a most intelligent and methodical manner, with little or no prompting on the part of their drivers. Anyone watching them at this occupation could also form some idea of their colossal strength, a power which they themselves are apparently incapable of appreciating, and which they willingly delegate to the service of man. Few animals are more easily tamed, and once domesticated, the desire for liberty seems to die out in them for good and all. The Burmese turn them into the jungle to browse, just as we do horses into a field; when they require one, they have but to walk a short distance and call any one of them by name, when the pachyderm leaves off feeding and follows his master like a dog. The mention of these sagacious animals brings to mind an omission. On our march to Mendoon, that I related some chapters back, we lost a number of the finest specimens; but on careful examination, I could find no specific cause beyond enormous distension of the colon. To administer poison is in itself no easy matter, for anything in the shape of medicine, however adroitly concealed, is usually rejected. Yet some powerful and subtle vegetable alkaloid must have gained an entrance, and we became positively alarmed at the frequency with which such losses recurred, for in them was our trust to carry our camp baggage.

From this emporium of teak, I went down to the docks, where I spent a considerable time. The art of ship-building has, from boyhood upwards, ever exercised a peculiar fascination over me; and only very recently I designed a five-foot model of a steamer, which I hope, ere long, to build with that most excellent of antipodean woods, the cowry pine, the chief characteristics of which are close grain and elasticity.

There were a number of fair sized vessels in different stages of construction, others in course of repair.

Chinamen predominated, as might have been expected, among the carpenters, [and they certainly appeared to me to take matters remarkably easy. I neglected to inquire whether they were paid by time or by work accomplished; if the latter, their earnings must have been insignificant.

What they undertake, however, is done well; though slow and easy going, they are on occasion painstaking, accurate and steady.

The practice of opium-smoking may induce lethargy, but not impairment of the faculties as with alcohol.

One vessel, which was just receiving the finishing touches, looked so trim that I was tempted on board, and her recent history was of a nature to open my eyes to certain phases of the ways of man, of which I had previously been totally ignorant.

About six weeks before, she had sailed with a large cargo of timber, but had not proceeded far when she was *discovered* to be extremely leaky, and everything was made ready in case she should founder. On one occasion indeed the crew took to the boats, but as it became evident that the buoyancy of her cargo would keep her afloat, she was again boarded and brought back for repairs. The individual who took upon himself to acquaint me with these thrilling facts expressed such unconcealed disgust at the way in which she had floated when she *ought* to have sunk—" She'd a' been worth a load more at the bottom!"—conjured up visions of a snug insurance, and on reading between the lines, I found it unnecessary to inquire into the *origin* of the leak!

Taking leave of my very outspoken companion, I emerged from the docks a sadder, yet a wiser man, than I had entered them. Already, in the old days, Shylock arrived at certain practical conclusions anent "land-rats and water-rats, and the peril of waters, winds and rocks," but such calculated villainy as the above is one of the fruits of the grand march of civilization.

The sight of all others, upon which the good people of this place above all prided themselves, was that of the "Caves," and I firmly believe that my newly-acquired friends and hospitable entertainers were rather nettled at my electing to visit the timber-yard and docks first. But the horizon soon cleared, when my friend and self arranged to go there on the morrow. Although not far off, they were difficult of approach at this season of the year, owing to the intervening expanse of water that had to be traversed, for the caves were located in some rocks that stood in the midst of that element.

Our intention evidently pleased our host, for besides a whole volume of instructions and warnings, every preparation was made for our comfort, and we started after breakfast with a hamper large enough for six, an extra coat apiece, an umbrella and a supply of torches. A Madrassee Jehu drove us through two or three miles of country under-timber, until we brought up at the edge of a swamp. Here occurred a pause of half an hour, after which a Burmese, who had sallied forth in quest of his elephant, returned with it.

The "howdah" was most ingeniously constructed of

P

bamboo and cane, very light and comfortable, as much so, at least, as anything can be on the back of one of those animals. Lashing everything securely, we plunged at once into the wilderness of waters, the margin of which was surrounded by large trees, creepers, and undergrowth.

Cautious as usual, the animal threaded its way, bearing direct for the two rocks, which stood out conspicuously about equidistant from dry land on either side. The distance looked nothing at starting, though, measured by the time it took to accomplish, it must have been considerable. Of course the animal had to proceed with extreme caution, plumbing the depth with its fore foot at every step, before trusting so enormous a weight to an uncertain bottom. In our progress we perceived numbers of elephants among the trees, from which they were breaking off suitable branches, first employing them with their trunks to whisk off numerous insect tormentors, and afterwards consigning the leafy morsels to their mouths.

As we approached the rocks, the water became gradually shallower, until we again emerged on dry land and stood before the mouth of the principal cave. The entrance was by way of a short passage some ten feet high, profusely adorned with images of Gautama, but otherwise unaltered by the hand of man. This abruptly expanded into a huge, vaulted chamber, damp, cold and dark as Erebus. Here we donned our extra coats and lighted the torches. As the flames dispelled the gloom, a very beautiful sight burst upon us. From the roof depended enormous masses of stalactites of every size, over which water trickled, exhibiting prismatic colours as the torchlight fell upon them at various angles; and they seemed studded with innumerable precious stones of exceeding brilliancy, the gems of Golconda, rubies from "the mines" and emeralds from Santa Fé. It was like being suddenly ushered into the abode of some fairy, the deception being heightened by the fantastic shapes of the rocks beneath, the result of the trickling water. Around and about the rocks were narrow paths covered with a soft substance, which took the impression of our feet, and though we could distinctly hear the murmur of flowing water, it was nowhere visible.

Moreover, it suddenly ceased, until we entered cave number two—like the first in every particular, only smaller—when it recommenced, puzzling me as much as before. By the time we had entered the third recess, it again ceased; and in extreme perplexity I asked our guide what it meant. The reply was almost as surprising as the mysterious sound itself—it proceeded from the wings of countless numbers of bats, fleeing before the light of our torches. We explored all the caves; I forget their number now, their beauty—never!

That same sound as of running water—really the gentle flapping of bats' wings—pioneered our retreat. I was rather ahead of the others, when my torch suddenly went out, leaving me in profound darkness. I tried to grope my way, but a few tumbles over those by no means soft rocks brought me to a standstill. I sat, therefore, like Patience on a rock, until my friend came up with the guide; otherwise, I believe I should be there now!

When we finally quitted the caves the light of the sun dazzled us so uncommonly, that some moments passed ere we could regain our normal vision. We at once sought out the shady side of the rock, and proceeded to open the hamper. Everything had been thought of ; and as the trip had sharpened our appetites, the cold fowls and ham soon disappeared, and the bottles of claret cup leaked alarmingly.

The elephant found no difficulty in stowing away all the bread that was left, while his master was content with a smoke. And so we chatted on, until the lengthening shadows of the rock warned us to set out on our homeward way.

That evening our glowing account of the lovely caves, and genuine praises of the contents of the hamper, reinstated us in the good opinion of our hostess. This alone was conducive to a good night's rest; and a day's outing under a sun removed only sixteen and a half degrees from the Equator, and the lurching and jolting on the back of a terrestrial leviathan, supplied what was wanting.

I was not sorry, therefore, when the retiring hour came round, and I could pass straight into dreamland.

Caves are exceedingly common in this part of the country, more especially on the upper reaches of the river. They are considered, in some measure at least, sacred by the Burmese, who endeavour to ornament their entrances with images, flags and other devices; but what ideas they entertain with regard to their origin and formation I never remember hearing. These particular caves were evidently formed in the ordinary way; by the action, that is, of water and possibly some chemical action on oolitic limestone. But how this solitary rock resisted the violent forces in operation when the principal mass was removed, would require an expert geologist to explain.

Even here, such a doctor might be as much at fault as his *confrères* have shown themselves with regard to those singular detached rocks at Tunbridge Wells, at which they have laboured in vain. Their grooved, fluted bases unquestionably denote the action of violent currents at some period or other; and being the fittest, they have survived the general overthrow. And certainly they have been put to the utmost use as a show place at that fashionable resort, and much ingenuity has been expended on making them appear more extensive than they really are.

CHAPTER XVI.

AMHERST.

"Oh! that a dream so sweet, so long enjoyed,
Should be so sadly, cruelly destroyed."

THE glory of this place had departed. As Moulmein rose in importance this once busy centre fell into decay, assuming for the most part its primeval condition of luxuriant vegetation.

It was, nevertheless, the spot chosen for a sanatorium during the second Burmese war, and it certainly fulfilled the requirements of all concerned. Being built on the seashore, and at the mouth of the river, it combined great salubrity with easiness of approach.

At the extreme point of a ledge of rocks that ran some distance out to sea stood the lighthouse, from which a submerged reef stretched obliquely towards the shore, enclosing an area of water in which the soldiers used to bathe, although the mouth of the river was infested with sharks.

According to the testimony of the oldest inhabitant, none of these monsters had ever been known to stray inside the reef; though how soon this immunity ceased to be, the reader will learn before the close of the present chapter.

There were several barracks facing the sea, and close to the shore, which was composed of alternate stretches of sand and rock. They were built on piles, very roomy and comfortable, having thick roofs and broad verandahs; and although unoccupied for several years, they were soon rendered habitable by a little vigorous sweeping and scrubbing, the eviction of extensive colonies of bats, spiders, and other insects, which were in possession, and had multiplied after their kind.

Amherst was, in fact, to Moulmein much what Brighton is to the Metropolis—a convenient place to run down to for a brief respite from drudgery and a breath of sea air.

The only particular, however, in which it could compete with the "Queen of Watering-places" was the absolute perfect rest which it afforded, and which is the only commodity that England cannot supply. No; our island is *facile princeps* a land of unrest, and is becoming more so day by day. Not more than five years ago I lighted on a primitive seaside place, where one could be free as air and, if so minded, wear out all one's old clothes. But, lo and behold! the ubiquitous builder scented it from afar, and now it is simply—ruined! A pier now desecrates its hitherto pure waters, round the bulbous extremity of which lounges the gorgeous Cockney, listening to indifferent music, and tainting the air with cigars that must have been home-made! Ere long there will be Ethiopians, winkle sellers, and photographers to fright the place from its propriety.

Amherst was just the reverse of this, and charming in its naked simplicity.

My friend and self decided on spending two or three days there, partly because we thought that a sea bathe would brace us up, and partly for the sake of tasting a certain small fish which abounds only in this neighbourhood, and which is so delicate as to spoil in transit, even so short a distance as that to Moulmein, ice being in those days an unknown luxury in remote Eastern stations.

The praises of this wonderful fish had been sung to us so often that, even with me, simple as my tastes are as to what I should "eat, drink, and avoid," the anticipation of its flavour alternated with impatience to bathe once more in the blue sea; while I do not think I am doing an injustice to the memory of my dear old friend when I say that with him the fish preponderated, the bathe being but as skim milk compared to the cream.

People at home would be extremely "put about" if, whenever they intended spending a few days at Brighton, they had to send on ahead beds and bedding, furniture, crockery, etc.; and if such were necessary, the place would probably welcome fewer visitors.

Yet this is what any lover of whitebait would have to do when bent on visiting the Burmese Greenwich. In the East, however, your factotum saves you all the trouble; you have but to tell him where you are going and how long you intend to stay, and, with a quickness acquired by long practice, he grasps the situation and forgets nothing.

In this case, especial stress was laid on the absolute necessity of procuring *the* fish for dinner, to which end he started the day before, thus making assurance doubly sure.

Failing therein, heavy penalties were darkly hinted at, to which he listened without moving a muscle, salaam'd, and disappeared.

The following afternoon we were borne quickly down stream in a roomy boat, provided with an awning astern. The conversation had reference to the Mutiny and all that we had seen since; but ever and anon the "fish" would crop up, showing what was uppermost in our minds.

When we landed at our destination there was still some little daylight before us, so we resolved on a preliminary tour of inspection, first of our quarters, and then of the shore.

The former we found in a very satisfactory condition; the latter was composed of hard sand, pleasant to walk on, while large rocks abutted into the sea covered with seaweeds and a variety of molluscs and crustaceans, especially small oysters. The scene brought vividly to the fore days now numbered with the past and oft looked back upon; but as darkness was coming on apace, as is its wont in the tropics, we retraced our steps, guided by the light that streamed from our room through the venetian blinds.

The supreme moment was now near at hand. We had scarcely performed our ablutions and made some slight change in our dress, when my friend gave the order for dinner, in a voice which might have been heard half way up to Moulmein, and, with customary punctuality, our domestic announced it almost immediately with an air of intense satisfaction.

It was a trying moment: there stood the dish, beneath the cover of which peeped out a snow-white napkin. My friend helped both of us liberally, and the attack commenced. After a few mouthfuls we looked up and our eyes met; on both our faces stood mute disappointment. We neither thought anything of the fish, and we confessed as much.

It was certainly aggravating. Day after day our friends had instilled into the porches of our ears the exquisite delicacy of a fish to be met with nowhere else, and we might just as well have masticated a few lumps of gelatine!

I did my best to dispel my friend's gloomy looks by perpetrating a few mild jokes, the effect of which was, strangely enough, not beneficial or soothing; and it was not before dinner was nearly over, and the claret had made several journeys, that his drooping spirits revived and the storm burst. He consigned the unhappy fish to —well, not back into their native element, at any rate. As soon as we had adjourned to the verandah to smoke the pipe of peace he fell asleep, and I was left to my own meditations. I might have followed his example, but for an impudent mosquito that buzzed round me sufficiently to keep me awake; he was evidently in quest of a meal, and I shrewdly suspect he got one, for I soon fell into a reverie. Just a zephyr coming seaward wafted to my corner the smell of the sea, fragrant as "the sweet south upon a bed of violets." The happy frame of mind it produced was very similar to what I had experienced off Madeira, the few extra degrees of temperature being differentiated by my light clothing. The waves, shimmering in the fitful moonlight, rolled in steady succession over the sandy shore, and again returned to the mass of waters.

My thoughts winged their way back to a primitive seaside place on the Welsh coast, where I had often gazed out upon such a scene as this, though listening to the dulcet accents of a siren, instead of being roused ever and anon by a snore louder than usual, which in so far resembled the murmur of the wild waves, in that every seventh was of greater dimensions than those that had gone before.

More vivid grew the vision; we were now leaning hand in hand over the balustrade, when, suddenly, the lissom figure by my side seemed to fall into the water, and I actually started up from my chair in agony.

That broke the spell; my friend awoke with a grunt, and asked what the time was. I told him it was already 2 a.m., and that we must be getting to bed; but, being sleepy and supremely comfortable, he "would not let belief take hold of him." Argument being of no avail, more energetic measures had to be employed, and I at last succeeded in getting him indoors, when, with mutual vows to be up early for a bathe, we turned in and fell asleep.

All the residents with whom we had spoken on the subject were agreed that bathing was perfectly safe within the triangular area of water bounded by the visible ledge of rocks leading to the lighthouse and the sunken reef that joined it, at an angle, with the shore.

Soldiers had bathed there times without number; though a hand dangled in the water outside the reef would have been snapped off in a trice. Provided, therefore, with towels, we were soon stripped, placing our clothes well beyond the reach of the flowing tide. There being, moreover, no audience but the sea-birds, who were in this place scarcely more untrammelled by conventionalities than ourselves, we dispensed with bathing-drawers, which are, however, used in India in deference to the prejudices of the natives, who consider it an indecent habit to dispense with them. More impatient than my companion, I was the first to traverse the intervening strip of sand and throw myself into the water. Rising again, I began to swim parallel with the shore, when I saw my friend, who was on the point of following, stop short, while he called out, "Come in as fast as you can"! Fully comprehending what his eyes were fixed on, I made for the shore with all the strength I could muster, crying out to him to throw in the largest stones he could lay hands on.

I knew that he had seen the back fin of a shark, aroused doubtless by my splash to the expectation of a meal. It makes me shudder even now, when I think of that moment.

Fast as I could swim on the wings—or fins—of fear, it was at best but crawling compared to the dart of the fish, which presently laid hold of my ankle, his serrated teeth cutting to the bone like a razor. I thought I was in my depth and endeavoured to touch the bottom, and sank. The shark had instantly relinquished his hold, but I fully expected another attack, though I managed to reach the shore without further molestation, for the creature was darting on all sides, confused by the pieces of rock which my friend continued flinging at him with unflagging energy.

In great pain and rather faint from loss of blood, I scrambled on to the sand and lay down exhausted. On coming round, I found my foot tightly bandaged, and my doctor-friend standing over me.

He presently helped me up to the rock, where we slowly dressed ourselves and had a chat about my narrow escape. One precaution of his was characteristic; and that was avoiding the mention of the terrible object he had seen when he gave me the alarm, from fear that the shock might incapacitate me.

The appearance of a shark in this hitherto safe expanse of water is easily to be accounted for by ingress during an abnormally high tide, and inability to get back over the reef after the sea had sunk to its ordinary level.

More unintelligible was the brute's failure to nip off so much as a foot; and I can only hazard a theory in explanation, that he must have come at me at right angles instead of straight on end.

There are moments in the lives of all of us which simply defy description. This was one of them. When the Sepoys fired and the commanding officer fell dead in my arms, was another! Meeting that tiger when out shooting was a third; and a fourth occurred years afterwards in India, when a tigress chased my pony for upwards of a mile.

All were bad enough, but this was perhaps the worst; for all was fair above, while the terrible danger lurked beneath.

With my foot well bound up, I managed to accept my friend's support to our quarters. Had there been at hand any means for so doing, I should have set up a notice-board opposite the spot, warning intending bathers somewhat after the manner of the Apostolic injunction:—" Beware of——sharks! "

But we had to be content with impressing on Europeans and natives alike the necessity of cautioning venturesome visitors.

It was the second grave disappointment in the brief span of twelve hours!

And I fear the sense of thankfulness was ephemeral, and the grumbling of far longer duration. It did seem *not* quite on a par with the fitness of things that such smooth, tempting, blue water should henceforth be forbidden, and that the principal object of our visit, seabathing, should at the outset be nipped in the bud in such an unmistakable manner. But though it sparkled in the rays of the sun, with its bosom quietly heaving in a midday siesta, " noli me tangere " was in our eyes written on its unruffled surface as indelibly as on that fabled tree, whose golden fruit tasted exceeding bitter.

We had to confine our attention to things terrestrial; and many a time as we walked among the rocks examining the creatures which adhered to them, a feeling of anger would come over me, and in my peevish opposition to the decrees of Providence, I would fling stones into the water in childlike resentment. What feeble puny creatures we men are! Once the spring of anger is allowed to well up, and the desire for retaliation comes to the surface, there is no limit to the petty acts to which we will descend!

In those unrighteous moments, I considered not the instincts implanted in the creature; and was moreover thoroughly ungrateful for having emerged from a ghastly fate by the skin of my foot. I furthermore devised a plan for capturing the *fons et origo* (syntax!); but the necessary gear was not forthcoming, nor could I derive any assistance from the native fishermen, who have an invincible dread of the creature, having learnt from experience not to meddle with it. Besides the undeniable satisfaction of landing and despatching him, his armoury of teeth would have been well worth preserving, and a portion of the spine would have made a valuable walking-stick.

It is strange that sharks do not frequent the harbour at Aden; the more so, as they swarm just outside its mouth. As soon as a steamer drops anchor there, she is surrounded by numbers of little Arab boys, amphibious brats and experts at diving, who clamour for coins to be thrown overboard, which they at once retrieve with amazing dexterity. So nice is their sense of touch under water, that they can at once discriminate between a coin of the realm and a piece of tin cut the exact size. I have often tried the deception, and the diver invariably came to the surface uttering unmistakable exclamations of disgust. The absence of sharks may be accepted as fact, since I never heard of an accident happening to any of these children. Yet boats were constantly coming in with several small sharks on board, taken in the nets, which readily sold for native consumption.

The environs of Amherst proved unsatisfactory, especially as dangerous snakes abounded in the rank undergrowth that had almost obliterated what had once been roads and footpaths.

Everything told of decay: there were a few *Amherstias* being slowly killed by parasitic creepers, just as ivy or honeysuckle will sap the vitality of our trees at home.

I remember, too, the remains of a once prosperous sugar-factory, the walls of which had been forced asunder by vegetation, which was fast reclaiming the land. The only other points of interest were some enormous samples of sugar-cane, the largest examples of the saccharine bamboo that I had ever beheld.

Thankful at being able to return in company, and still smarting from our twofold disappointment, we re-ascended the river at a slow pace. Nevertheless the change had done us a deal of good.

CHAPTER XVII.

TAVOY.

" Like a dull actor now, I have forgot my part."

THE somewhat tedious journey up the river was to an extent beguiled by a review of our recent experiences, which, if not unique, were by no means commonplace. My friend, taking up the parable, contrasted our present position with what might have been, if he had perforce returned alone.

He made one of the longest speeches I ever heard from him, which for obvious reasons I shall not reproduce; remarking, *inter alia,* that he would not have had the courage to face the others without me, and making an unwarrantable pun about the bruising of my sole!

As originally arranged, the time of my departure was now drawing nigh. In two days more the steamer that had brought us would take me back, and I should make a fresh start from the "whited sepulchre," only in the reverse direction.

Once again my plans were altered. Sitting on a jetty one evening we saw the "mail" boat let go her anchor just opposite us. As all letters were to remain with my agents until my return, I had nothing to look forward to; and I therefore proposed that we should go on board and hear the news. We therefore hailed a boat, and were soon in the midst of all the commotion of letting off steam, orders and counter-orders. My friend found an old acquaintance in the captain, and while they were talking I drew aside to watch the busy scene that was being enacted.

I was then introduced to Captain B., who, after the customary observations, said: "Our mutual friend has informed me of the dilemma in which you were placed by the breaking down of the Straits boat. I am off with the mail to-morrow to Tavoy and Mergui, and if you will give me the pleasure of your company, I'll make you as comfortable as I can." I accepted the invitation without more ado, merely suggesting that I thought it would be more reasonable if I were permitted to—, but he interrupted me, insisting that I should come as his guest, or not at all.

The arrival of the English mail with letters and newspapers six weeks old, always creates a flutter among Europeans in the East, everyone waiting impatiently for his own budget. In the arrangements even of the "Post" the ways of the East are exactly opposite to those of the West, for, instead of having the letters, etc., delivered, we send a trusty man for them.

Dinner was just over when that worthy arrived with a goodly load, the contents of which soon found their way into the hands of their respective owners. I was left out in the cold, and would have given a trifle for certain communications; nevertheless, under the circumstances of my original arrangements, it would have been mere folly to have had them sent from pillar to post all round the Bay of Bengal with a great risk of losing them. A friend handed me a newspaper, and on opening it, almost the first news I saw was the death of a very dear member of the family. I was aboard the *Pluto*, with my small belongings early next morning, and had not long to wait ere we got under weigh and steamed down the river. She was a beautiful boat, built on graceful lines, combining speed with beam, and well armed, and employed by Government for every available purpose during peace and war; but she seemed "a cut above" carrying mails and stores.

In his desire to make me comfortable the skipper attempted to give up his own cabin, but I rebelled at this, and warned him against spoiling me at the outset. I reminded him, moreover, that I had grown accustomed to adversity in the East, and had probably many a stony path before me, and to give me a bed of roses to lie upon now would but make me feel the thorns more keenly afterwards. My arguments prevailed, and he contented himself with giving me the free run of the ship.

Rounding the lighthouse, our course lay to the southward, parallel to the land, which I do not think we ever lost sight of. Verdure-clad hills skirted the shore, while here and there a pagoda glistening in the sun betokened the proximity of an isolated village. The country was known to be sparsely populated, and in such places only where a river debouched on the sea. Of actual life we saw none; no boats, nor man, nor beast.

The changing scene was delightful, and I did not for a moment regret having accepted the invitation on the spur of the moment. Years of experience have shown me that such decisions turn out, as a rule, better than those arrived at after the process we are pleased to call deliberation. We are told to "look before we leap." *Cui bono?* when none of us can see a hair's breadth into the future. Moreover, thinking over anything generally confuses nine men out of every ten, and the judgment of man, in whatsoever direction he may exercise it, almost invariably arrives at an erroneous decision. No; as far as my individual experience goes, instinct, viewed in the light of subsequent events, has throughout been safer than reasoning, while I regret not having acted on first impressions on several memorable and critical occasions.

We continued our southward course for a time, when the ship's head was suddenly turned due east, and we were evidently making for a river. For some time I could distinguish no opening, having but a landsman's powers of observation; but at length a fissure appeared in the otherwise unbroken line of mangrove forest which marks this coast, and ere long we were in the river that flows past Tavoy. I at once noticed that it was very much narrower than the Salween, more muddy, and also more rapid, cutting its way through the web of mangroves, that alone prevented the earth silting up the river and forming the usual bar at its mouth.

I may, *en passant*, mention a peculiarity of the seeds of this plant; and that is, they enjoy the power of germinating while still attached to the tree; the radicle, bursting through the covering, imbeds itself in the mud, and is followed in due course by the seed.

Some species of mangroves are sweet and palatable, and the wood of some of them is hard enough to be in demand for a variety of purposes, while others are rich in an inferior quality of tannin.

The generality of rivers are characterized by the graceful curves described by their winding course; but this one formed an exception, indulging in an eccentric abruptness, depending, of course, on the lay of the land.

At one time it looked as if we were running right on to the bank; and I was expecting to hear the familiar "Let go the anchor!" when I noticed that the river turned sharp round to the nor'ard. Still we kept our course, until the bowsprit was right over the low, open land! I was on the bridge at the time, but I did not dare say a word to the captain, whose energies were concentrated on this trying and hazardous piece of navigation. I was clutching at the railing, almost unable to endure the suspense a moment longer, when suddenly the helm was altered, the bowsprit described an arc of 90°, and we were steaming up a deep channel parallel with the shore.

I could not help congratulating the captain on this masterly piece of steering; and he acknowledged that he always turned his back on the river with relief, as it was the worst he had to navigate in any of his voyages.

Tavoy was one of those small stations dotted about the Tenasserim provinces, which we held with a handful of men, so as to prevent any awkward mistake as to the actual ownership of the country. It was now occupied by part of a Madras regiment. As evening was descending upon the scene, I saw but little of the native town, and still less of the military quarters, which were so nestled among the trees as to be for the most part undistinguishable. At the best it must have been a very dreary, isolated spot, shut out from the rest of the world, and offering officers and men the dubious delights of penal servitude. It doubtless resembled Pegu in one particular, the facilities afforded for saving money, besides which it must, in the dry season, have been a veritable El Dorado to the sportsman. But then it is not everyone in whom dwells the spirit to go forth and shoot! In the days, too, of which I am writing, men were sent out to the East at sixteen or seventeen years of age, and rarely acquired a musical or scientific turn, so their resources in such a place were indeed limited. The educational structure was built on the primitive model; classics and mathematics were regarded as its foundation, plinth, superstructure, and roof; history, geography, and a smattering of French, were embellishments, and music, drawing, and science, would do at any time!

Here, as elsewhere, the twelve mail days in the year were looked forward to with longing, and their dates written up in letters of gold. One mail every month! The present generation cannot comprehend such a state of affairs; neither could we understand the conditions obtaining in Hindustan under Clive.

And yet in this matter, having to wait thirty days for each batch of news, the wind was, to some extent, tempered to the shorn lamb, for we had not yet arrived at the high-pressure age. Not only did the events of a year occupy less space and importance than do those of a month nowadays, but before the spread of steam and electricity half the events actually enacted never came to light.

Now, on a declaration of war being ventured, millions are brought into the field, in lieu of thousands, and campaigns that formerly occupied years are (now) a matter of weeks. A Revolution breaks out, and the entire order of Government is reversed in four and twenty hours. Accidents by sea and land are alarming in their frequency, and appalling in their magnitude; murders, committed on the slightest provocation, are known in our furthest possessions almost ere the victims are cold, and are served up in various ways by a sensational press. One by one, too, the various grades of the working classes are quarrelling with their bread and butter, set on by agitators, who eat the grain, leaving their sheep the husks.

Endless divorce cases, from the lowest rung to the top of the ladder, fraught with momentous and unlooked-for consequences, disfigure every newspaper. Speculation, which seems to have reached its furthest limits in every direction, is producing commercial panics; and on every side our affairs are trembling in the balance. Garbage is plentiful, and sensational events so unintermittent that it is surprising how editors still find the need of drawing on their inventive faculties!

If Tavoy existed at the present day under the old *régime*, few Europeans would survive the ordeal beyond a mail or two.

The captain was evidently not enamoured of the place; he took time by the "fetlock," landed the mails and cargo, and made everything ready to be off early next morning. As soon as sufficient light dawned upon us we backed to that "unriver-like" bend, and were soon out at sea again. Of all the places I ever stopped at, Tavoy remains enveloped in the most impenetrable haze, so far as my recollection of it is concerned. Times without number I have tried to conjure it up in detail; but beyond fragments of buildings, a dense mass of vegetation, and a few natives, I can make nothing of it. I fear, therefore, that the heading of this chapter may be taken as somewhat misleading; it will serve, however, as a halting-place, before the more interesting portion of the trip, with which I shall take leave of the reader.

What I do remember of the place is being struck with the fact that none of the officers came on board, whereas the rule is for them to come off in anything that will float as soon as the anchor is let go.

They resided but a short distance from the jetty, alongside which we were anchored; and it was therefore all the more curious that they should be conspicuous by their absence. Perhaps they did not care for such ephemeral excitement; what after all was a steamer to them as long as she landed the mail and mess-stores? Perhaps, too, the ordeal was too much for them; I myself knew the envy and misery attendant on seeing off a friend "homeward bound;" straining one's eyes after the ship that drops slowly down to the sea, and then returning to purgatory!

It is almost as bad as leaving home afresh, without the mitigating pleasures of anticipation.

Tavoy, as a whole, apart from any individual characteristics which may have distinguished its town, certainly struck me as a spot where those native to the place and "to the manner born," might lead a very peaceful existence. Nature had placed within their reach a supply of delicious food, to be had without the asking. The bright green leaves of the plantain rose up in every direction, growing and multiplying unaided, besides bearing huge clusters of fruit all the year round. The glossy, thick-leaved Jack-fruit was also conspicuous; palms reared their tufted heads aloft, among them the much esteemed cocoa-nut, useful in more ways than one; there, too, the leafy tamarind stood waving its pinnate foliage in the evening breeze, proof against the scorching rays of the sun, even at midday.

The women, as elsewhere, sat under their houses, busy with the looms, on which they spun garments of many colours and gorgeous design. The buffaloes grazed around, enjoying a peaceful existence, until summoned to the periodical contest in the arena. They found no lack of food, and were kept at night in a strong enclosure, secure from the prowling tiger.

Rice and tobacco were the principal articles under cultivation, requiring little trouble and insignificant outlay of capital.

Yes, the aborigines must have led a happy, contented life in such a place; while the European grumbled, growled, and vilified everything, after the manner of his kind.

CHAPTER XVIII.

THE MERGUI ARCHIPELAGO.

"Alone she sat—alone! that worn-out word,
So idly spoken and so coldly heard;
Yet all the poets sing, and grief hath known,
Of hope laid waste, knells in that word—alone!"

ANYONE glancing at a map of the world's two hemispheres, cannot fail to notice that all the continents end in more or less pointed extremities looking due south, and that most of the larger islands, showing length in lieu of breadth, also lie nearly due north and south. The first half of the above remark is pointed by such examples as South America, Africa, India, and the prolongation from China in the direction now under notice; while the latter finds expression in the larger islands of the West India group; also in Sumatra, Java, Flores, Timor, New Guinea, and many others. Any attempt at an explanation of this curious symmetry in the conformation of our earth would be more appropriate to a manual of geography; and as it would involve the balancing of the many theories in favour of a local or universal deluge, I shall not enter into it.

The islands of the archipelago we were now approaching partook much of the same character. After a run of three hundred miles we came to them, a group keeping remarkably equidistant from the mainland, as far as Wellesley in the Malay Peninsula. Exceedingly beautiful and tempting they looked, as we passed each in turn; all well wooded, their shores composed, as the mainland, of sand and rock, but the only signs of life came from a few birds flitting about the trees, and a stray turtle basking on the shore. Man had not set his mark on the place.

As the steamer could not put us ashore we had to satisfy our curiosity by the aid of the glass. One island, the largest we had yet passed, was, so the captain told me, associated with that historical period when the French and ourselves were still trying conclusions as to which power was to be predominant in the East.

An opening in the side facing the mainland led to a sort of basin in the interior of the island, a natural dock, which the French found very handy for their vessels under repairs. The British fleet was then in pursuit of them, and probably passed in sight of this identical island, never dreaming of the snug retreat within. Otherwise, it had gone badly with the French, who would have been caught in a trap; for a single British vessel would have sufficed to guard the entrance, until the enemy capitulated.

As we surveyed each island in turn, striving in vain to distinguish some signs of higher animal life, and wondering why such beautiful spots should continue uninhabited, my thoughts wandered into the region of fancy, and pictured many things.

So strong in me was the desire of leading a Robinson Crusoe kind of existence on one of them, that I must have given my thoughts audible expression, for I heard a voice beside me, "No, you wouldn't; and if you did you'd be sorry for it!" I saw that the speaker was a merchant, the owner of a coasting vessel; and as he refused to explain his interruption, I might have considered it an impertinence on his part, but that his face betrayed unwonted sadness. For two days he made no further allusion to the subject, and I was left to speculate upon the probable cause of his emotion; someone he loved, perhaps, fell overboard opposite that identical island into the jaws of a ravenous shark. Or maybe, a quarrel arose among his Lascars, who forthwith ran amuck, staining his decks with blood, and branding his good ship with an evil reputation.

Or, if both these conjectures were erroneous, he may have been driven ashore through carelessness or a storm, suffering thereby pecuniary loss as well as bodily injury.

As usual, my speculations were all at fault. One evening after dinner, my fellow-passenger told me his tale; and as it will serve as a warning to those of my readers who are given to dwelling in airy castles, besides affording a more specific description of the general characteristics of these islands than my own personal experience would enable me to give, I make no apology for reproducing it, while we are still in sight of the archipelago.

He was, as I have already mentioned, a trader, the owner of a sailing-vessel, in which he conveyed merchandise between the various ports along the coast. It was an independent and profitable method of doing business, and his Lascars were all hard-working, steady men.

Sailing to and fro past these islands, the idea of residing on one of them for a time, Crusoe fashion, grew upon him with such force, that it finally became irresistible.

The first move in the wrong direction was landing, and roaming about the island—the identical one that had attracted my attention two days previously—with one of his men.

Not content, however, he constructed a temporary abode on the side facing the mainland, which was fitted up in a rude way with some of the ship's furniture; and as nothing ever passed on that side of the island, save the mail steamer and his own vessel, he left everything there in perfect security, his mind occupied in thinking of the various essential articles which had to be taken out on successive trips, and eagerly looking forward to the time when he should take up his abode there.

At length, everything was ready, and he determined to try the experiment during the next voyage to Moulmein. His men, with the customary politeness of natives in respect of the actions of any European, forbore from questioning his intentions, which they may have guessed to some extent, though certainly not *in toto*.

It only remained to send for his head man, explain the state of affairs to him, and hand over the care of the ship. That worthy received the charge without a word of surprise or remonstrance; and, although he knew that he was about to commit a rash act, and would have given worlds to retract, he now felt that having shared his plans with a subordinate, he must go through with them at any cost.

It was his last night on board. He tossed about in his cabin, picturing to himself all manner of evils and unknown dangers, till thoughts became dreams, and he enjoyed a troubled sleep.

Next morning, however, Aurora's harbinger dispelled his gloomy fears; and he was more firmly wedded to his purpose than ever.

There was a good deal of whispering among the men, until one of them, acting as spokesman, endeavoured with native eloquence to dissuade him from his ill-advised purpose; but he threw away this last golden opportunity of retiring gracefully from a most awkward position, and was duly landed with a gun and some ammunition, together with such creature comforts as the occasion demanded.

After carrying the things up to the hut, the men salaam'd and returned to the ship, which soon sailed out of sight.

Then for the first time did he realize the significance of the word "solitude": the very voice of nature seemed hushed, and an unearthly silence pervaded the entire scene. Returning to the hut, he lit a lamp and sank into an easy-chair with his gun close at hand. Here he slept for some time, being visited by the most fanciful dreams, and was at length startled into consciousness by the falling of his shot-belt.

When he awoke, his usual supper hour was long past; but unable to eat anything, he uncorked a bottle of beer, and the noise seemed terrific in the midst of that deathlike silence—everything frightened him, the cry of a bird, the moaning of a larger wave than usual on the shore.

Next morning he busied himself about the hut, and tried fishing; but he could not settle down to any occupation. Above all, he dreaded the lonely evening and the wakeful night. He had food in variety and abundance, but the desire to eat was in abeyance. Another night of nervous anxiety: he kept his door securely fastened, although he knew that nothing was there to enter, even had it been left wide open.

His fears now took the form of savages visiting the island to feast, perchance, on prisoners captured in some recent encounter.

On the third night, he managed to fortify the hut in some measure; loaded both his guns, and saw to his revolver, which lay under his pillow, and which he grasped many times during the night, as his disordered imagination conjured up some visionary danger.

The fourth day, he awoke with the same ideas uppermost in his mind, opened the door of his hut cautiously and stole out on to the shore.

In vain he looked all ways for a sail, half expecting to see a canoe full of savages down by the beach. Standing on a lofty ledge of rock and looking down into the clear, deep water, he watched the fish darting to and fro; and a horrible propensity to throw himself in and end his troubles in the bowels of a shark rushed upon him. It was but ephemeral; yet he turned his back on the sea, for fear lest it should grow upon him.

The desire often came upon him to shout; but weighed down by the silence of his surroundings, he dared not even speak aloud.

But the consciousness of self-control in having resisted that fearful temptation had a good effect upon him, for he soon entered on a more peaceful and contented frame of mind.

One day, he bethought him of another attempt at fishing, and he managed with a couple of handlines to catch numbers of the unsuspecting fish, when suddenly he saw the back fin of a shark. Either the shock caused by this unwelcome sight, or a tug more violent than usual caused him to lose his footing on the slippery rock, and he fell into the water. Strange coincidence! to have almost succumbed by accident to the fate he had nearly courted by design! Half a dozen strokes placed him out of danger; and when he looked round there was the shark darting about in the very place, attracted no doubt by the commotion. Never again would he try fishing on that island.

He returned to the hut and changed his wet clothes; and on revisiting the spot the same afternoon, found several sharks there, all seeking the cause of the splash, hoping against hope that their diligence might be rewarded.

His attention was next directed to that interesting amphibian that visited the shore at this season for the purpose of depositing its eggs in the sand—the turtle.

He turned one and despatched it for the table; then following its footprints away from the sea, he came upon its eggs, pretty, waxy-looking specimens, and very good eating when properly baked. The turtle found in these parts doubtless belonged to the ordinary edible species, the *Chelonia virgata;* a variety lacking the green fat found in those peculiar to the West Indies, and therefore beneath the notice of an alderman.

At last, after many days of watching and weariness, during which he was utterly weakened in body and mind, this voluntary Crusoe espied a sail on the far horizon over towards Moulmein. Nearer and nearer it came, until he lit a huge bonfire of dry leaves and fired off several charges from his gun.

All this was unnecessary, for it was his own ship coming back for him. The joy of the meeting between master and men was mutual. It seemed ages since he had heard the sound of a human voice; and, surrounded by his trustworthy Lascars, he made his first hearty meal under that roof.

And the last; for after a stroll round the island,

during which he showed the men the rock from which he had fallen, they carried the chattels back to the ship and quitted the island for good and all.

His men—faithful souls—unable to bear the suspense any longer, had turned back for him, at the risk of incurring his displeasure, before they had got half way to Moulmein.

Such was the burden of his narrative, which occupied nearly two hours, so that it was late ere we turned in. Sounds issuing from the captain's cabin proved unmistakably that he was in the Land of Nod; and I soon joined in the melody, dreaming all manner of things connected with an island, a kind of "dream within a dream."

The captain asked me next morning what had kept us conversing up to so late an hour of the night, so that I shrewdly suspect the hum of our voices disturbed the first part of his rest.

I had, however, promised my fellow-passenger not to make any further allusion to the subject of his story within his hearing, so the captain had to be content with a promise that I would entertain him therewith as soon as Mr. —— had left the ship.

CHAPTER XIX.

MERGUI.

"It gives me wonder, great as my content,
To see you here before me."

"Whether we shall meet again, I know not,
Therefore our everlasting farewell take!"

THE anchorage off Mergui is guarded by an almost perpendicular rock, which in our case necessitated steering a point to starboard. Although destitute of even a blade of grass, this rock is extremely valuable on account of a certain species of swallow, thousands of which nest there year after year, their dwellings being the much prized edible nests, in such great demand among Chinese epicures, as a stock for their soups. They resemble those of our own species, though a trifle more elongated; and are composed of a peculiar kind of gelatinous seaweed, very palatable when boiled with the addition of a little mixed spice.

When the young ones are fledged, the nests are separated from the rock, to which they were attached by a secretion peculiar to the bird.

Soup flavoured with these nests is to the Chinese gourmand what green turtle is to the alderman. Both are expensive; I never had the courage to ascertain the price of *real* turtle, but I know that the nests fetch as much as £7 per pound, or, as each weighs about half an ounce, nearly 5*s.* apiece.

And thus it comes about that this otherwise valueless rock rents for one thousand rupees per annum; and a junk annually sails for China with its precious freight.

We had to keep clear of the rock, so that I had on that occasion no chance of examining the birds individually. They are little more than four inches in length, while their expanse of wing is nearly three times as much; on the back they are dark brown, which passes to lighter shades underneath. In ornithological parlance they have been christened *Collocatia Esculenta*. The fact that they are not scared away from the place by the men and boys employed in appropriating their nests, is presumably due to the abstinence of the natives in holding their hand until the young are on the wing.

Not long after passing the rock, we anchored opposite the military station of Mergui, now all alive with excitement. The smoke of the steamer had been seen from afar, and the residents were aware that it brought news—good to some, bad to others—from the dear ones at home.

The scene, as we let go the anchor, was striking in the extreme, and transferred to canvas would have found favour in the eyes of the most critical scenic painter of the modern school. In the foreground, the afore-mentioned rock, rising sheer out of the cerulean blue, that sent back the rays of an almost perpendicular sun, while a large opening through the rock resembled an irregular archway. The station of Mergui on elevated ground close to the sea, and backed by a primeval forest, was on the left; while to the right, the emerald isles dotted the sea southward.

Although we arrived somewhat early in the afternoon, certain adventurous spirits came off at once, protected with pith hats and Burmese umbrellas, and were on deck as soon as the anchor held and the gangway had been lowered.

Very different from their apathetic brother officers at Tavoy, they came off in quick succession; the captain was besieged, and bore the ordeal bravely as usual, with a kind word for everyone, though discriminating withal. They buzzed round him like bees, after the manner of mankind in general, where the nectar is mostly stored, though thirsting in this case for news.

Withdrawing from the group, I looked over the stern into the blue water, which was clear as crystal, and saw hundreds of fish gathering about the keel, darting hither and thither, and glistening with all the colours of the rainbow as the rays of light fell upon them at different angles. The smaller ones would get out of the way of the larger; *seniores priores* is the rule among the inhabitants of the deep. Absorbed in the contemplation of these creatures, that have ever interested me above all others, and wondering at the productiveness of these warm seas, and at the survival of a species always at war with each other, I did not at first notice that the captain was speaking to me.

He wanted to introduce me to one of the residents, whose name and face were equally familiar to me, and who turned out to be an old fellow-student, who had joined the Madras army and had been shunted with part of his regiment to this out-of-the-way place.

Considering that those were the halcyon days ere locomotion had carried the now ubiquitous British tourist to every nook and corner of the habitable globe, it was indeed a strange coincidence to encounter an old friend in the neighbourhood of the Mergui Archipelago, which not one out of a thousand at home had ever heard of; or if they had, the name had described that overland route across the brain, which is not uncommonly followed by the subjects taught at school.

Nowadays, of course, progress is setting its stamp upon all *five* quarters of the globe; the beautiful names of Jones, Brown, Smith or " Arry " may be seen carved on the Pyramids of Egypt; on the costly marble of the Taj at Agra; on the Pagoda at Rangoon; and will ere long doubtless ornament the giant trees in " Darkest Africa," to the astonishment of the Pigmies!

" *Cœlum non animum mutant*, etc. . . .," and whether in his own beloved Epping Forest, or in a tropical jungle, he will ferret out nature's gems and destroy them; and in both places the course of his peregrinations may be traced by empty beer bottles and greasy sandwich papers.

The proprietor of an estate on the Dorset coast, which was laid out for the convenience of the public, went so far as to supply printed quotations from various authors, and a special tablet for the names of visitors, but the latter remained black, while the rocks around were deeply scored in every conceivable direction. Such conduct can only be accounted for on the Darwinian theory, for the bump of mischief is unquestionably more developed in the apes than in any other animal.

I invariably pencil under such names " sentenced for felony to penal servitude for life!" or some equally agreeable sentence, which may, or may not, have the desired effect. I was likewise struck when visiting Stratford-on-Avon, and *the* house there many years ago, by the custodian requesting that we should not write our names, or even initials, anywhere about the room in which the poet for all time is said to have first seen the light.

The injunction was doubly superfluous; in the first place, my friends and self were not in the habit of publishing ourselves in this most objectionable manner; and secondly, even if so minded, we could not have found a clear space for any one of our names!

Any encounter with a face not seen for many years, is sure to touch the spring of recollection and set in motion the machinery of the past. Pacing the deck, we wandered once more over the well-trodden road of the past, recalling notable episodes, and conjecturing where sundry of our fellow-students might even then be fighting the battle of life.

Just as we had arrived at the conclusion, not uncommonly held by young men in respect of themselves, that nothing on earth was good enough for us, we were joined by the captain, who held in his hand an invitation for himself and me to dine and sleep ashore.

We accepted the invitation and entrusted the missive to my friend.

Rather nervous as to the limited state of my wardrobe, and hoping that our entertainers would be the reverse of hypercritical, I went ashore at the appointed time in the captain's gig, and we found a considerable party of ladies and gentlemen already assembled to meet us. The dinner had evidently been got up in the captain's honour, and it was on a par with his usual thoughtfulness to get his guest included in his own invitation.

To the relief of all parties, the ceremony of introductions was duly accomplished, and we adjourned to dinner, the same ordeal as elsewhere, but reflecting in this instance unbounded credit on their Madrassee cook. It was undeniably a very pleasant evening, one of the most sociable I can look back upon. Many of their faces I can see before me still, the names, alas! have become effaced.

One of the topics of conversation was the variety and profusion of orchids in the primeval forest close at hand; and, particularly struck by the apathy with which everyone seemed to mention these choicest of Nature's gems, I inwardly resolved to be off to the forest early next morning and bring back a load of the rarest kinds I could lay hands on.

Waking at an early hour, I partook of some tea and toast, and sallied forth with my gun, which I had brought ashore, and—the wherewithal to indulge in a smoke, if so inclined.

The station was composed of a few bungalows built on rising ground along the sea front; behind which intervened a strip of cultivated land, and then one arrived at the edge of the mighty forest. The dividing belt of open ground having been under rice, was now dry and hard; and I consequently traversed it in a few minutes.

As in the affairs of life generally, my eagerness in this instance to secure the coveted orchids had entirely warped my judgment; otherwise I should have taken counsel with those proficient in local topography, and should have brought with me a couple of Burmese with hatchets and bamboo ladders.

Walking was easy enough owing to the total absence of undergrowth, and fairly pleasant on the springy bed of leaves, which had accumulated there for untold ages; while overhead the impenetrable lacework of massive branches completely shut out the sun, leaving almost indescribable gloom and darkness all around me. On looking up, I could see huge branches literally covered with the unrivalled parasites, their colours exceedingly varied and delicate, and their leaves greener and more spotless than I had ever yet seen.

There was, however, one grave fault to be found with all of them—they were far beyond my reach! It was horribly tantalizing; but hoping to find others at a lower elevation, I plunged deeper into the forest and—lost my way.

I came to the conclusion that I might fare worse if I went any further, so I turned back.

I have already lost my way once in these pages, so I shall find it again now as quickly as possible.

Nevertheless, my wanderings to that end were far from pleasant. I deeply regretted not having told even the "bearer" whither I was going. The place began to have a terrible fascination for me; on that soft carpet, I reflected that any uncouth beast might creep upon me unawares; while I began to scan the branches now, not for orchids, but for pythons, which I almost fancied I could see, hanging down and surveying me with their hard, lustreless eyes.

Nay, I refrained from firing a shot, by way of signal to a possible search-party, from fear of awakening such monsters from their normal state of lethargy.

At last, after about five hours' wandering, I emerged into a sun, which at first almost blinded me.

My absence was beginning to cause some anxiety at the house where I was staying; and at breakfast, which had been put off on my account, I had to make a clean breast of everything.

I was reminded by my hostess, that, besides the necessity of taking natives on such an expedition, it would also have been more prudent to have taken a few grains of quinine—of which I now swallowed five, at her express solicitation—before setting foot in a place known to be deadly, owing to pent-up malaria. And this was why the orchids were left to waste their beauties on the forest air and blush unseen!

I saw but little of the native stockade, which, if my memory serves me right, stood on a kind of delta, some way from the European quarters. The inhabitants led a peaceful existence; the sea supplied them with quantities of fish, which were dried for export; the land with timber and "tuskers," the latter very valuable for their ivory. Pearls too were by no means rare, though not fished under any organized system.

Some of the islands further south are, I believe, several thousand feet in height and extremely volcanic; but I had to refuse the only offer to see them that was ever made to me. A few hours after our arrival, another and larger steamer put in an appearance *en route* to the Andamans.

I was offered a passage; a tempting proposition, but which had to be declined.

Besides being averse to leaving my host so abruptly, in short, making a convenience of him, I had to consider the scanty state of my wardrobe—I had left nearly everything at Moulmein, and the still lower ebb of my funds. Pay was very small in those days, while the bulk of what I received had to be remitted home forthwith. Fortunately the rate of exchange was then about par; what my position would have been under the present abnormally low rate, I tremble to think.

Having been thoroughly cleared out by the Mutiny, I found myself severely handicapped by having to support a wife and child at home.

Some folks, dazzled by the brilliant prospects of the Indian Service, refuse to see the reverse side of the medal; but they should take into consideration the fact that on retirement with, say a colonel's pension of 365*l*., 60*l*. is deducted towards the Widows' and Orphan's Pensions Fund, the same amount as he has paid for years from his full pay.

The accounts are never published, never go beyond the sacred precincts of the India Office, so we must take it on trust, that the funds could not be maintained in any other way. The calculation of what an officer has paid at this rate for forty years, with donations, interest, etc., would make the mouth of many an insurance agent water!

For the reasons already mentioned, I elected to return by the way I had come, and had no reason to regret doing so. What if I did not see the Andaman Islands! they were places of little or no interest. A curse seemed to have rested on them. To begin with, their orginal inhabitants were few and far between; wretched specimens of humanity, at least morally and intellectually, if not physically; differing from anything I had been accustomed to—Cannibals! Upon this promising soil we then grafted the noblest types of the scum of India—mutineers, murderers and Dacoits; That is to say, we focussed on one spot all that was worse than cannibalism, there to dream of vengeance, and pass the remainder of their lives feeding on their dire hatred of mankind in general, and every other passion likely to convert them into incarnate devils, ten times worse than they had been before. Many were sent there because they attempted to recover their country from the iron rule of the usurper; others, because they acted up to the teachings of their childhood.

Could we but form an idea of the evil passions which surged up in the bosoms of those Asiatics torn by force from their own land, I believe that even Dante's immortal conception of the Inferno would pale its ineffectual fire before that seething cauldron of pent-up human rage. Before the advent of these horrors, the islands, even if we throw cannibalism into the balance, must have been infinitely better than our convict system has since made them.

That such a distinct race of people should have been confined to these islands, part of the same chain as included the Nicobars, Sumatra and Java, was also passing strange. The researches of Prichard and Latham point to the origin of the various human types from a single pair, the differences being due to the influence of climate, food and a variety of other circumstances; and if this was the case, the divergence of the Andamanese from Malay characteristics, considering their geographical proximity, is still more unaccountable. But other ethnologists—Camper of the Dutch school, the originator of the *facial angle* test of intelligence; Blumenbach of the vertical system; and Morton of American fame—incline to the belief in separate origins and subsequent fusion by intercommunication.

Science has yet much to account for in this direction.

Such a late breakfast brought the time of departure very near, as the captain was anxious to leave as early as possible that afternoon. As it was, he had to account for several hours' delay, and would be taken to task for any such unnecessarily indulged in. We therefore took leave of our hospitable entertainers, and commenced the return voyage to Moulmein, with no other passenger on board than myself. He soon reminded me of my promise regarding the merchant's experience on the island, and I gratified his curiosity, narrating the facts much as they have been here set forth. Moulmein was "made" in due time; and I was heartily sorry to bid farewell to the captain, who had to proceed straight to Calcutta, whereas my steamer would follow in the wake of the *Pluto* ten days later. I was glad of the respite, being moreover in no hurry to change the clear, bright Salween for the muddy, depressing Hooghly, with its defunct Hindoos and carrion fowl.

Before leaving Moulmein, I consulted with my friend as to some suitable way of tendering my thanks to the captain for all the kindness and hospitality I had received at his hands; and a plan was devised and carried out on my return to India. This, while insignificant in intrinsic value, served as a slight *souvenir* of the time when he had done all in his power to render the voyage as comfortable and interesting as possible, and to wean me from brooding over the recent Cimmerian period of the Mutiny. For some time we corresponded. If he still lives, may we meet again on this side of the border!

CHAPTER XX.

AND LAST.

" My pen is at the bottom of a page,
   Which being finished, here the story ends
   'Tis to be wished it had been sooner done,
   But stories somehow lengthen when begun."

THE reader may mentally alter the title of this concluding chapter to "*At* Last!" and if he has found my reminiscences dull or humdrum, he will soon have his reward by closing the book and consigning it to oblivion —or to Mudie's cart!

Nevertheless, in glancing back over the foregoing pages—a retrospect of a retrospect—I seem to have fulfilled what I undertook at the outset—even though that be little.

Digressions there are, I know, "innumerable as the temples in Pagan," to borrow an old Burmese proverb; and the bare outline of my story, stripped of such embellishments, might easily be reduced to the dimensions of a certain celebrated signboard, which set forth the fame of one John Thompson.

That worthy man, a hatter by trade, composed it himself as follows: "*John Thompson, hatter; makes and sells hats for ready money,*" under which was depicted a large hat. This he submitted to half a dozen cronies, who modified it as follows. The first thought the word "hatter" unnecessary, because followed by the words "makes hats." It was therefore struck out.

The next objected to the word "makes," as no one, he argued, would care who made the hats, as long as they were good. That was also omitted.

A third found fault with the expression "sells," as no one imagined for a moment that he gave them away. "Sells," therefore, followed the fate of its predecessors. Another took exception at "hats," in consideration of the painting underneath. Hats was accordingly obliterated.

The fifth condemned the clause referring to ready money, since that was the custom of the place; while the sixth and last, vexed beyond measure at finding nothing left to erase, would have pulled the signboard down bodily, but for the remonstrances of the others.

To resume the beginning of the end.

The business in teak-wood was now drawing to a close, for ere long the rains would cease, and there would no longer be any means of floating the timber down to the coast on the swollen tributaries of the Salween. Few vessels therefore remained, and the river looked deserted, but for an unusually large craft painted white, and therefore conspicuous in more ways than one.

She proved, on inquiry, to be an American vessel of considerable burden, chartered for the purpose of transporting elephants to Bengal; and as she was anchored in mid-stream, we went off to watch the process of embarking the invaluable creatures.

They were brought from the shore one by one on stout rafts, on which they behaved with the utmost decorum, evidently in blissful ignorance of their ultimate destination—the ship's hold. If they thought about it at all, it was merely a case of transferring them to the opposite bank of the river, a proceeding frequently indulged in. The raft was then made fast to the further side of the ship ; and some specially constructed gear was next lowered from a crane on the yard arm, and the elephant was slung in the broad leather bands attached to massive chains. Being accustomed to the "howdah" and belly bands, no notice was taken of this ; but as soon as they found themselves hoisted off their feet and suspended in mid-air, mere words would fail to describe their puzzled expression.

On first rising, they trumpeted loudly, but as they reached greater altitudes, all power of uttering even a protest seemed to desert them, and anything more ludicrous I never beheld.

The tackle had been made very powerful, the average weight of the large elephants being calculated ; but to guard against any possible mishap, the rafts were removed as soon as the pachyderms were fairly "under weigh," so that, had the worst come to the worst, they would only have fallen into the water and swum ashore. When clear of the ship's side, they were swung round until exactly over the main hold, and then lowered. Sometimes a foot would be planted on the combings ; but a gentle tap from a capstan bar soon removed the impediment, and the leviathan disappeared below, there to be cabin'd, crib'd, confined, and ere long tossed about in the Bay of Bengal. I forget the exact number shipped on this occasion ; but believe it was not far short of ninety, all fine, large animals, very different to anything ever seen in this country, not excepting the late lamented "Jumbo."

It was impossible not to think of the pitiable condition of these poor beasts, should anything like bad weather overtake the ship out at sea : while the condition of the hold must have been anything but savoury at the best of times ; and indeed the effluvia arising thence during the process of embarking robbed me of all desire to inspect their quarters.

They were, I believe, arranged in rows, a position in which they could afford each other some support during the varied movements of the ship; while they were further helped through the ordeal by their great stability in circumference of legs and feet, and the long, prehensile trunks, with which they could hold on to any convenient stanchions.

Indeed, on inquiring soon after our arrival at Calcutta, we learnt that they had all arrived safely and in good condition, so that they must be far better sailors than horses. Anything like mutiny in the hold might have led to serious consequences, considering that each animal was ten feet high, weighed about five tons, and possessed strength centred, according to Cuvier, in 40,000 muscles with a distinct or combined action, according to circumstances! Well, a panic ensuing among these monsters in the hold, numbering from fifty to ninety, would have been a scene of indescribable terror, besides probably occasioning the foundering of the ship and the loss of something between 12,000*l.* and 22,000*l.* in cargo alone, the average commercial value of such elephants being 250*l.* apiece.

When that widespread epidemic of elephant-mania broke out in England some years ago on account of "Jumbo," who does not remember the sickening details of the ridiculous offerings at his shrine, and the no less idiotic fuss made over the paraphernalia for removing one such animal a few miles by land! Why, his "mahout" would have ridden him from the Zoo to the Docks in an hour at dead of night, and then walked him on board! Such things are managed differently in the East.

The process of embarking the elephants had such a fascination for me, that I should, if alone, in all probability have remained on board for the rest of the day. My friend, however, felt the pangs of hunger and insisted on returning. Dear old fellow! after nearly completing his career in India, without even the semblance of illness, he slipped from some vehicle and thereby contracted a troublesome malady which soon carried him off. He was a good husband, father, friend and doctor, regretted by all who knew him : and I have many a time stood by his grave near Cheltenham and thought of the pleasant times we had spent together in far-off climes, this trip in particular.

The distance intervening between Moulmein and the sea had already displayed to our admiring gaze some of the beauties of the well-wooded banks of the Salween; but an excellent opportunity now presented itself for exploring further up.

The Commissioner being about to start an inspection duty in his steam yacht, and very sensibly preferring company to solitude, organized a picnic party, in which I had the honour to be included. The affair was to be a kind of picnic by land and water, affording time to land at various places, with the performance of certain official duties, thus combining business with pleasure.

The commissariat devolved on the chief's wife, and, with the assistance of a native cook, certainly acquitted herself admirably—such mulligatawny, and such salads! The scene on either side, as the river gradually narrowed, was very beautiful. From the wooded heights in the background, a bright pagoda peeped out here and there among vegetation more profuse and luxuriant than any I had ever seen since my journey on the Pegu river.

We visited several of the villages, which were very neat and built, as usual, on piles; but we soon discovered that distance lent enchantment to the view, and that a closer acquaintance brought us in contact with a formidable amalgamation of odours, not of the eau-de-Cologne order, a *mélange* of Jack-fruit, mango, and that curious native delicacy, to which I alluded in a former chapter, and which consists for the most part of fish not remarkable for its freshness!

While their houses were canopied with the thickest of foliage, the space around was kept clear of anything like undergrowth. Only a few bamboos were allowed to grow in each clump, about which a man could thread his way with ease. The survivors were consequently of large size—the largest I ever came across—the specimens cut for us as *souvenirs* measuring nine inches in diameter. Three joints of such a one I took back to Calcutta, one of which I had prettily carved for a present, while the others served as wine-coolers. The price asked by the natives for a bamboo sixty or seventy feet in length, including the cost of cutting up, was not exorbitant, amounting to about four annas, or sixpence. The dexterity with which it was levelled and cut up was almost unequalled, reminding one—ghastly reminiscence!—of the manner in which a Ghoorka handled his *kookerie*, when cutting off the heads of his prisoners. I once witnessed thirty severed in a row; and there was no keeping the bloodthirsty little demons from so disposing of their captives.

The Jack-fruit and plantain both revelled in that fertile soil, attaining to a large size; but as for the mango—oh, what a falling off was there! not off the trees, but in point of size and flavour. The ubiquitous crow of course abounded; paroquets flew away uttering discordant shrieks; and squirrels gambolled from bough to bough, running up and down the stems spiral wise.

Extremely picturesque were the costumes of the men and women squatting about in front of their dwellings, and especially the artistic way in which the latter coiled their jet-black hair and embellished it with flowers of a waxy appearance.

It certainly occurred to me that here, of all places on earth, the inhabitants ought to be happy and contented; nature had lavished her choicest gifts on them in such profusion, leaving them but little in the way of arduous occupation. Perhaps they were happy; they certainly seemed so, for all were well dressed, and I do not remember seeing a single beggar. And, from a knowledge of both, I should say that such simple villagers have a much better chance of present and future happiness than the inhabitants of some of our own villages, where for the most part the Christian virtues seem conspicuous by their absence.

Living in one for seven years in a private capacity, my services, in virtue of my profession, were nevertheless very frequently asked for and given, and I consequently saw a great deal of their inner life, which often startled and shocked me.

With all respect to General Booth, " Darkest England" exists in the rural districts, and not in London, where are centred the wealth, enterprise, benevolence and clerical power of the land. The country, on the other hand, remains in the shadow of death; and there stands the vineyard that requires labourers, who work to please their Master, and not merely for the loaves and fishes!

The party consisted of three or four married couples, a young unmarried lady and myself, a grass-widower of some eighteen months' standing. Naturally, we two were thrown together during the day, and just as naturally we were accused of flirting. It was therefore with extreme concern that I attended to my torch, remembering my mishap in the same neighbourhood on a former occasion, as we presently explored some very pretty caves, which, for a reason which geologists may be able to explain, especially abound on the right bank.

This time, I reflected I was not alone, and if my torch were to go out, of course no one would believe that it was the result of accident. So at least I concluded, mindful of the proverbial charity that folks at large indulge in when criticizing their neighbours' proceedings.

After lunch on the yacht, temptingly laid out and thoroughly appreciated, the boat's head was turned, and we quietly steamed down to Moulmein. The day was full of interest from start to finish, and everyone thoroughly enjoyed it.

Something of the old schoolboy sensation, when his fleeting holidays are drawing to a close, stole over me as our steamer turned up a few days later to convey us back to a land associated with so many painful memories. Before the Mutiny, I could count my friends by scores; now most of them had perished, slaughtered with few exceptions by their own men in whom they reposed such blind and ill-requited confidence. Many of the old landmarks of the service were also to be swept away, and new ones set up in their place.

The prospect was uninviting to a degree; but as I could not afford to cut the painter for good and all, I had to make the best of a bad bargain. At any rate, we were, under our old masters, content and happy, and should have been prosperous as well, but for an event, for which those at home were more to blame than the people on the spot.

What were the chances of improvement now, with more home interference on the part of those who knew not the East? Time alone could show! I had certainly enjoyed myself, and in some measure my Burmese trip had done me good; but now the reaction was setting in, and I began to question whether it would not have been better after all to have stayed on the spot and lived down the disagreeables. Hard work is without a doubt the best panacea for all manner of troubles; and not, as so many aver, an unceasing round of pleasure and fictitious excitement.

My feelings had partaken very much of the same character as those of a party of young children I once upon a time escorted to their first seaside holiday, and then brought back after a month's enjoyment of the indescribable delights which any of our watering places afford such juveniles. Going, they were all sunshine and excitement, never ceasing to prattle about their coming excursions and amusements, and even setting the other occupants of the carriage in a roar of laughter by their ingenuous attempts to pronounce the dreadful Welsh names of the stations through which we passed.

Very different was the return journey; all was dark without and sad within; hardly a word spoken from beginning to end; stations unnoticed and uncared for, and even the " goodies " eaten in silence.

And I felt sad too at the prospect of returning to India. For a time, I was diverted by the fatiguing process of packing; though it was only by the aid of a zealous and painstaking domestic, who ignored the mosquitoes and the exertion, that I finally succeeded in stowing away all the vases, teapots, cups and saucers, heathen gods and goddesses, bamboos, etc., regretting the while that I had ever been prevailed upon to buy them. I was therefore not sorry at having failed to secure a couple of Pegu ponies for transmission to India. Their price alone—Rs. 300 for an animal that formerly cost one-tenth of that price—placed me out of the ring; and the trouble and expenses attendant on the transport of live stock must have been considerable. As a speculation, it might have answered; but whatever gifts Nature may have lavished broadcast upon me, the bump of "barter" was only developed in a very rudimentary state. After packing came the still more painful operation of leave-taking, and we were soon steaming down the river for the last time. Several handkerchiefs waving from a verandah grew less disdinct, until a bend in the stream hid them from view.

We were taken back by the same adventurous, independent captain, a buoyant person of the Mark Tapley order, who gave us one more proof of his undeniable force of will. We had reached the Sand Heads, about a hundred and twenty miles from Calcutta, when a dispute arose as to whether we should be up in time to land that evening. Two circumstances militated strongly against us, the strength of the outward current and the rule that forbade any navigation after sunset among the shipping that lay off the town. But the captain swore he would be ashore in time to dine with his wife; and he kept his word. The wheels revolved faster, the wave of cleavage rose higher; and the inquiries of the engineer were ever met with "Give her as much more as you can!" As the daylight began to ebb, the smell of fire was distinctly perceptible, and smoke was issuing from various chinks. A number of Lascars too might be seen emptying buckets over the deck. Still the captain kept his course; and at last, the observed of all observers, we passed the shipping and reached our moorings, and were at rest.

I took a boat and went ashore, and——Chaos came again!

FINIS.

INDEX.

A.

ADEN harbour, 222.
Akyab, 192.
Albatross, Catching an, 17.
Albicore, 27.
Alligators, 112, 164.
Amherst, 214.
Amherstia nobilis, 205.
Amsterdam, 32.
Amusements, Burmese, 52.
Andaman Islands, 249.
Architecture, Burmese, 57, 65, 202.
Argonauts, 18.

B.

BAMBOO, 47, 65, 164, 257.
Banana, 48, 170.
Bandicoot, 42.
Barrackpore, 44.
Bats, 211.
Beri-beri, 107.
Birds' Nests, Edible, 241.
Birds, 56, 63, 94, 99, 133.
Bonito, Catching, 16.
Brahmans, 73.
Buddha, 69.
Burmah, Fertility of, 47.
Burmese Character, 49.

C.

CALCUTTA, 36.
Camel, 172.
Camper, 250.
Cape Route, 24.
Caste, 78.
Caves, 209, 259.
Chelonia virgata, 239.
Children educated at home, 184.
China Bazaar, 42.
Chinese, 59, 71, 114, 202.
Chivalry, 176.
Cholera, 65, 181, 194.
Climate, Effects of, 40.
Cock-fighting, 52.
Collocatia esculenta, 242.
Cookery, Native, 90, 102, 121.
Cow-itch, 166.
Cremation, 58.
Custard, Apple, 48, 126.

D.

DANCING, 22, 44.
Dracunculus, 103.
Duck-shooting, 135.
Durian, 48.

E.

EDUCATION, 181, 229.
Egyptians, 72.
"El Dorado," 161.
Elephants, 167, 207, 253.
Embalming, 58, 72.
Emigrants, 29.
Exhibition of 1851, 19.
Expedition, A secret, 137.

F.

FIRE, 25, 65.
Fish and fishing, 13, 164, 215, 222, 243.
Flying-bugs, 103.
Flying-fish, 17.
Football, Burmese, 54.
Funeral, A Chinese, 203.

G.

GAMBLING, 52.
Gautama, 50, 69, 71.

Germicides, 107.
Golail, 105.
Govilon, 164.
Gua-pu, 60.
Gulf-Stream, 25.
Gynee-Clubs, 199.

H.

HIGH pressure, Modern, 229.
Hinduism, 72.
Holy-stoning, 11.
Hooghly, 33.
Huc, Travels of M., 203.

I.

IMAGES, 58, 70.
Incas, 74.
Intermittent fever, 176.
———————— causes of, 178.
———————— hypodermic treatment of, 180.
Irrigation, Native, 161.

J.

JACK-FRUIT, 48, 205.
Jackal, 44, 64, 100.
Jungle-fowl, 52, 165.

K.

KALONG, 49.
Kookerie, 257.
Koran, 75, 83.
Kyouk-Phyao, 193.

L.

LATHAM, 250.
Line, Crossing the, 13.
Looting, 56, 58.

M.

MACKEREL fishing, 16.
Madeira, 9.
Mango, 257.
Mangrove, 227.
Matrimony, 22, 45, 51.
Medicine, Native, 166.
Mediterranean, 16, 18, 20.
Mendoon, 174.
Mergui, 241.

Missionaries, 78, 83.
Mohammed, 75.
Monkeys, 93.
Monsoon, 67.
Morality, Native, 51.
Morton, 250.
Mosquitoes, 89, 100.
Moulmein, 201.
Mucuna pruens, 166.
Mud fish, 68.
Mudar, 107.
Music, 22, 62.
Mutiny, 29, 82, 96, 110, 117, 130.

N.

NAUTILI, 18.
Navigation, Art of, 24.
Nepaulese, 82.
Nirvana, 69, 76, 83.

O.

OCTOPUS, 151.
Opium *v*. Alcohol, 186, 208.
Orchids, 151, 246.

P.

PAGODAS, 55, 96.
Panglang Creek, 89.
Pariah dogs, 99, 105.
Peacocks, 64.
Pegu, 95.
Petrified trees, 168.
Phayre, Sir A., 61, 160.
Plantain, 48, 170.
Poinsiana regia, 205.
Pongyees, 57.
Pongyee houses, 97, 116, 123.
Ponies, Pegu, 53, 261.
Pooay, A, 54.
Porpoises, 15.
Post-mortem examinations, 81.
Prichard, 250.
Prome, 123.
Pythagoras, 72.

R.

RANGOON, 46, 66.
Rats, 42.
Religion, 58, 69 *et seq*.
Rice, 170.

INDEX. 265

Riding, 53.
Robinson Crusoe, A modern, 234.

S.

ST. HELENA, 10, 16.
Salween river, 196.
"Scandal Point," 193.
Sea-sickness, 5.
Sea Voyages, Benefit of, 181.
Shark, 13, 219.
"Shingles," 201.
Shipbuilding, 207.
Smells, 41, 60.
Snakes, 130, 135, 223.
Steamer, The first Cape, 30.
Stockades, 46, 59, 163, 248.
Stormy Petrel, 27.
Suttee, 82.

T.

TAMARIND, 231.
Tavoy, 224.
Teak, 197.
———, Ruthless exhaustion of, 146, 206.

Temples, 57.
Theyetmyeo, 116.
Three, Significance of the numeral, 76.
Thuggee, 82.
Tigers, 64, 104, 153.
Tobacco, 169.
Trade winds, 24.
Transmigration, 72.
Travel, Modern, 2, 12, 15.
Tunbridge Wells, 212.
Turtle, 239, 241.

V.

VITALITY, Instances of dormant, 67.
Vocabulary, Anglo-India, 39.
Vultures, 56.

W.

WATERSPOUT, 21.
Whale, 20.
Whirlwind, 21.

LONDON:
PRINTED BY GILBERT AND RIVINGTON, LIMITED,
ST. JOHN'S HOUSE, CLERKENWELL ROAD.

JUNE, 1894.

MESSRS. W. H. ALLEN & CO.'S
(Publishers to the India Office)
GENERAL CATALOGUE.

CONTENTS.

India, History, &c.	... ...	1–4
Miscellaneous	... ...	5–7
Military	... ...	7–9
Naval	... ...	9–10
Sport	... ...	10
Biography	... ...	11
Eminent Women Series	...	12
Statesmen Series	... ...	13
Books of Reference	... ...	14
Fiction	... ...	15
History, Political, &c. ...	...	16
Natural History, Botany, and Popular Science	16–21
Allen's Naturalist's Library...	28
Travel	...21–23
Theology	...24–26
Veterinary and Riding...	...26–27
Books issued by the India Office and Government of India	29
Map of India...	30
Index	...31–32

India—History, &c.

SIR W. W. HUNTER, K.C.S.I., C.I.E., LL.D.

The Indian Empire: Its People, History, and Products. 852 pages. Third and Standard Edition, revised to 1893. Demy 8vo. With Map. 28s.

E. D. CUMING.

In the Shadow of the Pagoda. Sketches of Burmese Life and Character. **Crown 8vo.** Illustrated. 6s.

GEORGE ABERIGH-MACKAY.

Twenty-one Days in India. Being the Tour of Sir Ali Baba, K.C.B. Post 8vo. 4s. An Illustrated Edition. Demy 8vo. 10s. 6d.

SIR EDWIN ARNOLD, M.A., K.C.I.E., C.S.I. Author of "The Light of Asia," &c.

The Book of Good Counsels, from the Sanscrit of the Hitopadésa. New Edition. With Illustrations by Gordon Browne. Crown 8vo. 7s. 6d.

An Edition in large paper, limited to 100 copies, bound in white vellum. 25s. each net.

London: 13, Waterloo Place, Pall Mall, S.W.

THE STANDARD WORK ON THE INDIAN MUTINY.
SIR J. W. KAYE and COLONEL G. B. MALLESON.

History of the Indian Mutiny of 1857-8. Cabinet Edition. 6 vols. Crown 8vo. 6s. each.

SIR J. W. KAYE.

History of the Sepoy War, 1857-8. Demy 8vo. Vol. I., 18s. Vol. II., 20s. Vol. III., 20s.—continued by COL. G. B. MALLESON, C.S.I. Demy 8vo. 3 vols. 20s. each.

Analytical Index to the Complete Work. By FREDERICK PINCOTT. Demy 8vo. 10s. 6d.

History of the War in Afghanistan. New Edition. 3 vols. Crown 8vo. 18s.

Lives of Indian Officers. 2 vols., crown 8vo, 6s. each.

SIR GEORGE BIRDWOOD, M.D., K.C.I.E., &c.

Report on the Old Records of the India Office. Royal 8vo, with Maps and Illustrations. 12s. 6d.

REV. A. J. D. D'ORSEY.

Portuguese Discoveries, Annexations, and Missions in Asia and Africa. Crown 8vo. With maps. 7s. 6d.

G. K. BETHAM, Indian Forest Department.

The Story of a Dacoity, Nagoji the Beder Naik, and the Lolapur Week. Crown 8vo. 6s.

MRS. GRACE JOHNSON, Silver Medallist Cookery Exhibition.

Anglo-Indian and Oriental Cookery. Crown 8vo, 3s. 6d.

HOWARD HENSMAN, Special Correspondent of the " Pioneer " (Allahabad) and the " Daily News" (London).

The Afghan War, 1879-80. Being a complete Narrative of the Capture of Cabul, the Siege of Sherpur, the Battle of Ahmed Khel, the March to Candahar, and the defeat of Ayub Khan. With Maps. Demy 8vo. 21s.

T. R. E. HOLMES.

A History of the Indian Mutiny, and of the Disturbances which accompanied it among the Civil Population. Fourth Edition. With Maps and Plans. Crown 8vo. 5s.

London: 13, Waterloo Place, Pall Mall, S.W.

HENRY GEORGE KEENE, C.I.E., B.C.S., M.R.A.S., &c.

History of India. From the Earliest Times to the Present Day. For the use of Students and Colleges. 2 vols., crown 8vo. With Maps. **16s.**

The Fall of the Moghul Empire. From the Death of Aurungzeb to the overthrow of the Mahratta Power. A New Edition, with Corrections and Additions. With Map. Crown 8vo. 7s. 6d.

This work fills up a blank between the ending of Elphinstone's and the commencement of Thornton's Histories.

Fifty-Seven. Some account of the Administration of Indian Districts during the Revolt of the Bengal Army. Demy 8vo. 6s.

The Turks in India. Historical Chapters on the Administration of Hindostan by the Chugtai Tartar, Babar, and his Descendants. Demy 8vo. 12s. 6d.

An Oriental Biographical Dictionary. Founded on materials collected by the late THOMAS WILLIAM BEALE. New Edition, revised and enlarged. Royal 8vo. 28s.

COL. G. B. MALLESON, C.S.I.

Final French Struggles in India and on the Indian Seas. New Edition. Crown 8vo. 6s.

History of the Indian Mutiny, 1857-1858, commencing from the close of the Second Volume of Sir John Kaye's History of the Sepoy War. Vol. I. With Map. Demy 8vo. 20s.—Vol. II. With 4 Plans. Demy 8vo. 20s.—Vol. III. With Plans. Demy 8vo. 20s.

History of Afghanistan, from the Earliest Period to the Outbreak of the War of 1878. Second Edition. With Map. Demy 8vo. 18s.

The Decisive Battles of India, from 1746-1849. Third Edition. With a Portrait of the Author, a Map, and 4 Plans. Crown 8vo. 7s. 6d.

Founders of the Indian Empire. Vol. I.—LORD CLIVE. With Portraits and 4 Plans. Demy 8vo. 20s.

History of the French in India. From the Founding of Pondicherry in 1674, to the Capture of that place in 1761. New and Revised Edition. Demy 8vo, Maps. 16s.

ILTUDUS PRICHARD, of Gray's Inn, Barrister-at-Law.

Chronicles of Budgepore; or, Sketches of Life in Upper India. New Edition. Crown 8vo, 6s.

MRS. MANNING.

Ancient and Mediæval India. Being the History, Religion, Laws, Caste, Manners and Customs, Language, Literature, Poetry, Philosophy, Astronomy, Algebra, Medicine, Architecture, Manufactures, Commerce, &c., of the Hindus, taken from their Writings. With Illustrations. 2 vols. Demy 8vo. 30s.

REV. G. U. POPE, D.D., Fellow of Madras University.

Text-Book of Indian History; with Geographical Notes, Genealogical Tables, Examination Questions, and Chronological, Biographical, Geographical, and General Indexes. For the use of Schools, Colleges, and Private Students. Third Edition, thoroughly revised. Fcap. 4to. 12s.

ALEXANDER ROGERS (Bombay Civil Service, Retired).

The Land Revenue of Bombay. A History of its Administration, Rise, and Progress. 2 vols. Demy 8vo. With 18 Maps. 30s.

ROBERT SEWELL, Madras Civil Service.

Analytical History of India. From the earliest times to the Abolition of the East India Company in 1858. Post 8vo. 8s.

CAPTAIN LIONEL JAMES TROTTER, late Beng. Fusiliers.

India under Victoria from 1836 to 1880. 2 vols. Demy 8vo. 30s.

MRS. M. GRIFFITH.

India's Princes. Short Life Sketches of the Native Rulers of India. 4to. With numerous Portraits and other Illustrations. 21s.

London: 13, Waterloo Place Pall Mall, S.W.

Miscellaneous.

Academy Sketches, 1894, a Volume of Sketches of Oil Paintings, Water Colours, &c., in the Royal Academy and other Exhibitions. 1s.

CAPTAIN J. H. LAWRENCE ARCHER, Bengal H.P.

The Orders of Chivalry, from the Original Statutes of the various Orders of Knighthood and other sources of information. With 3 Portraits and 63 Plates. 4to. Coloured, £6 6s.; Plain, £3 3s.

JOHN BRADSHAW, LL.D., Inspector of Schools, Madras.

The Poetical Works of John Milton. With Notes, Explanatory and Philological. Crown 8vo. Vol. I., 2s. 6d.; Vol. II., 3s. 6d.; or in one volume complete, 6s.

MAJOR-GENERAL J. T. BOILEAU.

A New and Complete Set of Traverse Tables, showing the Differences of Latitude and Departures to every Minute of the Quadrant and to Five Places of Decimals. Together with a Table of the Lengths of each Degree of Latitude and corresponding Degree of Longitude from the Equator to the Poles; with other Tables useful to the Surveyor and Engineer. Fourth Edition, thoroughly revised and corrected by the Author. 1876. Royal 8vo. 12s.

REV. T. F. THISTLETON DYER, M.A.

English Folk-Lore. Second Edition. Crown 8vo. 5s.

J. MORTIMER GRANVILLE, M.D.

1. Nerves and Nerve Troubles. 2. Common Mind Troubles. 3. How to Make the Best of Life. 4. The Secret of a Clear Head. 5. The Secret of a Good Memory. 6. Sleep and Sleeplessness. Fcap. 8vo. 1s. each.

G. H. D. GOSSIP.

Theory of the Chess Openings. Demy 8vo. 7s. 6d.

REV. H. R. HAWEIS.

Music and Morals. Seventeenth Edition. With Portraits. Crown 8vo. 7s. 6d.

My Musical Life. Fourth Edition. With Illustrations. Crown 8vo. 7s. 6d.

London: 13, Waterloo Place, Pall Mall, S.W.

RALPH DUNSTAN, Mus. Doc. (Cantab.)

Manual of Music. Thirteenth Edition. Revised and corrected in accordance with the latest requirements of the Education Department. Crown 8vo. 2s. 6d.

MRS. HAWEIS.

Chaucer's Beads: A Birthday Book, Diary, and Concordance of Chaucer's Proverbs or Sooth-saws. Crown 8vo, cloth, bevelled edges, gilt, 4s. 6d.; padded morocco, 7s. 6d.

JOHN H. INGRAM.

The Haunted Homes and Family Traditions of Great Britain. Crown 8vo. Illustrated. 7s. 6d.

LUCY JONES.

Puddings and Sweets. 365 Receipts approved by Experience. Fcap. 1s.

MRS. LANKESTER.

Talks about Health: A Book for Boys and Girls. Being an Explanation of all the Processes by which Life is sustained. Illustrated. Small 8vo. 1s.

C. J. MICHOD.

Good Condition. A Guide to Athletic Training for Amateurs and Professionals. Crown 8vo. 1s.

HEALTH PRIMERS.

1. Premature Death. 2. Alcohol. 3. Exercise and Training. 4. The House. 5. Baths and Bathing. 6. The Skin. 7. The Heart. 8. The Nervous System. 9. Health in Schools. Demy 16mo. 1s. each.

Byron Birthday Book. In Padded Morocco, rounded corners, gilt edges, boxed, 4s. 6d. Cloth, gilt edges, 2s. 6d.

Treasury of Choice Quotations. Selections from more than 300 Eminent Authors. With Index. Crown 8vo, 3s. 6d.

London: 13, *Waterloo Place, Pall Mall, S.W.*

W. H. Allen & Co.'s General Catalogue. 7

DAVID THOMSON.

Lunar and Horary Tables. For New and Concise Methods of Performing the Calculations necessary for ascertaining the Longitude by **Lunar** Observations, or Chronometers; with directions for acquiring a knowledge of the Principal Fixed Stars and finding the Latitude of them. Sixty-fifth Edition. Royal 8vo. 10s.

M. A. WALFORD.

Holidays in Home Counties. With numerous Illustrations. Crown 8vo. 5s.

Pleasant Days in Pleasant Places. Illustrated with numerous Woodcuts. Second Edition. Crown 8vo. 5s.

J. C. WRIGHT.

Readings from Great English Writers. With Biographical Notes. Crown 8vo. 3s. 6d.

Military.

Moltke's Tactical Problems, 1858 to 1882. Edited by the Prussian Grand General Staff, Department for Military History. Authorised Translation, by KARL VON DONAT, late Lieutenant East Prussian Fusilier Regiment. Royal 8vo. With 27 Plans and 9 Sketch Maps. 28s.

CAPT. H. R. GALL, late 5th Fusiliers.

Modern Tactics. Third Edition. Royal 8vo. 15s. net.

This Edition has been almost entirely re-written in accordance with the New Drill Books, and contains upwards of 50 plates and worked-out schemes.

LIEUT.-GENL. SIR W. BELLAIRS, K.C.M.G.

The Military Career. A Guide to young Officers, Army Candidates, and Parents. Crown 8vo. 5s.

F. V. GREENE, Lieut. U.S. Army, and lately Military Attaché to the U.S. Legation at St. Petersburg.

The Russian Army and its Campaigns in Turkey in 1877-1878. Second Edition. Royal 8vo. 32s.

Sketches of Army Life in Russia. Crown 8vo. 9s.

London: 13, *Waterloo Place, Pall Mall, S.W.*

COL. G. B. MALLESON, C.S.I.

Battlefields of Germany. With Maps and Plan. Demy 8vo. 16s.

Ambushes and Surprises: Being a Description of some of the most famous Instances of the Leading into Ambush and the Surprise of Armies, from the time of Hannibal to the Period of the Indian Mutiny. With a Portrait of General Lord Mark Kerr, K.C.B. Demy 8vo. 18s.

IRVING MONTAGU (late Special War Correspondent "Illustrated London News").

Camp and Studio. Illustrated by the Author. Crown 8vo, 6s.

Wanderings of a War Artist. Illustrated by the Author. Crown 8vo, 6s.

Where Glory Calls. The Soldier's Scrap Book. 4to. 1s. Illustrations by R. SIMKIN.

Campaigns in Virginia, 1861-2. Royal 8vo. Paper Covers. With Maps. 3s. 6d. By T. MILLER MAGUIRE, M.A. LL.D.

Single - Stick Exercise of the Aldershot Gymnasium. Paper Cover. Fcap. 8vo. 6d.

Notes on Military Topography. By MAJOR WILLOUGHBY VERNER, Rifle Brigade. With Plans. Royal 8vo. 5s.

Rapid Field Sketching and Reconnaissance. By MAJOR WILLOUGHBY VERNER. With Plans. Royal 8vo. 7s. 6d.

London: 13, Waterloo Place, Pall Mall, S.W.

W. O'CONNOR MORRIS.

Great Commanders of Modern Times, and the Campaign of 1815. Turenne—Marlborough—Frederick the Great—Napoleon—Wellington—Moltke. With Illustrations and Plans. Royal 8vo. 21s.

The Nation in Arms. From the German of Lieut.-Col. Baron von der Goltz. Translated by PHILIP A. ASHWORTH. Demy 8vo. 15s.

CAPTAIN E. O. WATHEN, *Fifth Lancers.*

Field Service Pocket Book. 5s. *net.*

COL. F. A. WHINYATES, *late R.H.A., formerly commanding the Battery.*

From Corunna to Sevastopol. The History of "C" Battery, "A" Brigade, late "C" Troop, Royal Horse Artillery. With succession of Officers from its formation to the present time. With 3 Maps. Demy 8vo. 14s.

The Young Soldier in India: His Life and Prospects. By H. S. Crown 8vo. 3s. 6d.

Naval.

HARRY WILLIAMS, R.N. (*Chief Inspector of Machinery*).

Dedicated, by permission, to Admiral H.R.H. the Duke of Edinburgh.

The Steam Navy of England: Past, Present, and Future. Contents: Part I.—Our Seamen; Part II.—Ships and Machinery; Part III.—Naval Engineering; Part IV.—Miscellaneous, Summary, Conclusion. Second Edition. Medium 8vo. 12s. 6d.

CAPTAIN MONTAGU BURROWS, R.N.

Life of Edward, Lord Hawke; Admiral of the Fleet and First Lord of the Admiralty from 1766 to 1771. Demy 8vo. 21s.

London: 13, Waterloo Place, Pall Mall, S.W.

VICE-ADMIRAL P. H. COLOMB.

Naval Warfare, its Ruling Principles and Practice Historically Treated. Royal 8vo. 21s.

Essays on Naval Defence. Crown 8vo, with plates, 6s.

The Book of Knots. Illustrated by 172 Examples, showing the manner of making every Knot, Tie, and Splice. By "TOM BOWLING." Third Edition. Crown 8vo. 2s. 6d.

Sport.

G. P. SANDERSON, Officer in Charge of the Government Elephant Keddahs.

Thirteen Years among the Wild Beasts of India; their Haunts and Habits, from Personal Observation. With an account of the Modes of Capturing and Taming Wild Elephants. With 21 full-page Illustrations. Reproduced for this Edition direct from the original drawings, and 3 Maps. Fifth Edition. Fcap. 4to. 12s.

LIEUT. G. J. YOUNGHUSBAND, Queen's Own Corps of Guides.

Polo in India. Crown 8vo. 2s.

COLONEL PARKER GILLMORE ("Ubique").

Encounters with Wild Beasts. Third Edition. Crown 8vo. Illustrated. 3s. 6d.

Prairie and Forest: A Guide to the Field Sports of North America. Second Edition. Crown 8vo. Illustrated. 3s. 6d.

Gun, Rod, and Saddle. A Record of Personal Experience. Crown 8vo, 6s.

Leaves From a Sportsman's Diary. Crown 8vo. With Portrait. 6s.

London: 13, Waterloo Place, Pall Mall, S.W.

Biography.

H. G. KEENE, C.I.E., M.A.

An Oriental Biographical Dictionary. New Edition, Enlarged and Revised. Royal 8vo, 28s. (Published under the patronage of the Secretary of State for India in Council.)

SYED AMEER ALI, M.A., C.I.E., Barrister-at-Law.

The Life and Teachings of Mohammed; or, the Spirit of Islam. Demy 8vo. 18s.

MONSEIGNEUR BESSON.

Frederick **Francis Xavier de Merode**, Minister and Almoner to Pius IX. His Life and Works. Translated by Lady Herbert. Crown 8vo. 7s. 6d.

CAPTAIN MONTAGU BURROWS, R.N., Retired List, Chichele *Professor of Modern History in the University of Oxford.*

Life of Edward Lord **Hawke**, Admiral of the Fleet, Vice-Admiral of Great Britain, and First Lord of the Admiralty from 1766 to 1771. Demy 8vo. 21s.

MRS. E. F. CHAPMAN.

Sketches of **some Distinguished Indian Women.** Crown 8vo. 2s. 6d.

Rev. H. R. HAWEIS, M.A., Author of " Music and Morals."

Sir **Morell Mackenzie**, PHYSICIAN AND OPERATOR. A Memoir. Compiled and Edited from Private Papers and Personal Reminiscences. Crown 8vo. 3s. 6d.

New and Cheaper Edition. With Portrait and copy of Autograph Letter from the Queen.

MISS K. O'MEARA.

Life of Thomas Grant, First Bishop **of Southwark.** Third Edition. Crown 8vo. 5s.

London: 13, Waterloo Place, Pall Mall, S.W.

EMINENT WOMEN SERIES. Edited by JOHN H. INGRAM. Crown 8vo. 3s. 6d. each.

George Eliot.	By MATHILDE BLIND.
Emily Brontë.	,, A. MARY F. ROBINSON.
George Sand.	,, BERTHA THOMAS.
Mary Lamb.	,, ANNE GILCHRIST.
Maria Edgeworth.	,, HELEN ZIMMERN.
Margaret Fuller.	,, JULIA WARD HOWE.
Elizabeth Fry.	,, MRS. E. R. PITMAN.
Countess of Albany.	,, VERNON LEE.
Harriet Martineau.	,, MRS. FENWICK MILLER.
Mary Wollstonecraft Godwin.	,, ELIZABETH ROBINS PENNELL.
Rachel.	,, MRS. A. KENNARD.
Madame Roland.	,, MATHILDE BLIND.
Susanna Wesley.	,, ELIZA CLARKE.
Margaret of Navarre.	,, MARY A. ROBINSON.
Mrs. Siddons.	,, MRS. A. KENNARD.
Madame de Staël.	,, BELLA DUFFY.
Hannah More.	,, CHARLOTTE M. YONGE.
Elizabeth Barrett Browning.	,, JOHN H. INGRAM.
Jane Austen.	,, MRS. CHARLES MALDEN.
Mary Shelley.	,, MRS. ROSETTI.

G. BARNETT SMITH, *Author of "History of the English Parliament."*

Leaders of Modern Industry. Biographical Sketches. Contents:—THE STEPHENSONS, CHARLES KNIGHT, SIR GEORGE BURNS, SIR JOSIAH MASON, THE WEDGWOODS, THOMAS BRASSEY, THE FAIRBAIRNS, SIR WILLIAM SIEMENS, THE RENNIES. Crown 8vo. 7s. 6d.

London: 13, *Waterloo Place, Pall Mall, S.W.*

STATESMEN SERIES. Edited by LLOYD C. SANDERS.

Lord Beaconsfield. By T. E. KEBBEL.
Viscount **Palmerston.** By L. C. SANDERS.
Daniel **O'Connell.** By J. A. HAMILTON.
Prince **Metternich.** By COL. G. B. MALLESON, C.S.I.
Sir Robert **Peel.** By F. C. MONTAGUE.
The Prince **Consort.** By MISS YONGE.
Henry **Grattan.** By ROBERT DUNLOP.
Marquis **Wellesley,** K.G. By COLONEL G. B. MALLESON, C.S.I.
Viscount **Bolingbroke.** By ARTHUR HASSALL, M.A.
Lord **Derby.** By T. E. KEBBEL.
Marquis of **Dalhousie.** By CAPT. L. J. TROTTER.
Charles **James** Fox. By H. O. WAKEMAN.
Leon Gambetta. By FRANK T. MARZIALS.

G. BARNETT SMITH, Author of " History of the English Parliament."

Women of Renown. Nineteenth Century Studies. Contents:—FREDERIKA BREMER, COUNTESS OF BLESSINGTON, GEORGE ELIOT, JENNY LIND, MARY SOMERVILLE, GEORGE SAND, MARY CARPENTER, LADY **MORGAN** RACHEL, LADY HESTER STANHOPE. Crown 8vo. 7s. 6d.

The Life **and Enterprises of Ferdinand de** Lesseps. Crown 8vo, with Two Portraits. 7s. 6d.

CAPTAIN LIONEL JAMES TROTTER, late Beng. Fusiliers.

Lord **Lawrence.** A Sketch of his Career. Fcap. 8vo. 1s. 6d.

Warren Hastings, a Biography. Crown 8vo. 9s.

London: 13, *Waterloo Place, Pall Mall, S.W.*

Books of Reference.

New Edition. 8vo. 25s.

Dedicated by permission to the RIGHT HON. W. E. GLADSTONE, M.P.

Book of Dignities, containing lists of the Official Personages of the British Empire, Civil, Diplomatic, Heraldic, Judicial, Ecclesiastical, Municipal, Naval, and Military, from the Earliest Periods to the Present Time, together with the Sovereigns and Rulers of the World from the Foundation of their respective States; the Orders of Knighthood of the United Kingdom and India, and numerous other lists. Founded on Beatson's "Political Index" (1806). Remodelled and brought down to 1851 by the late JOSEPH HAYDN. Continued to the Present Time, with numerous Additional Lists, and an Index to the entire Work, by HORACE OCKERBY, Solicitor of the Supreme Court.

"The most complete official directory in existence, containing about 1,300 different lists."—*Times.*

"The value of such a book can hardly be over-rated."—*Saturday Review.*

Cooper's Hill Royal Indian Engineering College, Calendar of. Published (by Authority) in November each year. Demy 8vo. 5s.

London in 1894. Its Suburbs and Environs. Illustrated with 20 Bird's Eye Views of the Principal Streets, and Maps. Fourteenth year of publication. Revised and Enlarged. Crown 8vo. 1s.

India List, the—Civil and Military. Issued yearly. By permission of the Secretary of State for India in Council. Demy 8vo. Cloth, 10s. 6d.

A Gazetteer of the Territories under the Government of the Viceroy of India. Revised and Edited by SIR ROPER LETHBRIDGE, C.I.E., formerly Press Commissioner in India, &c., and ARTHUR N. WOLLASTON, C.I.E., of H.M.'s Indian (Home) Civil Service, Translator of the "Anvár-i-Sahaili." Demy 8vo. 28s.

London: 13, *Waterloo Place, Pall Mall, S.W.*

Fiction.

LOUISA M. ALCOTT.
Little Women. 200 Illustrations. 4to. 18s.

Mrs. W. K. CLIFFORD.
A Grey Romance, and Stories by GILBERT PARKER, FRANK R. STOCKTON, FREDERICK GREENWOOD, and others. Crown 8vo. 6s.

J. R. COUPER.
Mixed Humanity. A Story of Camp Life in South Africa. Crown 8vo. Boards. 2s.

GEOFFREY DRAGE.
Cyril, a Romantic Novel. Sixth Edition. Crown 8vo. 3s. 6d.

JULIAN HAWTHORNE.
An American Monte Cristo. A Romance. By JULIAN HAWTHORNE. New Edition. Crown 8vo. 6s. Boards, 2s.

FERGUS HUME.
The Harlequin Opal. A Romance. By FERGUS HUME, Author of "The Island of Fantasy." New Edition. Crown 8vo. 6s. Boards, 2s.

IRVING MONTAGU (late Special War Correspondent "Illustrated London News").
Absolutely True. A Novel. By IRVING MONTAGU, late Special War Correspondent "Illustrated London News" With numerous Illustrations by the Author. New Edition. Crown 8vo. 6s. Boards, 2s.

From the French of EDOUARD ROD.
The Private Life of an Eminent Politician. New Edition. Crown 8vo. 6s. Boards, 2s.

J. W. SHERER, C.S.I.
Alice of the Inn : A Tale of the Old Coaching Days. New Edition. Crown 8vo. 6s.

FRANK R. STOCKTON.
The Shadrach and other Stories. Crown 8vo. 6s.

SARAH TYTLER.
War Times ; or, The Lads of Craigross ; and In the Cannon's Mouth. Crown 8vo. 3s. 6d.

London : 13, *Waterloo Place, Pall Mall, S.W.*

History, Political, &c.

D. C. BOULGER.

A Short History of China. An Account for the General Reader of an Ancient Empire and People. Demy 8vo, and New Map. 12s. 6d.

PERCY M. THORNTON.

Foreign Secretaries of the Nineteenth Century. Lord Grenville, Lord Hawkesbury, Lord Harrowby, Lord Mulgrave, C. J. Fox, Lord Howick, George Canning, Lord Bathurst, Lord Wellesley (together with estimate of his Indian Rule by COL. G. B. MALLESON, C.S.I.), Lord Castlereagh, Lord Dudley, Lord Aberdeen, and Lord Palmerston. With 10 Portraits and a View showing interior of the old House of Lords. Second Edition. 2 vols. Demy 8vo. 32s. 6d.

Vol. III. Second Edition. With Portraits. Demy 8vo. 18s.

Harrow School and its Surroundings. Maps and Plates. Demy 8vo. 15s.

W. M. TORRENS.

History of Cabinets. From the Union with Scotland to the Acquisition of Canada and Bengal. 2 vols. Demy 8vo. 36s.

Natural History, Botany, &c.

Allen's Naturalist's Library (*see page* 28).

E. BONAVIA, M.D., Brigade-Surgeon, Indian Medical Service.

The Cultivated Oranges and Lemons of India and Ceylon. Demy 8vo, with Atlas of Plates, 30s.

R. BRAITHWAITE, M.D., F.L.S., &c.

The Sphagnaceæ, or Peat Mosses of Europe and North America. Illustrated with 29 Plates, coloured by hand. Imp. 8vo. 25s.

B. CARRINGTON, M.D., F.R.S.

British Hepaticæ. Containing Descriptions and Figures of the Native Species of Jungermannia, Marchantia, and Anthoceros. Imp. 8vo, sewed, Parts 1 to 4, each 2s. 6d. plain; 3s. 6d. coloured.

London: 13, *Waterloo Place, Pall Mall, S.W.*

M. C. COOKE, M.A., LL.D.

The British Fungi: A Plain and Easy Account **of.**
With Coloured Plates of 40 Species. Fifth Edition, Revised. Crown 8vo. 6s.

Rust, Smut, Mildew, and Mould. An Introduction to the Study of Microscopic Fungi. Illustrated with 269 Coloured Figures by J. E. Sowerby. Fourth Edition, with Appendix of New Species. Crown 8vo, 6s.

A Manual of Structural Botany. Revised Edition, with New Chemical Notation. Illustrated with 200 Woodcuts. Twenty-fifth Thousand. 32mo. 1s.

A Manual of Botanic Terms. New Edition, greatly Enlarged. Illustrated with over 300 Woodcuts. Fcap. 8vo. 2s. 6d.

Handbook of British Hepaticæ. Containing Descriptions and Figures of the Indigenous Species of Marchantia, Jungermannia, Riccia, and Anthoceros. Crown 8vo. Illustrated. **6s.**

Our Reptiles and Batrachians. A Plain and Easy Account of the Lizards, Snakes, Newts, Toads, Frogs, and Tortoises indigenous to Great Britain. New and Revised Edition. With original Coloured Pictures of every Species, and numerous Woodcuts. Crown 8vo, 6s.

M. C. COOKE, M.A., A.L.S., et L. QUELET, M.D., O.A., Inst. et Sorb. Laur.

Clavis Synoptica Hymenomycetum Europæorum.
Fcap. 8vo. 7s. 6d.

BARON CUVIER.

The Animal Kingdom. With considerable Additions by W. B. CARPENTER, M.D., F.R.S., and J. O. WESTWOOD, F.L.S. New Edition, Illustrated with 500 Engravings on Wood and 36 Coloured Plates. Imp. 8vo. 21s.

THOMAS DAVIES.

The Preparation and Mounting of Microscopic Objects. New Edition, greatly enlarged and brought up to the Present Time by JOHN MATTHEWS, M.D., F.R.M.S., Vice-President of the Quekett Microscopical Club. Fcap. 8vo. 2s. 6d.

London: 13, Waterloo Place, Pall Mall, S.W.

GEORGE E. DAVIS, F.R.M.S., F.C.S., F.I.C., &c.

Practical Microscopy. Illustrated with 257 Woodcuts and a Coloured Frontispiece. Demy 8vo. 7s. 6d.

COL. HEBER DRURY, late Madras Staff Corps.

The Useful Plants of India, with Notices of their chief value in Commerce, Medicine, and the Arts. Second Edition. Royal 8vo. 16s.

SIR JOHN F. W. HERSCHEL, Bart., K.H., &c., Member of the Institute of France, &c.

Popular Lectures on Scientific Subjects. Crown 8vo. 6s.

SIR W. J. HOOKER, F.R.S., and J. G. BAKER, F.L.S.

Synopsis Filicum; or, a Synopsis of all Known Ferns, including the Osmundaceæ, Schizæaceæ, Marratisceæ, and Ophioglossaceæ (chiefly derived from the Kew Herbarium) accompanied by Figures representing the essential Characters of each genus. Second Edition brought up to the present time. Coloured Plates. Demy 8vo. £1 8s.

J. HUNTER, late Hon. Sec. of the British Bee-Keepers' Association.

A Manual of Bee-Keeping. Containing Practical Information for Rational and Profitable Methods of Bee Management. Full Instructions on Stimulative Feeding, Ligurianising and Queen-raising, with descriptions of the American Comb Foundation, Sectional Supers, and the best Hives and Apiarian Appliances on all systems. With Illustrations. Fourth Edition. Crown 8vo. 3s. 6d.

W. SAVILLE-KENT, F.L.S., F.Z.S., F.R.M.S., formerly Assistant in the Nat. Hist. Department of the British Museum.

The Great Barrier Reef of Australia: Its Products and Potentialities. Super Royal 4to. 16 Chromo Plates and 48 Plates. £4 4s. net. (*See page* 30.)

A Manual of the Infusoria. Including a Description of the Flagellate, Ciliate, and Tentaculiferous Protozoa, British and Foreign, and an Account of the Organisation and Affinities of the Sponges. With numerous Illustrations. 3 vols. Super Royal 8vo. £4 4s. net.

G. H. KINAHAN.

A Handy Book of Rock Names. Fcap. 8vo, cloth. 4s.

MRS. LANKESTER.

British Ferns: Their Classification, Arrangement of Genera, Structures and Functions, Directions for Out-door and In-door Cultivation, &c. Illustrated with Coloured Figures of all the Species. New and Enlarged Edition. Cr. 8vo. 3s. 6d.

Wild Flowers Worth Notice: A Selection of some of our Native Plants which are most attractive for their Beauty, Uses, or Associations. With 108 Coloured Figures by J. E. SOWERBY. New Edition. Crown 8vo. 5s.

E. LANKESTER, M.D., F.R.S., F.L.S.

Our Food. Illustrated. New Edition. Crown 8vo. 4s.

Half-Hours with the Microscope. With 250 Illustrations. Seventeenth Thousand, enlarged. Fcap. 8vo, plain, 2s. 6d.; coloured, 4s.

Practical Physiology: A School Manual of Health. With numerous Woodcuts. Sixth Edition. Fcap. 8vo. 2s. 6d.

The Uses of Animals in Relation to the Industry of Man. Illustrated. New Edition. Crown 8vo. 4s.

How to Choose a Microscope. By a Demonstrator. With 80 Illustrations. Demy 8vo. 1s.

JOHANN NAVE.

The Collector's Handy-Book of Algæ, Diatoms, Desmids, Fungi, Lichens, Mosses, &c. Translated and Edited by the Rev. W. W. SPICER, M.A. Illustrated with 114 Woodcuts. Fcap. 8vo. 2s. 6d.

The Late EDWARD NEWMAN, F.Z.S.

British Butterflies and Moths. With over 800 Illustrations. Super Royal 8vo. Cloth gilt. 25s.

The above Work may also be had in Two Volumes, sold separately. Vol. I., Butterflies, 7s. 6d.; Vol. II., Moths, 20s.

Notes on Collecting and Preserving Natural History Objects. Edited by J. E. TAYLOR, F.L.S., F.G.S., Editor of "Science Gossip." With Numerous Illustrations. Crown 8vo. 3s. 6d.

Ornithology in Relation to Agriculture and Horticulture. By Various Writers. Edited by JOHN WATSON, F.L.S., &c. Crown 8vo. 3s. 6d.

London: 13, Waterloo Place, Pall Mall, S.W.

RICHARD A. PROCTOR, B.A., F.R.A.S.

Half-Hours with the Stars. Nineteenth Thousand. Demy 4to. 3s. 6d.

Half-Hours with the Telescope. Illustrated. Fcap. 8vo. 2s. 6d.

Other Suns than Ours. A Series of Essays on Suns, Old, Young, and Dead, Science Gleanings, &c. Second Edition. Crown 8vo. 6s.

The Southern Skies. A Plain and Easy Guide to the Constellations of the Southern Hemisphere, &c. True for every year. 4to, with 12 Maps. 5s.

Rev. ALEXANDER KYD NAIRNE, late Bombay Civil Service.

The Flowering Plants of Western India. Crown 8vo. 7s. 6d. net.

MARY A. PRATTEN.

My Hundred Swiss Flowers. With a Short Account of Swiss Ferns. With 60 Illustrations. Crown 8vo, plain 12s. 6d.; coloured, 25s.

R. RIMMER, F.L.S.

The Land and Fresh Water Shells of the British Isles. Illustrated with Photographs and 3 Lithographs, containing figures of all the principal Species. Second Edition. Crown 8vo. 5s.

J. SMITH, A.L.S.

Ferns: British and Foreign. Fourth Edition, revised and greatly enlarged, with New Figures, &c. Crown 8vo. 7s. 6d.

J. E. TAYLOR, F.L.S., F.G.S., &c.

The Aquarium: Its Inhabitants, Structure, and Management. With 238 Woodcuts. Second Edition. Crown 8vo. 3s. 6d.

Flowers: Their Origin, Shapes, Perfumes, and Colours. Illustrated with 32 Coloured Figures by Sowerby, and 161 Woodcuts. Second Edition. Crown 8vo. 7s. 6d.

London: 13, Waterloo Place, Pall Mall, S.W.

Nature's Bye-paths: A Series of Recreative Papers in Natural History. Crown 8vo. 3s. 6d.

Half-Hours at the Seaside. Illustrated with 250 Woodcuts. Fourth Edition. Crown 8vo. 2s. 6d.

Half-Hours in the Green Lanes. Illustrated with 300 Woodcuts. Fifth Edition. Crown 8vo. 2s. 6d.

Travel.

D. T. ANSTED and R. G. LATHAM.

The Channel Islands. Revised and Edited by E. TOULMIN NICOLLE. Third Edition. Profusely Illustrated. Crown 8vo. 7s. 6d.

STEPHEN BONSAL, Junr. (Special Correspondent "Central News").

Morocco as it Is. With an account of the recent Mission of Sir Charles Euan Smith to Fez. Second Edition. Crown 8vo, with Map and numerous Illustrations. 7s. 6d.

CAPTAIN JAMES ABBOTT.

Narrative of a Journey from Herat to Khiva, Moscow, and St. Petersburg during the late Russian Invasion of Khiva. With Map and Portrait. 2 vols. Demy 8vo. 24s.

S. BARING-GOULD, M.A., Author of "Mehulah," &c.

In Troubadour Land. A Ramble in Provence and Languedoc. Medium 8vo. With Illustrations by J. E. Rogers, 12s. 6d.

MISS SOPHIA BEALE.

The Churches of Paris from Clovis to Charles X. Crown 8vo. With numerous Illustrations. 7s. 6d.

GEORGE DOBSON.

Russia's Railway Advance into Central Asia. Notes of a Journey from St. Petersburg to Samarkand. Crown 8vo. Illustrated. 7s. 6d.

London: 13, *Waterloo Place, Pall Mall, S.W.*

H. SWAINSON COWPER, F.S.A.

Through Turkish Arabia: a Journey from the Mediterranean to Bombay by the Euphrates and Tigris Valleys and the Persian Gulf. Demy 8vo. Maps and Illustrations. 18s.

MAJOR S. LEIGH HUNT, Madras Army, and ALEX. S. KENNY, M.R.C.S.E., A.K.C., Senior Demonstrator of Anatomy at King's College, London.

On Duty under a Tropical Sun. Being some Practical Suggestions for the Maintenance of Health and Bodily Comfort, and the Treatment of Simple Diseases; with remarks on Clothing and Equipment. Second Edition. Crown 8vo. 4s.

Tropical Trials. A Handbook for Women in the Tropics. Crown 8vo. 7s. 6d.

E. F. KNIGHT, Author of "The Cruise of the Falcon."

The Falcon in the Baltic: A Voyage from London to Copenhagen in a Three-Tonner. With 10 full-page Illustrations. New Edition. Crown 8vo. 3s. 6d.

COL. T. H. LEWIN, Dep. Comm. of Hill Tracts.

Indian Frontier Life. A Fly on the Wheel, or How I helped to govern India. Map and Illustrations. Demy 8vo. 18s.

T. W. M. LUND, M.A., Chaplain to the School for the Blind, Liverpool.

Como and Italian Lake Land. With 3 Maps, and 11 Illustrations by Miss Jessie Macgregor. Crown 8vo. 10s. 6d.

London: 13, Waterloo Place, Pall Mall, S.W.

CHARLES MARVIN.

The Region of the Eternal Fire. An Account of a Journey to the Caspian Region in 1883. New Edition. Maps and Illustrations. Crown 8vo. 6s.

The REV. SAMUEL MATEER, of the London Missionary Society.

Native Life in Travancore. Illustrations and Map. Demy 8vo. 18s.

EDWARD ROPER, F.R.G.S.

By Track and Trail. A Journey through Canada. Demy 8vo. With Numerous Original Sketches by the Author. 18s.

SIGNORA LINDA VILLARI, Author of "On Tuscan Hills and Venetian Waters," &c.

Here and There in Italy and Over the Border. Crown 8vo. 5s.

S. WELLS WILLIAMS, LL.D., Professor of the Chinese Language and Literature at Yale College.

The Middle Kingdom. A Survey of the Geography, Government, Literature, Social Life, Arts, and History of the Chinese Empire and its Inhabitants. Revised Edition, with 74 Illustrations and a New Map of the Empire. 2 vols. Demy 8vo. 42s.

LIEUT. G. J. YOUNGHUSBAND, Queen's Own Corps of Guides.

Eighteen Hundred Miles in a Burmese Tat, through Burmah, Siam, and the Eastern Shah States. Illustrated. Crown 8vo. 5s.

BY THE AUTHORS OF "AN IRISH COUSIN," Illustrated by W. W. RUSSELL, from Sketches by EDITH Œ. SOMERVILLE.

Through Connemara in a Governess Cart. By the Authors of "An Irish Cousin." Crown 8vo. Illustrated. 3s. 6d.

In the Vine Country. Crown 8vo. Illustrated. 3s. 6d.

London: 13, Waterloo Place, Pall Mall, S.W.

Theology.

HENRY ALFORD, D.D., the late Dean of Canterbury.

The New Testament. After the Authorised Version. Newly compared with the original Greek, and Revised. Long Primer, Crown 8vo, cloth, red edges, 6s.; Brevier, Fcap. 8vo, cloth, 3s. 6d.; Nonpareil, small 8vo, 1s. 6d., or in calf extra, red edges, 4s. 6d.

HON. A. S. G. CANNING.

Words on Existing Religions. Crown 8vo. 3s. 6d.

DR. DOLLINGER.

The First Age of Christianity and the Church. Translated from the German, by H. N. OXENHAM. Third Edition. 2 vols. Crown 8vo. 18s.

THEODOR GRIESINGER.

The Jesuits; a Complete History of their Open and Secret Proceedings from the Foundation of the Order to the Present Time. Translated by A. J. SCOTT, M.D. Third Edition. Demy 8vo. 10s. 6d.

REV. T. P. HUGHES.

Notes on Muhammadanism. Third Edition, revised and enlarged. Fcap. 8vo. 6s.

A Dictionary of Islam. Being a Cyclopædia of the Doctrines, Rites, Ceremonies, and Customs, together with the Technical and Theological Terms of the Muhammadan Religion. With numerous Illustrations. Royal 8vo. £2 2s.

S. H. JEYES, M.A.

The Ethics of Aristotle. Nich. Eth. Books 1—4, and Book 10, ch. vi.—end. Analysed, Annotated, and Translated for Oxford Passmen. Demy 8vo. 6s.

Keble College Sermons. Second Series, 1877-1888. Crown 8vo. 6s.

London: 13, *Waterloo Place, Pall Mall, S.W.*

REV. F. G. LEE, D.D. (*Vicar of All Saints', Lambeth*).

The Church under Queen Elizabeth. An Historical Sketch. By Rev. F. G. LEE, D.D. (Vicar of All Saints', Lambeth). Second Edition. **Crown 8vo. 7s. 6d.**

Sights and Shadows. Being Examples of the Supernatural. Crown 8vo, 6s.

REV. HENRY NUTCOMBE OXENHAM, M.A.

Catholic Eschatology and Universalism. An Essay on the Doc'rine of Future Retribution. Second Edition, Revised and Enlarged. **Crown 8vo. 7s. 6d.**

Catholic Doctrine of the Atonement. An Historical Inquiry into its Development in the Church, with an Introduction on the Principle of Theological Development. Third Edition and Enlarged. 8vo. **14s.**

The First Age of Christianity and the Church. By JOHN IGNATIUS DÖLLINGER, D.D., Professor of Ecclesiastical History in the University of Munich, &c., &c. Translated from the German by H N. OXENHAM, M.A. Third Edition. **2 vols Crown 8vo. 18s.**

VERY REV. R. W. RANDALL (*Dean of Chichester*).

Life in the Catholic Church. Its Blessings and Responsibilities. Third Edition. **Crown 8vo. 6s.**

Addresses and Meditations for a Retreat of Four or Six Days. Second Edition. With Preface by the Bishop of Lincoln. Part I.—Union with God; Part II.—From Life to Life. Second Edition. **Crown 8vo. 5s.**

WILFRED RICHMOND.

Economic Morals. Four Lectures, with Preface by the Rev. H. S. HOLLAND, M.A., Canon of St. Paul's. Crown 8vo. 3s. 6d.

ARTHUR PENRHYN STANLEY, D.D. (Dean of Westminster).

Scripture Portraits and other Miscellanies collected from his Published Writings. By ARTHUR PENRHYN STANLEY, D.D. Crown 8vo. 5s.

Uniform with the above.

VERY REV. FREDERICK W. FARRAR, D.D., F.R.S. (Archdeacon of Westminster).

Words of Truth and Wisdom. By VERY REV. FREDERICK W. FARRAR, D.D., F.R.S. Crown 8vo. 5s.

Uniform with the above.

SAMUEL WILBERFORCE, D.D. (Bishop of Winchester).

Heroes of Hebrew History. Crown 8vo. 5s.

Uniform with the above.

CARDINAL NEWMAN.

Miscellanies from the Oxford Sermons of John Henry Newman, D.D. Crown 8vo. 5s.

Veterinary and Riding.

EDWARD L. ANDERSON.

How to Ride and School a Horse. With a System of Horse Gymnastics. Crown 8vo. 2s. 6d.

A System of School Training for Horses. Crown 8vo. 2s. 6d.

GEORGE GRESSWELL.

The Diseases and Disorders of the Ox. Second Edition. Demy 8vo. 7s. 6d.

London: 13, *Waterloo Place, Pall Mall, S.W.*

JAMES LONG.

The Dairy Farm. Illustrated. Crown 8vo. 3s. 6d.

JAMES IRVINE LUPTON, F.R.C.V.S.

The Horse, as he Was, as he Is, and as he Ought to Be. Illustrated. Crown 8vo. 3s. 6d.

EDWARD **MAYHEW, M.R.C.V.S.** (*Revised and Improved by* JAMES **IRVINE LUPTON, F.R.C.V.S.**, *Author of several works on Veterinary Science and Art*).

The Illustrated Horse Doctor. **Being an Account** of the various Diseases incident to the Equine **Race; with the Latest** Mode **of** Treatment and Requisite Prescriptions. By EDWARD MAYHEW, M.R.C.V.S. (Revised and Improved by JAMES IRVINE LUPTON, F.R.C.V.S., Author of several works on Veterinary Science and Art.) Demy 8vo. 400 Illustrations. 10s. 6d.

Illustrated Horse Management. **Containing descrip**tive Remarks upon Anatomy, Medicine, Shoeing, Teeth, **Food,** Vices, Stables; likewise a plain Account of the situation, **nature,** and value of the various points; together with Comments on Grooms, Dealers, Breeders, Breakers, and Trainers. With more than 400 Engravings from original designs made expressly for this work. A New Edition, revised and improved by J. I. LUPTON, M.R.C.V.S. Half-bound. Demy 8vo. 7s. 6d.

MRS. POWER O'DONOGHUE.

Ladies on Horseback. Learning, Park Riding, and Hunting. With Notes upon Costume, and Numerous Anecdotes. With Portrait and Illustrations. New Edition. Crown 8vo. 3s. 6d.

WILLIAM PROCTOR, Stud Groom.

The Management and Treatment of the Horse in the Stable, Field, and on the Road. New and Revised Edition. Crown 8vo. 6s.

London: 13, *Waterloo Place, Pall Mall, S.W.*

ALLEN'S
NATURALIST'S LIBRARY.
Edited by R. BOWDLER SHARPE, LL.D., F.L.S., &c.

THE extraordinary favour which Jardine's Naturalist's Library has enjoyed during the last fifty years, has induced the proprietors of the copyright to issue a series of volumes, written by some of the most eminent naturalists of the day, under the title of "Allen's Naturalist's Library."

The Publishers have secured for the Editorial work the services of Dr. R. BOWDLER SHARPE, of the British Museum, whose long and honourable connection with that Institution, coupled with his experience of the Editorship and publication of many of the most important of modern works on Natural Science, entitle him to be considered one of the fittest men in England for the task.

The Editor has obtained the co-operation of the following eminent naturalists:—

Mr. R. LYDEKKER, M.A. (Mammalia).
Mr. H. O. FORBES (Mammalia and Birds).
Mr. W. R. OGILVIE GRANT (Birds).
Mr. W. F. KIRBY (Insects).
Professor R. H. TRAQUAIR, F.R.S. (Fishes),

while the Editor undertakes several of the Ornithological volumes.

Over 1,000 steel-plate engravings, many of them by the most eminent artists of the time, will be utilized for the purposes of the present work, and will be produced in the highest style of modern chromolithography, in addition to which the services of Mr. KEULEMANS and other leading artists of the day have been secured for the illustration of those forms of animal life which it has been found necessary to depict, in order to bring the present work up to the standard of Modern Science.

The volumes will be published at the popular price of 6s. Each volume containing about 320 pages of letterpress, together with from 20 to 40 coloured plates.

The volumes now issued consist of:—

A HANDBOOK TO THE BIRDS OF GREAT BRITAIN, Vol. I.,
by R. BOWDLER SHARPE, LL.D., Zoological Department,
British Museum;

A HANDBOOK TO THE MARSUPIALIA AND MONOTREMATA,
by R. LYDEKKER, F.L.S.;

and will be followed by

MONKEYS, by H. O. FORBES, F.R.G.S.

BUTTERFLIES (with special reference to British species), by
W. F. KIRBY, F.L.S.

London: 13, *Waterloo Place, Pall Mall, S.W.*

List of Books

Issued by the **Secretary of State for India in Council** and the Government of **India**, on **Sale by Messrs. W. H. ALLEN & CO.**

Edited by GEORGE W. FORREST, *B.A., Director of Records of the Government of India, &c.*

The Indian Mutiny, 1857-58. Selections from the Letters, Despatches, and other State Papers preserved in the Military Department of the Government of India. Royal 8vo, with Map and Plans, 12s. 6d. Vol. I.

GEORGE WATT, *M.B., C.M., C.I.E., Reporter on Economic Products with the Government of India. Assisted by numerous Contributors.*

A Dictionary of the Economic Products of India. In Six Volumes, Royal 8vo, half-bound, £3 3s.

F. C. DANVERS, Registrar and Superintendent of Records, India Office, London.

Report to the Secretary of State for India in Council on the Portuguese Records relating to the East Indies, contained in the Archivo da Torre de Tombo, and the Public Libraries at Lisbon and Evora. Royal 8vo, sewed, 6s.

C. H. SAMPSON, Registrar, Home Department, Government of India.

A Manual of Rules and Regulations applicable to the Members of the Indian Civil Service, including certain information as to existing appointments for which members of the Indian Civil Service are eligible. Imperial 8vo, boards, 2s. 6d.

J. FORBES WATSON, M.A., F.R.A.S., Reporter on the Products of India to the Secretary of State for India in Council.

The Textile Manufactures and the Costumes of the People of India. Imperial 4to. With 11 full-page Plates of Costumes. Half-bound. 21s.

ALEXANDER CUNNINGHAM, C.S.I., C.I.E., Major-General, Royal Engineers (Bengal Retired); Director-General Archæological Survey of India.

The Stupa of Bharhut. A Buddhist Monument Ornamented with numerous Sculptures illustrative of Buddhist Legend and History in the Third Century B.C. 4to, 57 Plates, cloth gilt. £3 3s.

Mahabodhi; or, the Great Buddhist Temple under the Bodhi Tree at Buddha-Gayâ. Royal 4to, Cloth, with 31 Illustrations. £3 3s.

London: 13, *Waterloo* Place, *Pall Mall, S.W.*

Super-Royal 4to, with 16 Chromo Plates and 48 Plates in Photo-mezzotype. £4 4s. net.

THE
GREAT BARRIER REEF OF AUSTRALIA:
ITS PRODUCTS AND POTENTIALITIES.

Containing an Account, with Copious Coloured and Photographic Illustrations (the latter here produced for the first time), of the Corals and Coral Reefs, Pearl and Pearl Shell, Bêche-de-Mer, other Fishing Industries, and the Marine Fauna of the Australian Great Barrier Region.

By W. SAVILLE-KENT, F.L.S., F.Z.S., F.I.Inst., &c.,
Author of "A Manual of the Infusoria."

"A veritable romance of the sea; the whole work is a labour of love and enthusiasm."—*The Times.*

"The first thought that strikes one in glancing through this magnificently illustrated volume is the diligence and skill of the author in photography, and the enterprise of the publisher. Never before has a semi-scientific work been illustrated with such a wealth of plates. . . . The illustrations are unique for beauty, trustfulness, and number, and the descriptions are short and to the point."—*Nature.*

"A deeply instructive and attractive book."—*Manchester Examiner.*

"Is marvellously comprehensive, and by far the best ever written on its subject. The production is beyond all praise."—*Publishers' Circular.*

Carefully corrected to 1893 from the latest Authorities and showing Railways already finished and in progress.

In Six Sheets, size 5 ft. 6 in. by 5 ft. 8 in., Coloured, £2.
In Cloth Case, mounted on Linen, £2. 12s. 6d.
Mounted on Rollers, varnished, £3. 3s.

MAP OF INDIA
SHOWING THE BRITISH TERRITORIES SUB-DIVIDED INTO COLLECTORATES

AND INCLUDING

BURMA,

WITH THE POSITION AND BOUNDARIES OF EACH NATIVE STATE.
Chiefly compiled from Trigonometrical Surveys.
Executed by Order of the Government of India by
JOHN WALKER,
Geographer to the India Office.

London: 13, Waterloo Place, Pall Mall, S.W.

LIST OF AUTHORS.

	PAGE		PAGE
Abbot's "Herat to Khiva"	21	"Eminent Women Series"	12
Aberigh-Mackay's "Twenty-one Days"	1	Farrar's "Words of Truth"	26
"Academy Sketches"	5	Gall's "Modern Tactics"	7
Allcott's "Little Women"	15	Gillmore's "Gun, Rod, and Saddle"	10
Alford's "New Testament"	24	,, "Prairie and Forest"	10
Alf's (Ameer) "Mohammed"	11	,, "Sportsman's Diary"	10
Allen's "Naturalist's Library"	16	,, "Wild Beasts"	10
Anderson's "How to Ride"	25	Goltz's "Nation in Arms"	9
,, "School Training"	26	Gossip's "Chess Openings"	5
Ansted's "Channel Island"	21	Granville's Works	5
Archer's "Orders of Chivalry"	5	Greene's "Army Life"	7
Arnold's "Book of Good Counsels"	1	,, "Russian Army in Turkey"	7
		Gresswell's "Diseases of the Ox"	26
Baring-Gould's "Troubadour Land"	21	Griesinger's "Jesuits"	24
Beale's "Churches of Paris"	21	Griffith's "India's Princes"	4
Bellair's "Military Career"	7	Haydn's "Book of Dignities"	14
Besson's "Merode's Life"	11	Haweis' "Chaucer's Beads"	6
Betham's "Story of a Dacoity"	2	,, "Sir Morell Mackenzie"	11
Birdwood's "Old Records of India Office"	2	,, "Music and Morals"	5
Boileau's "Traverse Tables"	5	,, "My Musical Life"	5
Bonavia's "Oranges and Lemons"	16	Hawthorne's "American Monte Cristo"	15
Bonsal's "Morocco as it is"	21	Health Primers	6
"Book of Knots"	10	Hensman's "Afghan War"	2
Boulger's "Short History of China"	16	Herschel's "Lectures"	18
Bradshaw's "Milton"	5	Holmes' "Indian Mutiny"	2
Braithwaite's "Sphagnaceæ"	16	Hooker's "Synopsis Filicum"	18
Burrows' "Life of Lord Hawke"	9	"How to Choose a Microscope"	19
"Byron Birthday Book"	6	Hughes' "Dictionary of Islam"	24
		,, "Muhammadanism"	24
Canning's "Existing Religions"	24	Hume's "Harlequin Opal"	15
Carrington's "Hepaticæ"	16	Hunter's "Bee-Keeping"	18
Chapman's "Indian Women"	11	Hunter's "Indian Empire"	1
Clifford's "Grey Romance"	15	Hunt's "Tropical Sun"	22
Colomb's "Naval Warfare"	10	,, "Tropical Trials"	22
Cooke's "Botanic Terms"	17	India List	14
,, "Botany"	17	,, Maps	30
,, "British Fungi"	17	Ingram's "Haunted Homes"	6
,, "Clavis"	17	Jeyes' "Aristotle"	24
,, "Hepaticæ"	17	Johnson's "Cookery"	2
,, "Reptiles"	17	Jones' "Puddings and Sweets"	6
,, Rust, Smut"	17	Kaye's "Afghanistan"	2
"Cooper's Hill Calendar"	14	,, "Indian Officers"	2
Couper's "Mixed Humanity"	15	,, "Sepoy War" and "Index"	2
Cowper's "Through Turkish Arabia"	22	Kaye and Malleson's "Mutiny"	2
Cuming's "In the Shadow of the Pagoda"	1	"Keble College Sermons"	24
Cuvier's "Animal Kingdom"	17	Keene's "Biographical Dictionary"	3
Davies' "Microscopic Objects"	17	,, "Fifty-seven"	3
Davis' "Microscopy"	18	,, "History of India"	3
Dobson's "Russian Railway"	21	,, "Moghul Empire"	3
Dollinger's "First Age of Church"	24	,, "Turks in India"	3
D'Orsey's "Portuguese in Asia"	2	Kent's "Great Barrier Reef"	18
Dunstan's "Manual of Music"	6	,, "Infusoria"	18
Drage's "Cyril"	15	Kinahan's "Rock Names"	18
Drury's "Useful Plants of India"	18	Knight's "Falcon in the Baltic"	22
Dyer's "Folk Lore"	5	Lankester's "Animals"	19

London: 13, Waterloo Place, Pall Mall, S.W.

LIST OF AUTHORS (continued).

	PAGE
Lankester's " Ferns "	19
,, " Microscope "	19
,, " Our Food "	19
,, " Physiology "	19
,, " Talks about Health "	16
,, " Wild Flowers "	19
Lee's " Church under Elizabeth "	25
,, " Sights and Shadows "	25
Lethbridge's " Gazeteer of India "	14
Lewin's " Frontier Life "	22
" London in 1894 "	14
Long's " Dairy Farm "	27
Lund's " Como "	22
Lupton's " Horse "	27
Maguire's " Campaigns in Virginia "	8
Malleson's " Ambushes and Surprises "	8
,, " Battlefields of Germany "	8
,, " Afghanistan "	3
,, " Clive "	3
,, " Decisive Battles of India "	3
,, " French in India "	3
,, " Final French Struggles "	3
,, " Indian Mutiny "	3
Manning's " India "	4
Marvin's " Region of Eternal Fire "	23
Mateer's " Travancore "	23
Mayhew's " Horse Doctor "	27
,, " Horse Management "	27
Michod's " Good Condition "	6
Moltke's " Tactical Problems "	7
Montagu's " Absolutely True "	15
,, " Camp and Studio "	8
,, " War Artist "	8
Morris's " Great Commanders "	9
Nairne's " Flowering Plants "	20
Nave's " Algæ "	19
Newman's " Butterflies and Moths "	19
,, " Miscellanies "	26
O'Donoghue's " Ladies on Horseback "	27
O'Meara's " Life of Bishop Grant "	11
Oxenham's " Atonement "	25
,, " Eschatology "	25
Pope's " Indian History "	4
Pratten's " Swiss Flowers "	20
Prichard's " Chronicles of Budgepore "	4
Proctor's " Horse "	27
,, " Southern Skies "	20
,, " Other Suns "	20
,, " Half-hours with the Stars "	20
,, " Half-hours with the Telescope "	20
Randall's " Catholic Church "	25
,, " Retreat Addresses "	25
Richmond's " Economic Morals "	26
Rimmer's " Shells "	20
Rod's " Eminent Politician "	15
Roger's " Land Revenue of Bombay "	4
Roper's " Track and Trail through Canada "	23
Sanderson's " Wild Beasts of India "	10
Sewell's " History of India "	4
Sherer's " Alice of the Inn "	15
Singlestick Exercises	8
Smith's " De Lesseps "	13
,, " Modern Industry "	12
,, " Women of Renown "	13
,, " Ferns "	20
Somerville's " Through Connemara "	23
,, " In the Vine Country "	23
Stanley's " Scripture Portraits "	26
" Statesman Series "	13
Stockton's " The Shadrach "	15
Taylor's " Aquarium "	20
,, " Bye-Paths "	21
,, " Flowers "	20
,, " Green Lanes "	21
,, " Notes on Collecting "	19
,, " Seaside "	21
Thomson's " Lunar Tables "	7
Thornton's " Foreign Secretaries "	16
,, " Harrow School "	16
Torrens' " History of Cabinets "	16
" Treasury of Quotations "	6
Trotter's " India under Victoria "	4
,, " Lord Lawrence "	13
,, " Warren Hastings "	13
Tytler's " War Times "	15
Verner's " Field Sketching "	8
,, " Topography "	8
Villari's " Here and There in Italy "	23
Walford's " Home Counties "	7
,, " Pleasant Days "	7
Wathen's " Field Service Pocket Book "	9
Watson's " Ornithology "	19
" Where Glory Calls "	8
Whinyate's " Corunna to Sevastopol "	9
Wilberforce's " Heroes "	26
Williams' " Middle Kingdom "	23
,, " Steam Navy "	9
Wright's " Great Writers "	7
Younghushand's " Polo in India "	10
,, " Burmese Tat "	23
" Young Soldier in India "	9

London: 13, Waterloo Place, Pall Mall, S.W.

www.ingramcontent.com/pod-product-compliance
Lightning Source LLC
Chambersburg PA
CBHW022027240426
43667CB00042B/1220